PEER GROUPS

No one is immune from peer pressure.
Everyone has been a part of it.
No one has failed to learn from its power.

Peer Groups

Expanding Our Study of Small Group Communication

Dr. SunWolf
Santa Clara University

Los Angeles • London • New Delhi • Singapore

For information:

SAGE Publications, Inc.
2455 Teller Road
Thousand Oaks,
California 91320
E-mail: order@sagepub.com

SAGE Publications Ltd.
1 Oliver's Yard
55 City Road
London EC1Y 1SP
United Kingdom

SAGE Publications India Pvt. Ltd.
B 1/I 1 Mohan Cooperative
Industrial Area
Mathura Road, New Delhi 110 044
India

SAGE Publications Asia-Pacific
Pte. Ltd.
33 Pekin Street #02-01
Far East Square
Singapore 048763

Printed in the United States of America

Library of Congress Cataloging-in-Publication Data

SunWolf, Dr.
Peer groups: Expanding our study of small group communication/SunWolf.
p. cm.
Includes bibliographical references and index.
ISBN 978-1-4129-2686-7 (pbk.)
1. Age groups. 2. Small groups. I. Title.

HM721.S86 2008
303.3'27—dc22 2008001109

This book is printed on acid-free paper.

08 09 10 11 12 10 9 8 7 6 5 4 3 2 1

Acquisitions Editor:	Todd R. Armstrong
Editorial Assistant:	Aja Baker
Production Editor:	Astrid Virding
Copy Editor:	Alison Hope
Typesetter:	C&M Digitals (P) Ltd.
Proofreader:	Ellen Brink
Indexer:	Nara Wood
Cover Designer:	SunWolf
Marketing Manager:	Carmel Schrire

Contents

Prologue

a cowardice of curs • a kindle of kittens • a murder of crows • an aurora of polar bears • a brace of ducks • a charm of finches • a scare of ghosts • a knot of toads • a wake of buzzards • a gaggle of geese • a hover of trout • an army of ants • a crash of rhinoceroses • an ostentation of peacocks • a sleuth of bears • a leap of leopards • a clowder of cats • a quiver of cobras • a romp of otters • a huddle of penguins • a wedge of geese • a drove of sheep • a shrewdness of apes • a squabble of seagulls • a bevy of roebucks • a prickle of hedgehogs • an exaltation of larks • a route of wolves

One of the oddities of the English language is that there are so many different collective nouns that all mean "group"—but each word is specific to the particular things *in* that group. Collective nouns were originally either terms of *venery* (from the sport of hunting) or terms of *husbandry* (having to do with farming or livestock).* Whatever you may think of hunting as a social sport, in the fifteenth century it was socially acceptable—generating a delightful language, full of words indicating collections of beasts or birds.**

Collective nouns remain a vibrant linguistic force today. They are still being created, and now these new collective nouns imaginatively extend to groups of *people:* an eloquence of lawyers, an illusion of

---

*Medieval collective nouns are found in Shakespeare. The most important record of such nouns is known as the *Book of St. Albans,* "A Treatyse Perteynynge to Hawkynge, Huntynge and Coote Armiris," published in 1486. To illustrate how specific the collective nouns from hunting were: a *gaggle* (a flock of geese when not flying), a *skein* (geese in flight), and a *wedge* (denoting geese in flight and in formation); ducks on the water are a *paddling,* but when they take flight, they are a *team;* a *sounder* of wild swine, but a *dryft* of tame swine. Wolves were commonly said to go about in *routes* or routs, with a "route of wolfes" being 12 or more (jury-ish).

**If you are interested in delving into this topic, I urge you to get a copy of James Lipton's *An Exaltation of Larks;* also, *A Crash of Rhinoceroses: A Dictionary of Collective Nouns* by Rex Collins.

painters, a rascal of boys, a circus of clowns, a stack of librarians, a geek of engineers, a pan of reviewers, a blarney of bartenders, a babble of linguists, a yard of gardeners, a clergy of priests, a discord of experts, or a shrivel of critics.

This book explores the customs, oddities, rituals, symbols, language, and behaviors of a GROUP OF PEERS.

> If you are now (or have dedicated plans to be) a hermit, isolate, or lone dweller-on-mountain-tops, read no further.
> This book has nothing for you.

❖ THE GROUPS THAT MATTER MOST (PEERS)

For the strength of the pack is the wolf and the strength of the wolf is the pack.

—Rudyard Kipling
(English author and poet, 1865–1936)

peer n. 1. a person who is the equal of another in abilities, qualifications, age, background, responsibilities, or social status 2. a person of the same legal status, privilege, or rights as another

The first thing to know about behavior in peer groups is that we are talking about *us,* not just about others. This point is important to establish, right at the beginning. We are talking about other people, sure, but we are talking (a whole lot) about *us.* You are a member of at least one—and probably several—peer groups: clans, cliques, clubs, or choirs; teams, travelers, taskers, or tribes.

Our experiences in peer groups may be rewarding or hurtful (or a confusing combination of both). One project team member described the euphoric culture of his experience in a group:

> We even walked differently than anybody else. We felt we were way out there, ahead of the whole world.[1]

In fact, when we work on projects with others, we are members of peer *work groups* that tend to develop unique cultures, in which the work of one is considered to be the work of all:

> And if he's too big for one man to handle, we'd get down together, and we'd catch him by the tail and hold him right tight to keep him from jumpin' on that fella, then they say, "Hora sí." And down we go. Then we got him. That's teamwork. (African American cowboy from Texas, age 90, reflecting on how it once was with cowboys and cows.)[2]

However, peer group experiences may be infuriating, as evidenced by this juror's description of the fifth day of deliberations:

> I screamed that I couldn't believe this was happening, that we were possibly going to be a hung jury when in my mind the case was so obvious. Everything was there, DNA evidence, witness testimony. There was no room for interpretation. I was angry. There were words of profanity that came out of my mouth.[3]

Peer groups can hurt us even when we are *not* members of them. Our experiences of being excluded, for example, are painful—as one 14-year-old African American teen poignantly pointed out,

> They said I couldn't be in the group because I was too ugly and I wasn't german [*sic*] which made me not good enough to be in the group. I was really hurt and I thought I was ugly and I wished I looked german [*sic*]. I thought I was the ugliest person alive.[4]

We are embedded in groups, from the moment we are born: families, sports teams, classes, task groups, special interest groups, support groups, neighborhoods, clubs, churches, friendship circles, faculty, orchestras, choirs, committees, sibling groups, scout troops, professional groups, living groups, and lost-on-an-island-together groups, to name only a few. Some groups are voluntary (clubs), while others are involuntary (juries); some are a bit of both (biological families or chosen families; military troops); some groups may have existed before we joined them (cliques), while we choose to organize other groups ourselves (hot groups). Some groups seem to cripple our thoughts (cults), while others help us move beyond our personal best (superteams). Which groups, however, are considered *peer* groups?

❖ DEFINING AND DISTINGUISHING PEER GROUPS

Members of peer groups perceive that they are like one another, in one or more salient ways. Here, the term *peer groups* draws on on the definition of "peer" offered at the outset of this prologue and, furthermore, suggests a working framework for distinguishing *peer groups* from many other groups in our lives:

> **Peer groups** are composed of members who consider one another to be equals, in terms of abilities, background, age, responsibilities, beliefs, social standing, legal status, or rights. *Not all group members agree about the equality of all other members at all times*, but there is overt consensus that members of the group are primarily equal.

That is, there may be a "sliding scale" when it comes to measuring enacted *equality* in various peer groups.*

*Some "peers," it turns out, may seem to be more equal than others.

Are all small groups, then, essentially peer groups, as long as the members have something in common? As this book will describe throughout, having "something in common" with others is qualitatively different from being with other people who share the perception that each of them is an equal, in some important way. For example, the people in many small, spontaneous groups all have something in common: eating in a small restaurant, folks on an elevator, locals waiting for a bus, students attending a university, or fans of a sports team (but these are not peer groups). Some groups are distinguished by hierarchy, privilege, power, or status, such that even the members do not consider themselves to be equal (so these are not peer groups, either). Consider, for example, the president of a country and government cabinet members, a military commander and soldiers, a coach and team members. Subtract the members who have extraordinary power, however, and the remaining members, when engaged in their shared goal, might be peers. When a losing sports team is dressed down by the coach and the coaching staff in the locker room after a game, only the players are group peers (both players and coaching staff realize this). A family that includes parents, grandparents, brothers, and sisters is a group worth studying—but some family members have more power, control, knowledge, and privilege than others. Within that family, however, only the siblings, generally, can be considered a peer group, as conceptualized in this book.

It follows that when members of a small group enjoy different status, power, privilege, decision-making rights, tenure, pay, opportunities, or rewards—particularly at multiple levels—they might not, in a useful sense, be peers (even if someone has labeled them a "team"). Players on a sports team can usefully be studied as a peer group, even though some are rookies and others veterans. The team owner, manager, and coaches, however, have such vastly different powers and decision-making privileges, and so are not peers of the players. Members of a cross-functional work team that includes both supervisors and line workers are, generally, not peers for our thinking here, nor are hospital surgical teams in which there may be surgeons, various certification levels of nurses, medical students, or interns. Performing members of the Rolling Stones, Wu-Tang Clan, or Alabama may be part of a small peer group, but when they meet with their agents,

> One of the first useful tasks of peer group scholarship, consequently, would be to operationalize* "peer group" *for the population of interest* to be studied, and then to acknowledge the *peer member differences* that may make a difference within that group.

business managers, stage crew, and road drivers, the "sameness" of power, pay, status, and responsibility are significant and threaten any image of member-perceived equality.

A university faculty of tenured English professors may be the peer group that we choose to study, but it would be useful, for example, to acknowledge at the outset that some of the faculty may be "associate professors," others "full professors," whereas some faculty may hold an "endowed chair." These English professors are paid differently, but may share voting privileges, departmental or professional service obligations, teaching responsibilities, and scholarly goals. Consequently, if we study such a group, we acknowledge, first, the differences; subsequently, we focus on the specific peer qualities that make these groups and their members appropriate for understanding the communication processes of peer groups.

❖ PREMISE BINDING EVERY PEER GROUP

The glue-like premise of a peer group is primarily member *sameness*—sameness in some way that is important to the members of that particular group. *How this sameness is evaluated by the peer members of a group may not be apparent to outsiders.* Furthermore, perceived member sameness may change over time and across situations.

Real-world *peer groups* are different, in significant ways, from the more-frequently studied problem-solving task groups (in organizations) or even laboratory or experimental groups (comprising college students earning course credits). *Peer groups* may have goals that are social (friendship), rather than task (generating ideas or competing against other teams), or both (monthly book clubs). Success may be measured by members' enjoyment or support of one another over time, rather than by their tendency to tackle a problem quickly. Membership may be short term ("We've got to find a way out!") or long term ("One for all and all for one!"). Real-world peer groups are naturally occurring—rather than artificially assembled—and, as a result, they are embedded in communities, surrounded by other groups, and their members have multigroup loyalties.

---

*"Operationalize," here, refers to the careful process by which we set specific boundaries on what is included or excluded for a specific term, construct, or population of interest. If we want to ask people about the top three rules for being a good friend, for example, we need to give each person we ask the *same* definition of "friend," so that everyone is answering from a similar perspective. If we want to study high school *cliques,* at the outset, we need to create a working definition we will use that makes it clear what observable characteristics we require for a group of adolescents to be considered a "clique," as opposed to a loose group of friends. Which high school groups will we count as a clique, and, furthermore, on what basis?

❖ EMBEDDEDNESS OF PEER GROUPS ACROSS THE LIFE SPAN

Peer relationships are worth more of our attention today because for many people multiple peer groups consume more of their lives than such groups did in earlier times. Children will spend considerable time with similar-age peers throughout childhood and adolescence; they are immersed in a world of peer groups.[5] The social structure of childhood peer groups is complex and demanding, requiring children to develop communication skills to successfully enter a new peer group, maintain coordinated play, coordinate competing goals with others, process novel social information, and respond appropriately to diverse situations. A child's inability to succeed with peer groups is a source of anguish and stress for some children and teens (as well as their families and teachers).[6] In fact, school days are anxiety ridden and lonely for those children and adolescents who are frequently rejected by peer groups.[7]

> I think that they excluded me because they just judge people by the outside, but those people are wrong. You should get to know people more.*

The successes (or hurts) of our childhood peer group experiences are stored in our memories and, consequently, are available to affect our behaviors, perceptions, and expectations of other people when we join new peer groups:

> Today everybody's going to Mary Ann's party in the group. I'm sort of the one that gets left behind. I'm not invited to the party so I won't do anything on the weekend. Anywhere the whole group goes, I don't. . . . I'm just the person that gets left back. Maybe they don't realize that I get left, that I'm there, but it happens all the time. (sixth-grade female student)[8]

Studying the various communication subcultures and outcomes of peer groups in childhood, adolescence, and adulthood is an important endeavor, in part because it illuminates the powerful influence on our satisfactions, anxieties, and behavior choices. This perspective is missing from a more limited study of the problem-solving or task groups that are typically embedded in organizations.

---

*Words of an Asian American adolescent female (SunWolf & Leets, 2003, p. 355).

❖ OVERVIEW

Peer groups construct their boundaries, socialize members, create identity, engage in tasks, resolve conflicts, enact rituals, adopt symbols, exclude outsiders, and even disband through *communication.* The talk and the symbols of peer groups help these groups create and recreate themselves across time and across tasks. Consequently, this book takes a communication focus concerning the study of peer groups.

This book offers a broad spectrum of theories, research findings, concepts, and predictions about what happens (or what does not happen) in groups of peers. It then uses those conceptual lenses to explore some of the peer group processes in early childhood ("Peer Groups in Childhood: Learning the Rules of Peer Play," Chapter 2), adolescence ("Peer Groups in Adolescence: The Power of Rejection," Chapter 3), neighborhoods ("Peer Groups in Neighborhoods: Hoodies, Homies, and Gansta Girls," Chapter 4), work ("Peer Groups That Super-Task: Hot Groups," Chapter 5), and community ("Peer Groups as Decision Makers: Juries," Chapter 6).

What's in it for me? (And what's not?) In short, this book offers the possibility of a bit more pleasure, a bit less pain in the (unavoidable) time you will spend with myriad future peer groups; more understanding, less confusion about what goes right and what goes wrong. If you are also someone who thinks about group processes, there's this added value: a whole lot of intriguing (empty) spaces are revealed (dots no one has connected, yet), that would benefit from your mindful attention. Select research findings are highlighted that involve various peer groups throughout—although no attempt is made here to review all of the research in these areas. This is not a comprehensive handbook, but rather a thinking guide to display some intriguing peer-paths.

The purpose here is to alter your consciousness about what is possible concerning the peer groups that impact your life—and, in doing so, perhaps to stimulate new thinking about your own behaviors and reactions in such groups; new understandings about the norms, rules, and dynamics of your peer groups; and, finally, to suggest additional avenues for research or theory-building.

Furthermore, all of the concepts and theories you may be familiar with from studying problem-solving groups, meetings, and input-throughput-output groups can be applied to *peer groups,* which may increase understanding of both. The groups you know best from your own life may cast new light on concepts you learned from studying groups with which you may have no personal experiences.

Peer groups attempts to function as both a window and a door: designed to let you *see* processes and consequences that may have been invisible to you, and, at the same time, allow you to *enter* and behave differently, with different results. This book is designed to showcase existing knowledge about several specific peer groups, as well as to offer theoretical perspectives that could serve as springboards for further inquiry into all small group communication processes.

Throughout, this book intends to challenge your current ideas about what does happen and what *can* happen in peer groups. This book flows from a profound belief that our satisfactions with and contributions to the multiple peer groups in our social worlds can be vastly enhanced.

Peer groups matter most because they are pervasive and because they impact our lives in multiple ways, throughout our life spans.

We will never be without them.

Critical Thinking About Peer Groups

- If, as argued here, the first useful task of peer group scholarship might be to "operationalize" what you mean by *peer group* for a specific group you are interested in understanding, consider the following groups and determine in what ways they do (or do not) meet this book's definition of peer groups: a Little League baseball team, a Girl Scout troop, a cardiac surgical team, members of a local university fraternity, and a group of tourists on a bus trip through the Amazon.
- Generate a list of several groups of people who may have something in common, yet who you believe would not usefully be considered "peer groups" as used here.
- If the second useful task for studying a specific peer group is to acknowledge at the outset the "peer member differences" that may make a difference within that group under various circumstances, consider with others what might be significant differences between the members of a certain peer group. First, agree with others about several groups that everyone believes are "peer" groups; second, consider, together, the differences that might exist between the members that might emerge under certain circumstances. How could they "make a difference?"
- Expand this critical thinking from hypotheticals to *your* real world. Consider several peer groups in your life and focus on (a) the ways you believe members consider themselves all to be equals, and (b) specific member differences that exist within each group of peers.
- Consider a peer group you are a member of and another one that you do not belong to, but admire. What forms of communication do each of these groups regularly use to construct identity, perform tasks, resolve conflict, communicate norms, regulate conduct, and create shared group culture?

1

Peer Group Lenses

Theories and Perspectives

the•o•ry, n., ***1.*** *a coherent explanation for events, behaviors, or observations.* ***2.*** *a proposed explanation or opinion, whose status can be tested.* ***3.*** *a guess or idea about what causes certain things to happen.*

We are all theorists. Our ideas about why things happen, or what causes people to behave in certain ways, are integral parts of our everyday thinking. Our theories might be mistaken, of course, but they often help us feel in control of our social worlds. Our everyday theories also guide our choices—mental tools that can make other people seem (a little) more predictable and life events seem (somewhat) less uncertain. Our personal theories organize our thinking, for better or for worse.

Social science theories operate in much the same way. Their goal is to increase understanding about the world around us. Scholars agree, however, that what distinguishes social science theories from personally held theories is that we attempt to test scientific theories with research, and then to extend or refine these theories in systematic ways.[1] *Formal* theories and models about social behaviors attempt to fulfill one or more purposes:

to describe behaviors,

to explain behaviors,

to predict future behaviors, or

to offer variables that may change behavior in the future.

For example, Decisional Regret Theory[2]

1. *describes* how people talk and think about significant decisions,
2. *explains* how the counterfactual imagining of possible outcomes appears when people face decisional choices,
3. *predicts* that people who cannot imagine a positive outcome of a decisional choice will reject it, and
4. *offers variables* that affect behavior (importance of the decision, unwanted outcomes of past decisions, resolution of imagined unwanted outcomes, anticipation of decisional regret, to name a few).

When a theory or model performs any of these four functions well, helping us understand our own behaviors and those of others around us, it can be argued that such a theory is a practical theory.

Groups can be frustrating places in which to find ourselves (yet they are entirely impossible to avoid), so it is not surprising that formal theories have emerged that attempt to explain group processes and group behaviors. Group research was recently described by leading scholars Poole and Hollingshead as a "fragmented and discipline bound," with few attempts to connect theory and research across disciplinary boundaries.[3] Aptly reflecting the vagaries of real life, however, not all group theories have received their fair share of attention from scholars. Furthermore, some theories that have managed to grab the lion's share of academic ink have devoted little, if any, attention to explaining or describing what happens in peer groups. *We spend most of our life-span group time communicating in peer groups.**

---

*And some of the behaviors of our peers in those groups seem to need a lot of explaining.

Seven useful perspectives are set forth to guide new thinking about peer group processes, drawing on the latest cross-disciplinary thinking about group dynamics. The specific assumptions of each is described to illustrate how each one is valuable in divergent ways, illuminates different constructs, and contributes to new knowledge about peer group communication, although each contributes differently. A visual tool is offered in Table 1.1 that sets out these theories and perspectives in a way that allows them to be more easily compared and contrasted. In Table 1.1, for each theoretical perspective included, the following is described:

- Key assumptions about groups from that perspective
- Applications to peer groups
- Challenges of studying group dynamics from that perspective

❖ THEORETICAL LIGHTS THAT ILLUMINATE PEER GROUP DYNAMICS

This book shines a spotlight on intriguing (and useful) theories or perspectives that have something to say about communication in peer groups—even though (or perhaps especially because) these newer perspectives have received less attention. These theoretical perspectives can help us understand more about group communication processes in general—and peer group dynamics in particular—because they invite more events to the scholarly group-thinking party.

Symbolic-Interpretive Perspective: The Effects of Symbol Usage

Symbols are one of the primary forms of communication that all people use to share meaning with others. Rituals, objects, colors, music, silences, humor, rewards, punishments, and language are symbolic tools for human communication.

Recently, Frey and SunWolf offered the Symbolic-Interpretive (S-I) Perspective as a useful theoretical framework for understanding small-group dynamics.[4] An S-I Perspective is concerned with

(a) understanding how group members use symbols,

(b) the effects of symbol usage on individual, relational, and collective processes and outcomes, and

(Text continues page on 14)

Table 1.1 Group Theories and Perspectives that Apply to Peer Groups

Theory or Perspective	Key Assumptions
Bona Fide Group Perspective	• Argues that a group cannot be understood as a fixed entity apart from the contexts and environments within which it is embedded. • Groups are characterized by permeable boundaries that are symbolic socially constructed; that can be negotiated, defined, and redefined through the members' interactions. • A group's boundaries are interdependent with its relevant contexts (financial, political, social, temporal, and cultural) and change as group membership changes.[1] • Relevant contexts, in turn, affect internal group symbolic activity (which can also affect the contexts).
Decisional Regret Theory	• Faced with making a meaningful decisional choice with uncertain outcomes, people experience anxiety, as they anticipate choice-regret. • Anxiety is uncomfortable. • People attempt to reduce that anxiety by imagining narratives about what might happen with each anticipated choice. • This story-thinking allows people to anticipate outcomes through self-talk (counterfactual thinking) or talk with others (counterfactual dialogue), as people search for a decision that has an *imagined* positive outcome.[2]

Applications to Peer Groups	Challenges of Studying Group Dynamics From That Perspective
• Focus on the symbolic aspects of communication within a group. • Focus on the effect of environmental issues, events, changes on peer group vitality, membership, satisfaction, or conflict. • Gives attention to the effects of multigroup loyalties of members on specific peer groups. • Rich explanation of peer group events by taking into account multiple situational variables. • Allows consideration of the relationship between various community peer groups.	• Acquiring access to bona fide groups in natural settings. • Context-bound findings may be applicable only to particular groups and situations. • Multiple variables make it difficult to reach certainty about cause-and-effect outcomes. • Dense data require complex gathering techniques. • Context-sensitive variables suggest a need for longitudinal research, examining peer groups over time.
• Peer groups facing important decision-choices will experience anxiety about uncertain outcomes. • Members will attempt to reduce their anxiety by imagining how choice-alternatives would play out, storying possible outcomes. • Members may attempt to reduce anxiety about outcomes from choices by talking with other members before making a decision, using group dialogue to anticipate imagined positive and negative outcomes of gift choices. • Peer groups or members with past experiences with those decisions will provide the primary pool from which members draw in creating imagined outcomes (positive or negative) for group decision-choices. Their secondary pool draws from shared stories others tell during counterfactual dialogue about possible choice outcomes.	• Acquiring access to real-world peer groups. • Gaining reliable access to mental processes in which regret is anticipated and storied. • Collecting distorted data in which group members did not accurately recall either their own thoughts or their dialogue with others. • Unwillingness of people to discuss their anxieties. • Collecting dense multilevel data, involving individual thoughts of multiple members, as well as group dialogue over more than one occasion. • Collecting data about negative emotions.

(Continued)

Table 1.1 Group Theories and Perspectives that Apply to Peer Groups

Theory or Perspective	Key Assumptions
Decisional Regret Theory	
Group Dialectical Perspective	• Tensions experienced by group members are both inevitable and pervasive. • Dialectical tensions will occur between contradictory elements that demand at least temporary resolution (wanting closeness and distance, for example). • Tensions will involve struggles with dependence and independence), as well as how to manage those tensions. • Tensions will be managed in a group through symbolic means of communication. • Groups are created in the dynamic interplay of dialectical tensions and communicative responses to those tensions among members.[3]

Applications to Peer Groups	Challenges of Studying Group Dynamics From That Perspective
• In addition to group decisions, individual members facing choices about communication will feel uncertain when they are anxious about unknown outcomes (how other members will react). • Members may choose to speak or remain silent, how to frame what they say, or the timing of their communication, based on the regret they anticipate as they story and imagine the reactions to their choices. • Some group members will have a greater tolerance for the anticipation of regretted choices than will others, which may result in disagreement or lack of support within the peer group.	
• Suggests a focus on the challenges that peer groups face that are unavoidable and recurring. • Useful for understanding the simultaneous need peers have to conform to one another and to be acknowledged as special or unique in their groups. • Explains adolescent struggles with both dependence and independence within their own peer groups. • Offers explanations for symbolic behaviors, dress, signals, and nonverbal behaviors as ways of managing natural peer group tensions within and without the group. • Suggests reasons why some peer groups are more cohesive, successful, and desired than others. • Suggests areas for intervention to improve peer group life.	• Member tensions are subjective and challenging to measure. • Tensions change over time and within single episodes. • It is difficult for a group outsider to gain access to or fully understand within-group tensions. • Individual group members will have idiosyncratic perspectives, tolerances, and understandings of any dialectical tensions experienced by other members.

(Continued)

Table 1.1 Group Theories and Perspectives That Apply to Peer Groups

Theory or Perspective	Key Assumptions
Social Comparison Theory	People have a basic need to know how they are doing, so they compare themselves to others they believe are similar (or slightly better) on dimensions such as same/different or superior/inferior.[4]
Social Identity Perspective	• Assumes groups provide a source of identity common to all members (social identity). • Members are motivated to sustain a positive social identity, which is accomplished through positive differentiation between their group and other groups.[5] • Group goals, norms, stereotypes, and influence are defined by the intergroup context (which can be implicit or explicit).

Applications to Peer Groups	Challenges of Studying Group Dynamics From That Perspective
• People are uncertain about how they are viewed by peer group members, so they compare their experiences to those of other members: What privileges did others receive at the same event? What rewards or punishments did other people receive for similar behaviors or omissions? • Peer group members will continually engage in two levels of thinking: Was my behavior or my effort *better or worse* than my peers in this group? In what ways am I similar to or different from my peers in this group? • Peer groups and individual members will continually engage in comparisons between their groups and perceived similar groups: better or worse, same or different? • Satisfaction with peer groups will be affected by these continual comparisons. • Peer group members may differ in the frequency and mental outcomes of their comparison to others.	• Social comparisons are not always highly conscious to individual members, thus it is difficult to accurately assess them. • The degree to which social comparison is healthy or dysfunctional in a peer group involves value judgments. • Social comparisons are painful for members to acknowledge. • Social comparisons of same-different or better-worse are not static or singular, but rather are dynamic and multidimensional. • Negative comparisons may produce fractured relationships with a group and lessen commitment and cohesion, even when accurate.
• Explains members' sense of the social groups to which they belong. • Describes members' identification with these groups and how members construct social identity based on this identification. • Explains what drives the dynamics that occur between ingroups and outgroups, based upon members' identification with their groups.	• Requires some measurement of inner cognitive processes. • Requires fieldwork in natural settings, rather than laboratory work. • Suggests attention to multiple groups to understand a single group.

(Continued)

Table 1.1 Group Theories and Perspectives That Apply to Peer Groups

Theory or Perspective	Key Assumptions
Social Identity Perspective	Groups that share identity are cohesive. This identity affects cohesiveness more than other variables (conflict, status, attraction, conformity, or relationships). • Face-to-face interaction is not necessary for social influence to occur within a group since group action will be activated by prototypical group position.[6]
Structuration Theory	• Assumes that social systems (groups) become patterned with respect to collective practices. • Assumes that group processes must be understood through analysis of the structures that underlie them. Underlying group structures will include rules (how things should happen) and resources (materials, knowledge, or skills) members create or bring, in order to sustain the group system. • Group processes are produced and reproduced through members' use of rules and resources.[7]
Symbolic-Interpretive Perspective	• Any group is a significant symbol to its members and to outside others. • The symbolic meaning of a group is created through the members' symbolic activities. • A group's symbolic activities are the predispositions of its members, its group practices and processes, and the products of those practices and processes. • Predispositions, practices, processes, and products of a group are influenced by the environments in which a group is embedded.[8]

Applications to Peer Groups	Challenges of Studying Group Dynamics From That Perspective
• Casts light on the effect of the groups in which a peer group is embedded on the behavior, cohesiveness, and identity of peer group members. • Offers an explanation for the function some peer groups perform for their members and the attractiveness of belonging to some peer groups.	• Benefits from a multivariable approach in which many factors (such as norms, language, status, roles, or dress) are examined within a single study.
• Casts light on the creation and emergence of rules within a peer group. • Acknowledges the resources each peer brings to the group. • Suggests that a peer group contains observable structures that, in turn, are produced and reproduced by peer members. • Takes both a macro view (group processes and environment, for example) and a micro view (rules and resources of individual members) of peer groups. • Makes room for the changes that occur as peer group membership shifts.	• Requires a focus on multiple variables that influence one another (such as words, behaviors, and outcomes) over time in a group. • Benefits from studies that involve real-world groups and is difficult to apply to short-term artificially constructed peer groups. Requires a knowledge of a group's history.
• Increases the importance placed on understanding relational dynamics of peer groups. • Suggests a focus on rituals within groups. • Illuminates individual practices of peer members, such as symbolic dress, language, signage, or colors. • Increases understanding of peer group behaviors as having symbolic meaning to members that may be invisible to, or misunderstood by, outsiders.	• Acquiring access to natural real-world groups and their communication processes. • Collecting the dense data needed to make claims about symbolic communication in groups. • Findings are context-bound, often limited only to particular situations. • Research is largely descriptive rather than predictive.

(Continued)

Table 1.1 Group Theories and Perspectives That Apply to Peer Groups

Theory or Perspective	Key Assumptions
Symbolic-Interpretivist Perspective	

[1] Putnam, L. L., & Stohl, C. (1990). Bona fide groups: A reconceptualization of groups in context. *Communication Studies, 41*, 248–265.
Putnam, L. L., & Stohl, C. (1996). Bona fide groups: An alternative perspective for communication and small group decision making. In R. Y. Hirokawa & M. S. Poole (Eds.), *Communication and group decision making* (2nd ed., pp. 179–214). Thousand Oaks, CA: Sage.

[2] SunWolf. (2006). Decisional regret theory: Reducing the anxiety about uncertain outcomes during group decision making through shared counterfactual storytelling. *Communication Studies,* 57(2), *1–29.*
Landman, J. (1993). *Regret: The persistence of the possible.* New York: Oxford University Press; and Roese, N. J., & Olson, J. M. (Eds.) (1995b). *What might have been: The social psychology of counterfactual thinking.* Mahwah, NJ: Lawrence Erlbaum.

[3] Smith, K. K., & Berg, D. N. (1987). *Paradoxes of group life: Understanding conflict, paralysis, and movement in group dynamics.* San Francisco: Jossey-Bass.
Johnson, S. D., & Long, L. M. (2002). "Being a part and being apart": Dialectics and group communication. In L. R. Frey (Ed.), *New directions in group communication* (pp. 25–42). Thousand Oaks, CA: Sage.

Applications to Peer Groups	Challenges of Studying Group Dynamics From That Perspective
• Useful to group leaders and facilitators by suggesting symbolic practices that create cohesion, satisfaction, and solve peer group challenges (for example, losing a group member or competing with other peer groups).	

[4] Festinger, L. (1957). *A theory of cognitive dissonance.* Stanford, CA: Stanford University Press.

[5] Tajfel, H. (1982). *Social identity and intergroup relations.* Cambridge: Cambridge University Press.

[6] Abrams, D., Hogg, M. A., Hinkle, S., & Otten, S. (2005). The social identity perspective on small groups. In M. S. Poole & A. Hollingshead (Eds.), *Theories of small groups: Interdisciplinary perspectives* (pp. 99–137). Thousand Oaks, CA: Sage.

[7] Poole, M. S., Seibold, D. R., & McPhee, R. D. (1996). The structuration of group decisions. In R. Y. Hirokawa & M. S. Poole (Eds.), *Communication and group decision making* (2nd ed., pp. 114–146). Thousand Oaks, CA: Sage.

[8] Frey, L., & SunWolf. (2005). The symbolic-interpretive perspective of group life. In M. S. Poole & A. Hollingshead (Eds.), *Theories of small groups: Interdisciplinary perspectives* (pp. 185–239). Thousand Oaks, CA: Sage.
Frey, L. R., & SunWolf. (2004). A symbolic-interpretive perspective on group dynamics. *Small Group Research, 35(3)*, 277–306.

(c) the manner in which groups and group dynamics themselves are the products of such symbolic activity.*

This perspective is particularly appropriate as a foundation at the outset of this chapter, because the S-I Perspective is a conceptual framework that holds or includes other group theories, including Symbolic Convergence Theory, Structuration Theory, the Group Dialectical Perspective, Decisional Regret Theory, and the Bona Fide Group Perspective (discussed individually below).

The S-I Perspective offers a dynamic understanding of two primary aspects of group life, the *use* of symbolic communication, and the *products* of such use. Group research that fits an S-I Perspective might investigate (1) the ways in which group members use *symbols* (words, objects, or actions that stand for or represent something else) to communicate, as well as the effects of symbol usage on individual, relational, and collective processes and outcomes; or (2) how groups and group dynamics themselves are *products* of this symbolic activity.

People (therefore, peers) may possess a basic need for symbols, which is said to distinguish them from animals. Even a cursory review of the underlying concepts behind the S-I Perspective demonstrates its applicability to peer groups. Frey has acknowledged the intellectual-philosophical-historical contributions to the S-I Perspective on group life. Symbols allow people to share meaning and to participate in collective action.[5]

Burke asserted that human beings were basically the "symbol-using (symbol-making, symbol-misusing) animal."[6] MacIntyre claimed that people are "essentially a story-telling animal."[7] Fisher offered an entire narrative theory of communication, based on understanding humans as *homo narrans* who organize experience into stories with plots, central characters, and action sequences that carry implicit and explicit lessons.[8] Furthermore, collectively, humans create and construct their realities. As people interact in social groups, new truths,

*The relationship between symbols, language, social interaction, and accomplishments (such as the construction of reality) was more fully articulated in *symbolic interactionism,* the study of how social interaction creates and maintains the self, shared meanings, and social structures. Mead (1934) concentrated on how symbols and communication give rise to the self, whereas his disciple, Blumer (1969), who coined the term "symbolic interactionism," focused on how having a common community of symbols allowed interactants to create shared meaning and to act together on the basis of that shared meaning.

perspectives, and "facts" emerge for the members of those groups. Social constructionism, therefore, is a basis for the S-I Perspective. Social constructionism has brought us concepts such as *transactive memory* (shared systems for encoding, storing, and retrieving information),[9] *shared mental models* (mental processes in which people create descriptions of how things function and predict future events), [10] and *negotiated order* (when group interaction does not proceed smoothly and individual behaviors do not mesh, individuals must adjust, through explicit or implicit negotiation).[11]

As a perspective, S-I makes certain assumptions about groups:[12]

1. Any group is, in reality, a concept socially constructed by its members and outside others, rather than an entity in an objective sense.
2. Groups are not fixed containers with static boundaries. They do not exist apart from their environments.
3. Groups are dynamic products resulting from the symbolic activities of their members, which are the primary means by which members create shared reality and groupness.
4. Studying the social construction of any group requires methods that focus on the use and interpretation of symbols.

Frey and SunWolf offered a visual model that articulated the symbolic nature of group dynamics and the constructs of interest to this perspective, reproduced as Figure 1.1.[13]

As portrayed in this model, an S-I Perspective on groups focuses on three aspects of symbolic activities that occur within a group, each of which contains specific constructs of interest:

1. symbolic *predispositions,*
2. symbolic *practices,* and
3. symbolic *processes and products.*

Symbolic predispositions are the tendencies a person may have to do something (that is, to act in a certain way), so symbolic predispositions include the ways in which people are initially inclined toward other people. As group members interact, the S-I Perspective suggests that they engage in *symbolic practices* (specific communication such as humor, metaphors, rituals, or stories). During symbolic practices, members

Figure 1.1 Symbolic-Interpretive Model of Group Predispositions, Practices, Processes, and Products

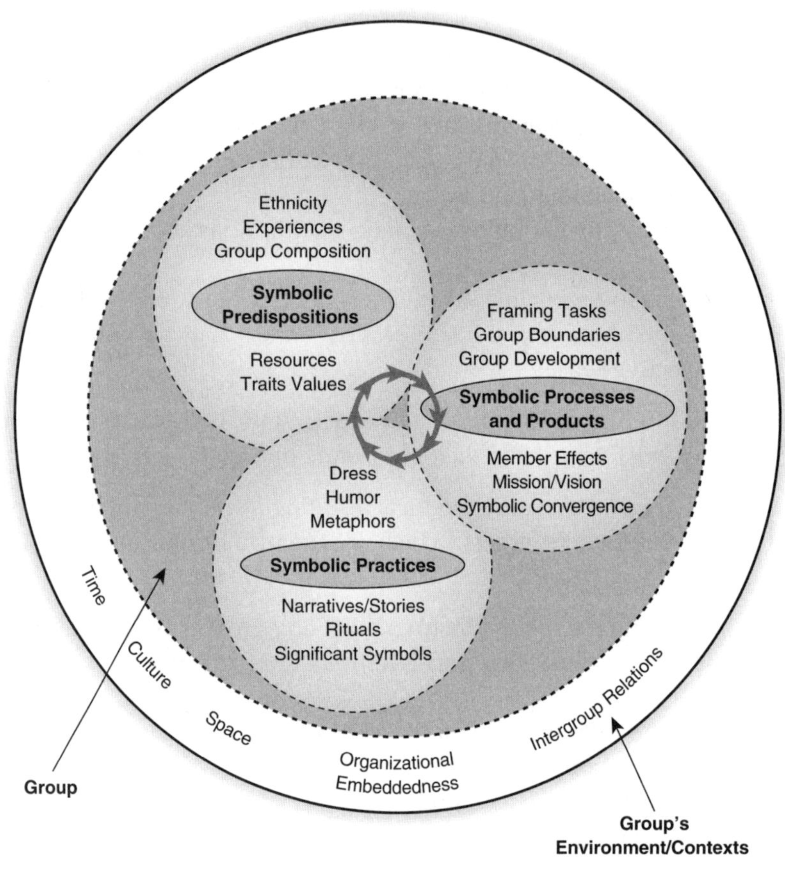

Source: Frey, L. R., & Sunwolf. (2005). The symbolic-interpretive perspective on group life. In M. S. Poole & A. Hollingshead (Eds.), *Theories of small groups: Interdisciplinary perspectives* (pp. 185–239, Figure 1). Thousand Oaks, CA: Sage. Reproduced with permission.

create *symbolic processes and products,* which refer to both macrolevel group dynamics (group identity and culture) and the specific outcomes of group symbolic activity (strategies, activities, or decisions). Frey noted that the linking together of processes and products, as opposed to treating them as separate entities, highlights their recursive and reflexive relationship, arguing that group culture is both a process and a product that results from and influences symbolic practices.[14]

The S-I model demonstrates that these domains are not mutually exclusive (as visually indicated by overlapping circles) and that they influence one another (as indicated by bidirectional arrows between circles). For example, ethnic diversity in a group (a symbolic predisposition) may create dialectical tensions in the group (symbolic processes and products) that need to be managed through particular rituals (symbolic practices) that subsequently affect how the diversity of new and current members is perceived and interpreted.[15] Symbolic predispositions, practices, processes, and products emerge and merge continually during group formation and, in fact, throughout the course of a group's life. Every group has permeable boundaries (as indicated by the broken circle surrounding the group, consistent with the Bona Fide Group Perspective, below) and is embedded in multiple environments and contexts that influence internal group dynamics and necessitate that a group interact with other individuals, groups, organizations, and communities in its environment.

When peer groups are studied through an S-I Perspective, the language, clothing, colors, rituals, music, writings, initiations, ceremonies, stories, metaphors, humor, or signage would be significant.

A classic study from the S-I Perspective would be that of Adelman and Frey in the 1990s, who described a peer group's grieving ceremony at a hospice.[16] They described how a balloon ceremony held for each resident who passed away (in which residents, staff, and loved ones stand together in a circle holding balloons tied to long ribbons, offer remembrances of the deceased, and then release the balloons simultaneously) not only helped members to remember the deceased but also to "re-member" as a group of peers, all of them, in this case, living with AIDS.

Using humor—which itself is a social phenomenon, generally requiring both a sharer and a recipient—is another symbolic practice engaged in by group members, often for the purpose of relieving the dialectical tensions associated with group life. One study, for instance, explored how humor was created in narratives of peers within work groups in a childcare center, in order to unify members in the face of divisive values and behaviors.[17] This study found that humorous stories, teasing, and jokes were employed to de-stress the work environment, create cohesion, and avoid miscommunication, and that shared humor provided a nonthreatening way of acknowledging group disagreement and diversity, and thereby promoted unity among group members by reinforcing the shared values. Negative humor can be targeted at one peer member, while intending to be symbolic of power, attraction, or entertainment. Children's sport teams constitute an underutilized but rich field for harvesting an understanding of dynamic processes in everyday peer groups. Fine, studying preadolescent culture in boys' Little League baseball, using taped accounts of instances of preadolescent verbal combat, reported the utility of the unfortunate victim to the group, as the lad unwittingly enabled his attackers to impress one another with their negative verbal skills.[18]

Social Comparison Theory: The Urge to Measure Up Against Others

Comparisons are odious.

—15th-century saying[19]

Throughout the last decade, Social Comparison Theory has reemerged as a popular area of inquiry for social psychologists, though researchers have begun to recognize the complexity of the comparison process and the theoretical significance of this complexity. According to Social Comparison Theory, people have a basic need to know how they are doing in their lives.[20] As a result, people continually compare themselves to others that they believe are similar (or slightly better), using dimensions in two general directions:

SAME/DIFFERENT

SUPERIOR/INFERIOR

This comparison to our *perceived* peers (or those we may consider slightly better than we are) begins in childhood. Children compare their appearance to that of children in their school classes, athletes compare their statistics to those playing similar sports or to those on the same team, students ask others in the class what grade they received on a test, workers check with coworkers to see if they are making more or less than they are, people compare the cars they drive to others' cars, people decide whether or not they have dressed appropriately by looking at others, and class reunions are replete with anxiety-producing social comparisons (some overt, some covert) about family, income, career, weight, and perceived general happiness, to name a few of the myriad everyday comparisons that season our lives. As a result of these comparisons, people trigger continual satisfactory or negative emotions for themselves. A large portion of our satisfaction with our own lives, in fact, is fragile—depending, as it does, on continual comparisons to our peers.

Members of peer groups perceive that they are *like one another,* in one or more salient ways; that is, group members are aware of their *peerness.* The working framework for distinguishing *peer groups* from other groups used in this book is particularly relevant for discussing Social Comparison Theory:

> **Peer groups** are made up of members who consider one another to be equals in terms of abilities, background, age, responsibilities, beliefs, social standing, legal status, or rights. *Not all group members agree about the equality of all other members at all times*, but there is overt consensus that members of the group are primarily equal.

In order to conclude that "sameness" exists, however, peers within the group must engage in both intragroup and extragroup social comparisons. Sometimes, in fact, other people do that task for us, pointing out how we measure up (or do not measure up) to our peers. Social Comparison Theory casts light on the dynamic intragroup and extragroup comparisons peer members continually make, resulting in a sense of belongingness, loyalty, superiority, exclusiveness, or satisfaction with peer group membership (or the lack thereof).

Using the lens of Social Comparison Theory, peer group researchers might see the manner in which member comparisons function to block or bond group relationships. Comparisons may occur at the individual member level (How do I measure up against her?) or at the group level (How does our group measure up against theirs?). Some groups, for example, purposefully isolate themselves from others, following comparisons that find others to be unacceptably "different," even among adults and within organizations. A case study of teams in a cooperative supermarket showed how the organizational hierarchy, the nature of the strong ingroup identity of some departments, and the lack of "living up" to the hoped-for cooperative principles resulted in relatively autonomous teams at the cooperative (teams that, essentially, attempted to treat themselves as separate containers).[21] The strong-identity peer teams avoided direct confrontation with team members they considered "external," including even those members who were assigned to their team.

It follows that when peers compare themselves to others in their group, jealously or envy may result. As one example, *group envy* (feelings of resentment or inferiority relative to other group members) was found to result between members, which can subsequently affect members' behaviors and even group outcomes. Duffy and Shaw documented the sabotaging nature of envy, which was directly and negatively related to group performance and cohesion, and which indirectly influenced members' absenteeism and satisfaction with the group by increasing their social loafing.[22] They offered the phrase "Salieri syndrome" to describe the emergence of peer envy in groups. Each member has a number of communication choices concerning how to manage that envy, when that emotion is recognized. It would be expected (but has not, to date, been widely investigated) that children and adolescents experience difficulty in choosing appropriate communication tools to cope with intragroup peer envy, for example.

Relevant for understanding of peer groups was a study that investigated how medical students compared themselves to their classmates.[23] The social comparison strategies of fourth-year medical students (peers) were surveyed to determine the influence of a student's gender when that student engaged in self-comparison within a peer group of mixed-gender others (in this case, those in the medical school class). Questions were included to see what comparisons were made about diagnostic ability, relationships with patients, clinical skills, writing of patient reports, and relationships with physicians. Results showed that women compared themselves to both male and female medical students in their peer class, while men tended to compare themselves only to male medical students in their peer class.

Other areas of study might include

- how peer groups regulate membership,
- how peer group leaders are chosen,
- how peers rely on the successes of outside peer groups to determine whether their group is worthy,
- how members "count" their value in a group,
- whether group satisfaction is based on negative social comparisons, and
- the degree to which social comparison leads members to leave or attempt entry into a peer group.

Group renewal rituals may occur after a member leaves a group, as the remaining members compare "what we were" to "what we are now." Sinclair-James and Stohl have described this group renewal among groups of peers as functioning to rejuvenate group identity.[24]

Structuration Theory: Creating and Recreating Group Rules or Structures

Structuration Theory attempts to explain the processes by which groups become patterned with respect to collective practices.[25] This theory starts by assuming that the key to understanding group practices is through analysis of the structures that underlie those practices. Structures are the *rules* (statements about how things ought to be done, the order of things, procedures, or consequences for infractions) and *resources* (such as materials, knowledge, experience, or skills) that members bring to generate and sustain the group system.

Structuration Theory, therefore, draws our attention to the processes by which group systems are produced and reproduced through members' use of rules and resources.[26]

The study of a peer group, using a structurational approach, might focus on

- the specific skills, networks, or resources members bring to the new group,
- the rules for behavior, communication, and tasking that members bring,
- the rules that are subsequently created during discussions (procedures, voting, or turn-taking),
- the structures suggested, rejected, or created to accomplish group goals,
- the manner in which leadership is enacted over the course of time and by various members,
- structure and rules to repair damages and cope with mistakes, and
- rules to govern member infractions of group rules or norms.

A structurational approach might examine both the initial structures of a peer group, and, later, the emergent structures and rules that are created or sustained during group communication processes. An ethnographic study of Alcoholics Anonymous (AA), for instance, is an excellent example of a peer group that relies on the perception that all members share similarity around their historical use and abuse of alcohol. In that study, the structures of the global organization (AA) were appropriated and reproduced in the local organizational (chapter), through recursive group practices and individual actions.[27]

Researchers using Structuration Theory have also focused on how small group members appropriate technology in their group interactions and how such appropriations mediate the impact of that technology.[28] Two aspects of technological structures have been distinguished that emerge during small group processes: the structural features built into a particular technology (for example, giving each group member one vote) and the symbolic spirit of a particular technology, the general goals and attitudes the technology promotes (for example, democratic decision making).[29] Poole and his colleagues have documented how different appropriations of the spirit of technology (group decision support systems) influenced the quality of team efforts.[30]

When peers disagree, those authors argued, and when this occurs in peer groups, a structure emerges to manage the argument. Scholars have used a structurational approach, for instance, to reveal the structuration of arguments in small groups, including how arguments are sometimes produced by "tag-team" discourse among members.[31] Meyers and Seibold analyzed the argument structures of many peer groups and concluded that group argument involves the production of interactive group discussion messages. These messages are patterned, rule governed, and collaboratively produced.[32]

Often, people enter new peer groups with preconceptions about what *structures or rules* ought to guide that group's processes. This is a structurational question of interest about group life. Researchers in one study used Structuration Theory to look at peers called for jury duty, for instance. The study reported that citizens waiting to be called for jury service in a courthouse jury assembly room had already brought with them (and were able to immediately describe and apply to hypothetical vignettes) specific *structuring rules* for their *anticipated* group verdict-rendering task, such as how time should be used and valued, how leadership should be created, what symbolic meaning should be contained in a note sent to the judge about the jury's competency to perform the task, and how dialectical tensions between loyalty to the group (jury) or loyalty to the organization (judicial system) should be resolved.[33]

Decisional Regret Theory: "Woulda/Coulda/Shoulda" Mental Minefields

> *I've never looked at the consequences of missing a big shot. When you think about the consequences, you always think of a negative result.*
>
> —Michael Jordan
> (retired American basketball player, 1963–)

I see it all perfectly. There are two possible situations—one can either do this or that. My honest opinion and my friendly advice is this: Do it or do not do it. You will regret both.

—Søren Kierkegaard
(Danish philosopher, 1813–1855)

The Decision is not the problem. The Outcome is the problem.

—Zen teaching

The outcomes of our decisions are not predictable, but that does not stop us from attempting to make future predictions before we settle on a decisional choice. In fact, decision tasks are not always welcomed (since decisions require complex cognitive effort), so it stands to reason that the more important any decisional outcomes, the greater the dislike of having to decide. Each time we make an important decision, we experience some uncomfortable dissonance—since there are often both advantages and disadvantages to all choices.*

People *do* reflect, it turns out, on roads not taken. Landman, a scholar who examined how people conceptualize and cope with "regret," described four destructive functions that regret can have for individuals:

1. Excessive regret can provoke excessive hesitation.
2. Specific regrets might be assigned excessive weight, resulting in distracting preoccupation.
3. Anticipation of regret interferes with future-oriented optimistic thinking.
4. Entertaining regrets entails an admission of personal deficiency or poor judgment.[34]

On the one hand, groups can be crippled by painful regrets (presently felt or remembered) that are being nurtured by *any* of their members. On the other hand, imagining alternative worlds (what-might-yet-be) is arousing, producing either soothing or discomforting feelings.

---

*One line of research describing mental processes *after* a decision has been made has pointed out that people often experience *post*-decisional dissonance. Further complicating decision-making challenges, immediately after making a decision some people have a tendency to focus on the *negative* aspects about the choice made, as well as the *positive* aspects of the choice rejected (Aronson, Wilson, & Akert, 1999).

The inevitability of *regret* creeping into our group decision-making tasks is more understandable when we pause to consider how the media surrounds us with reminders that trigger our fear of regretting a decision. Lottery advertising, for example, often exploits the normal human capacity for "what if" thinking ("It could have been you!"), inviting high personal involvement and perceived proximity of positive outcomes.[35]

Our everyday *pre*decisional thoughts and feelings of anticipated regret are also affected by consumer marketing strategies ("What if I find it cheaper someplace else?"), which attempt to anticipate a buyer's subsequent regret by offering price guarantees.[36] Personal ruminations may contaminate the enjoyment of life choices ("What if I had decided not to have children?"), while teams may become paralyzed by second-guessing strategies ("What if we hadn't traded our quarterback?"). There is something at once obsessively compelling and oddly unsettling about confronting the unrealities that *could have been.*[37]

Faced with decisions that are particularly important, a person can experience *anxiety* (while anticipating possible choice-regret in the future). Decisional Regret Theory (DERT)[38] describes a type of *communication* that emerges when someone is anxious about making a decision,* so DERT is useful for understanding a variety of decision events that occur among peers in decision-making groups:

> **The communicative dynamic of Decisional Regret Theory is the production, sharing, and reconstruction of predecisional imaginary narratives (stories about what might happen) that allow people to anticipate various alternative decisional outcomes before actually making the decision.[39]**

DERT predicts a specific type of shared communication (stories), hence it is useful for studying peer groups that face decision-making tasks. The type of communication DERT predicts is *counterfactual storytelling.* DERT predicts that under specific circumstances (having to make a meaningful decision), a person will talk to others about all of the imagined *unwanted* outcomes of the choices.

We all naturally engage in *thinking contrary to reality.* When we think, "If only I had been accepted at Harvard," we are thinking contrary to reality—the *reality* is that Harvard turned us down, yet we are imagining the wonderful things that might have followed, if we had

---

*Although DERT may be applicable to a number of communication contexts, including both intrapersonal (self-talk) decision making and dyadic (person-to-person) decision making, the theory conceptually emerged from a study of real-world peer group arguing (videotapes of jury deliberations).

been accepted. If we think, "I don't know the answer to question #7, so I am probably going to flunk this test, which means I will flunk the course, so I'll never graduate from college," the *reality* is that we just don't know the answer to question #7. The other thoughts are merely future dismal guesses that might not occur.

Thinking contrary to reality can be contagious in group settings, although some members may more often engage in it than others. As with the above examples of thinking contrary to reality, *counterfactual thinking* involves

- the mental creation (that is, imagining),
- of fictional story-plots (concerning either past events or anticipated future events),
- about *antecedent* facts that already occurred, and
- how an outcome might have been (or might still be) different.*

Social psychologists have investigated factors[40] that constrain or inhibit the production of counterfactual thoughts,[41] individual differences in counterfactual thinking,[42] the process of comparison during counterfactual thinking,[43] antecedents and consequences of upward and downward counterfactual thinking,[44] dysfunctional implications,[45] the impact of counterfactual thinking on emotion, attitudes, and behaviors,[46] superstitions resulting from anticipated regret,[47] gender bias and explanations for performance,[48] and counterfactual thinking in light of traumatic life events, to name a few. More recently, interaction between mood as a motivator to generate counterfactual production has been investigated. Scholars have reported that people in good moods generated the greatest number of downward (worse than reality) counterfactuals, while people in bad moods generated the greatest number of upward (better than reality) counterfactual stories.[49] Peers, it seems, have spent a lifetime engaging in what-if or if-only thinking, which would be expected to emerge, to some degree, during group decisional talk.

People who face making decisions generally want to avoid outcomes that might have them thinking afterwards with regret, "If only!" One way to avoid a bad decision is to engage in what-if thinking *before* the decision choice is made. DERT also predicts, however, how *listeners* might respond.

---

*For a full discussion (with group dialogue examples) of how counterfactual thinking emerges for peer group members during jury deliberations, see SunWolf (2006).

When someone who is trying to make a decision shares *imaginary narratives* (what might happen if), listener(s) might (1) reproduce the story, (2) alter the story, (3) create an alternative story, or (4) disconfirm the story. In particular, when we imagine unwanted outcomes from a decision and share our mental stories with others, some people will agree with us, while others, instead, will tell us different imaginary outcome stories that have more positive endings. Decisional Regret Theory argues that an individual will not make a decision unless that person can at least *imagine a positive outcome* from the decision, or, alternatively, *imagine a positive way of handling any imagined negative outcomes* of the decision.

How might regret or counterfactual thinking emerge during small group decisional talk? Figure 1.2 is a moving model (sequential), illustrating the emergence of shared (anticipated) decisional regret by members in a group. Figure 1.2 should be viewed from the bottom to the top, sequentially.

A complete model, visually describing the entire process of regret thinking and regret talk in groups appears in Figure 1.3.

Additionally, Figure 1.3 illustrates the emergence of groupregret (see also Appendix), decisional deadlock, the restorying of any imaginary outcome tales shared by group members, and, finally, the sequential nature of counterfactual thinking about decisions.[50] The next decision may be impacted by how counterfactual talk was handled by a group for previous decisions.

Since it is natural to evaluate our life events not simply by the reality of what comes to pass, but also by thoughts of *what might have been,* it follows that some peer group members may be constantly revisiting unwanted outcomes of their group decisions, as well as attempting to avoid future poor-decision-making outcomes.* Decisions are a pervasive part of every peer group's life.

Research adopting DERT to predict or explain group behavior, processes, or outcomes might focus on decisions peers make about

- how to best recruit new members,
- how to handle deviant group members,

*In fact, Sherman and McConnell (1995) compellingly argued that staying focused in the present is a challenge for people, since our minds constantly wander to the past (last night or years before), with floodings of nostalgia about people, relationships, or experiences.

Figure 1.2 Sequential Model of the Emergence of Shared Anticipated Decisional Regret in a Group

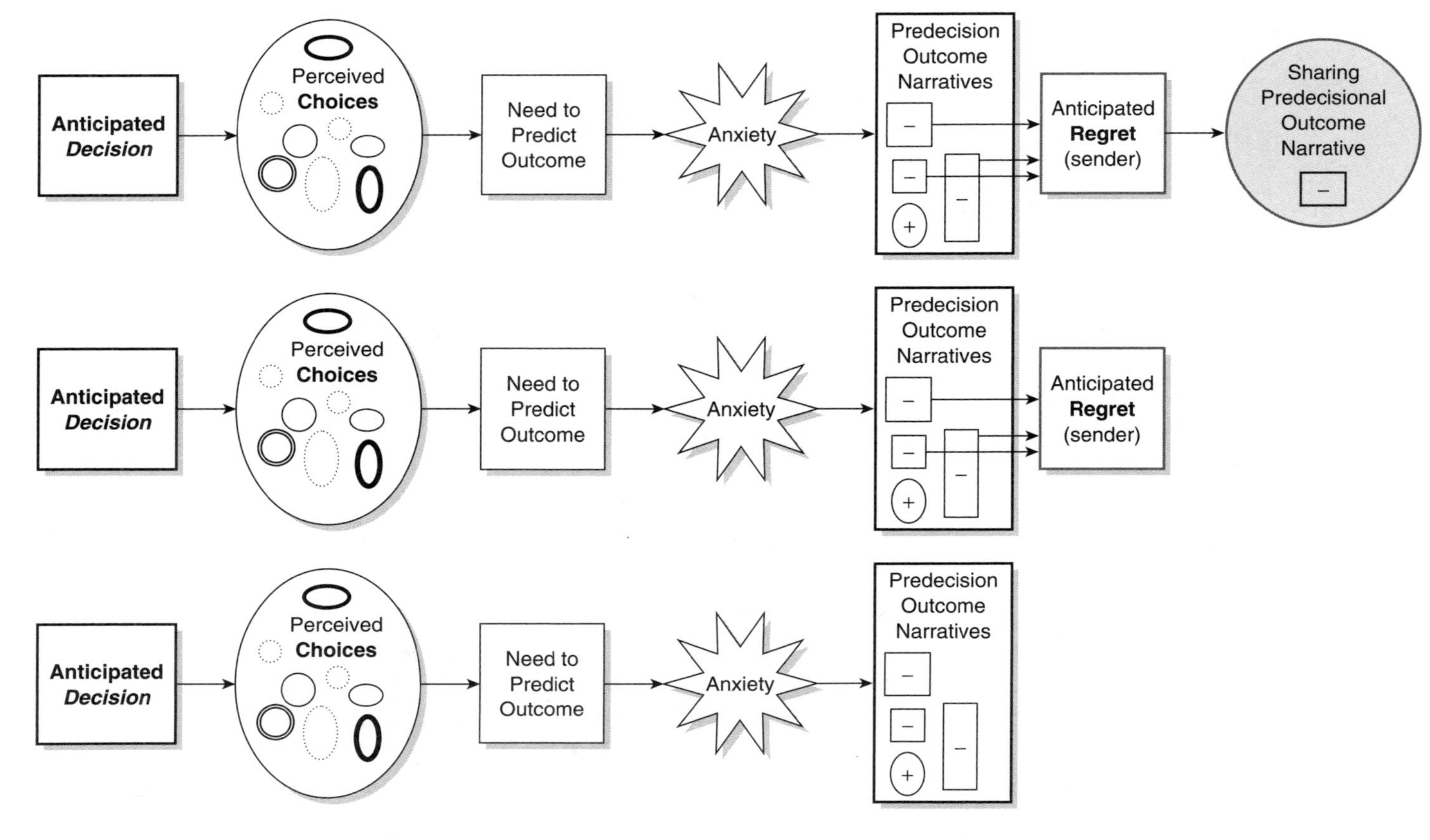

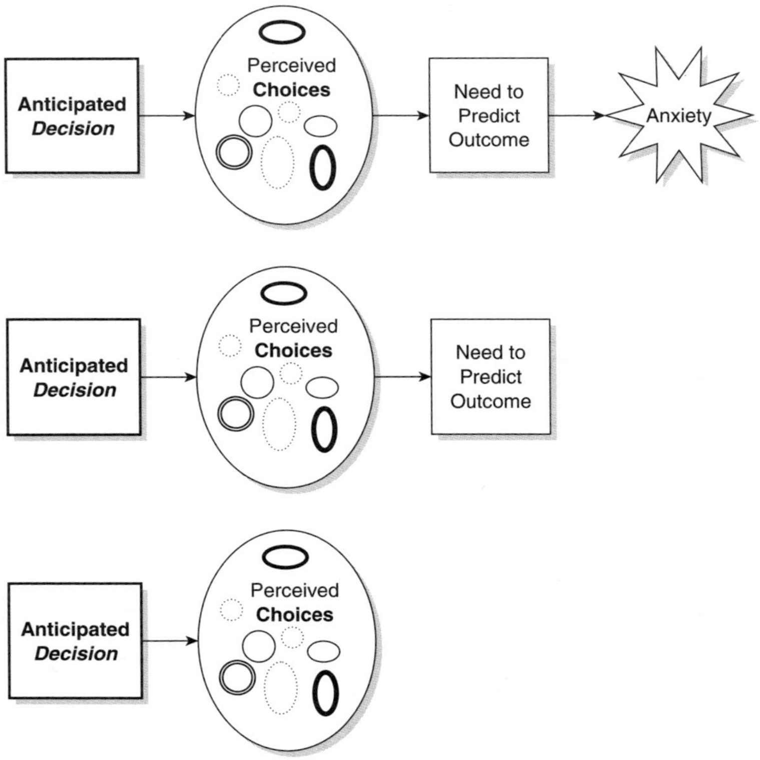

Anticipated ***Decision*** → Perceived **Choices** → Need to Predict Outcome → Anxiety

Anticipated ***Decision*** → Perceived **Choices** → Need to Predict Outcome

Anticipated ***Decision*** → Perceived **Choices**

Source: Author.

Figure 1.3 Decisional Regret and the Production of Shared Counterfactual Stories to Avoid the Decision

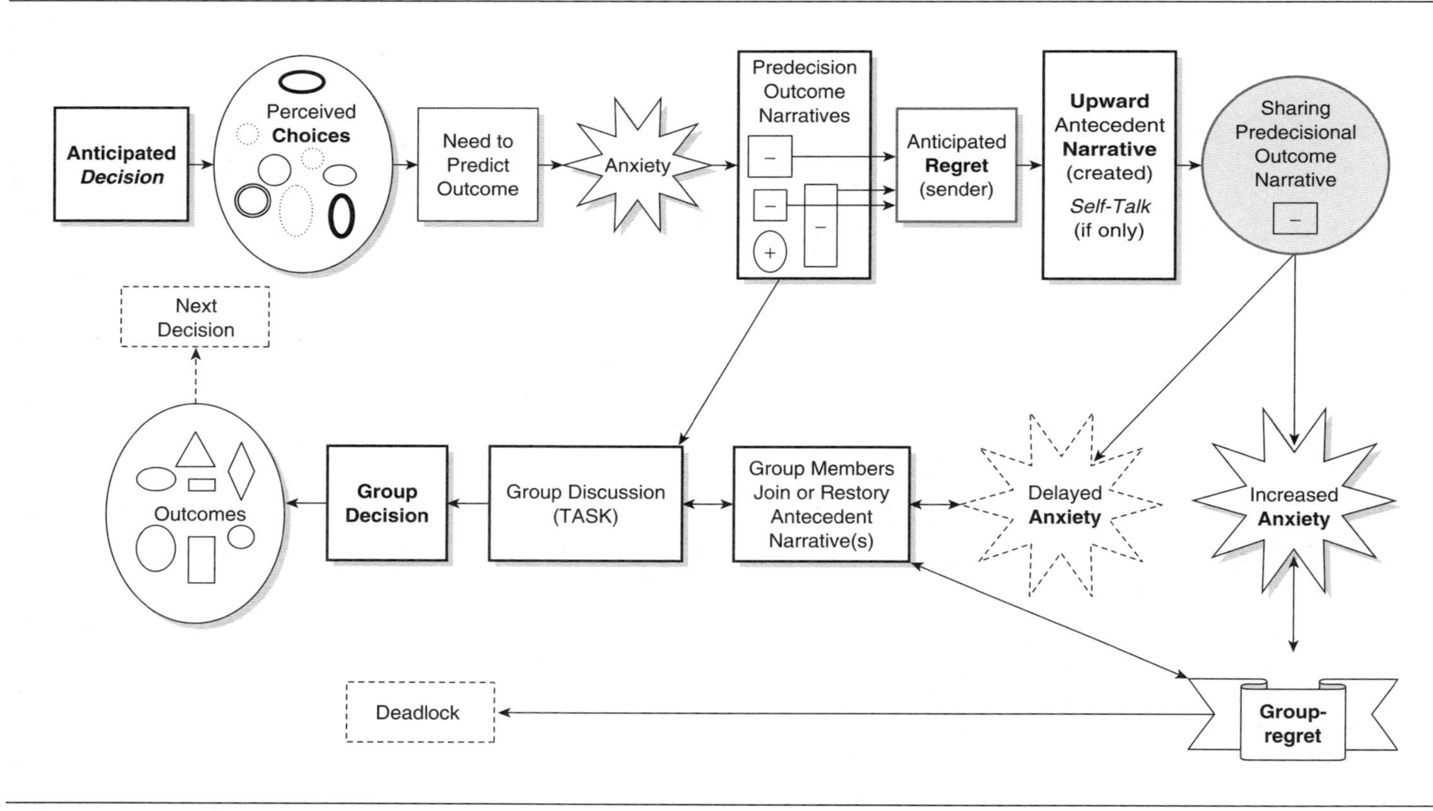

Source: Author.

- what activities deserve the group's commitment,
- what rules are needed,
- how to generate more ideas,
- who should lead,
- how to deal with member behaviors,
- what ceremonies to adopt,
- how to win (beat the competition) more often,
- how to deal with crises, threats, or challenges,
- how to do things faster,
- how to please more people,
- how to deal with slackers, or
- how to construct positive branding of their group to outsiders.

Decisions and decisional consequences are a part of every peer group's life, whether the group is on the playground, on a ball field, listening to evidence in a courtroom, hanging out together in a neighborhood, performing surgery, worshipping in a church, making music on a stage, flying planes, exploring new territories, sailing a boat, or trying to survive on a battlefield.

Social Identity Perspective: Identifying Us and Them

Father, Mother, and Me,
Sister and Auntie say
All the people like us are We,
And everyone else is They.

—Rudyard Kipling
(English author and poet,
1865–1936), *We and They*

Sometimes we define ourselves by exclusion. We may come to make sense of who we are, as individuals or as groups, by gaining clarity on who we are *not*—as well as who is *not* welcome in our groups.

A person's identity is shaped and reshaped by the groups to which he or she belongs. Peer groups, consequently, can have a powerful influence on our personal identities (whether we are members of these peer groups or whether we are outsiders looking in). An individual's identity is also shaped by the groups that exclude him or her, or the groups that person *chooses* not to join ("Include me out!"). Likewise, a small group defines itself, in part, by member exclusion and group boundaries. Unchecked inclusion, in important ways, blurs the clarity about who we are as individuals or as groups. Social Identity Perspective has been available since 1982, yet remains underutilized by scholars who study small groups. This perspective helps explain a specific social need to perform identity *by exclusion* of others.[52]

While frequently applied by multicultural and intergroup scholars,[53] the Social Identity Perspective has been used less by those who study small group processes—yet the perspective offers rich insight into peer group dynamics. Social Identity Theory argues that our social identities are primarily determined by the groups to which we belong. Consequently, we are motivated to join the groups we perceive to be most attractive. Once we are in the group, we give them our resources and evaluate them more positively than we evaluate groups to which we do not belong.[54] As a result, we develop a sense of "us" and "them," which influences, in turn, our sense of self.

Ingroups and outgroups are constructs of interest to the Social Identity Perspective. Social identities are said to be primarily based on the comparisons that people make between *ingroups* (groups we belong to) and *outgroups* (groups we do not belong to). The Social Identity Perspective is, as a result, consistent with Social Comparison Theory, though Social Identity Perspective narrows the focus of the comparison of interest to that of ingroups and outgroups. The basic premise is that, once a group is formed, subsequent pressures to evaluate one's own group positively (using comparisons to outside groups) leads peer groups to attempt to differentiate themselves from other similar groups.

Social Identity Perspective and the Theory of Thin-Slicing

The human brain's cognitive-thinking-associating activities take place at high speed, on multiple simultaneous levels, and are continual.

A key concept embedded in the Social Identity Perspective is the fact that our ingroup outgroup thinking, while inevitable, may be either *mindless* (we are unaware of it) or *mindful* (we know we think that way). We all hold on to (and are influenced by) more outgroup thinking than we realize.

Implicit associations, for example, are mental connections our minds make between two separate things. We are largely unaware of the way implicit associations happen in our thinking. Furthermore, it is difficult to turn off this implicit thinking. That is, when it comes to thinking about other people, we are often thinking unaware.

This mindless implicit social thinking nonetheless influences our experiences in peer groups—as well as our assumptions about groups to which we do not belong. One opportunity to obtain a glimpse of the thinking-unaware-about outgroups that your own mind experiences is available online at the Harvard University Web site in a study called, "Project Implicit."* First brought to my attention by author Malcolm Gladwell, I have shared this online exercise that measures our own mental associations with lawyers, judges, law students, and undergraduates, all of whom have been amazed about what they learned about their own "mindless" thinking:**

> We are all (often) willing to let a little bit of knowledge go a long way, when it comes to thinking about other people.

We get hunches about other people (especially those we know little about) and our brains love to leap to conclusions—rather than wade through unfamiliar murky thinking places.***

Malcolm Gladwell's *Blink* is an extraordinarily useful concept for understanding and strategizing about the snap judgment functioning

---

* Implicit.harvard.edu/implicit/demo. The demonstration tests, and *not the actual study,* give you feedback about how your thinking compares to that of other people. One of the most revealing demonstration tests is the RACE IAT, because we believe we know our biases. A wide variety of other tests are also available, including Arab-Muslim IAT, Sexuality IAT, Asian IAT, Gender-Career IAT, or Age IAT. Your measured bias on each scale that you choose will be immediately given to you. Share this Web site with friends, family, coworkers, and colleagues to gain great insight into the outgroup and ingroup thinking of people you know. (Feel free to participate, later, in the full Harvard study, rather than just the "demo." Due to the methodological requirement of random assignment, however, you cannot pick which sub-tests you will do on the full study.)

**One of the most frequent results, in fact, of exposing people to this intriguing exercise is that a law student, judge, or undergraduate returns to report that they insisted that their roommate, coworkers, colleagues, parents, or true love take the same test! It appears that we are equally fascinated with the mindless thinking and associations of those with whom we work, live, or love. (Social Comparison Theory, discussed earlier, suggests that we evaluate our own test results about our thinking by seeing the results of those with whom we associate.)

***The human brain loves a short-cut. Our **social hunches** are the modern manifestation of the *evolutionary adaptive unconscious,* acting like a giant computer that quickly and quietly processes large quantities of novel data. The brain's decision-making parts are capable of making quick judgments based on little information when sizing up the world, in order to warn us of danger: this is a good thing. However, making quick judgments about other people: not so good.

of a human's thinking brain.* In the everyday world, "snap judgment" carries a negative connotation (as in, "*Hold on, don't make any snap judgments, here.*"). We assume that the quality of a decision is directly related to the time and effort that went into making it. "Haste makes waste." "Don't judge a book by its cover."

What if, instead, some of our most profound judgments about other people were the products of rapid cognition (snap judgments)? What if our spontaneous impressions and conclusions about a new person happen in *two seconds?* The Theory of Thin-Slicing (see Appendix) explains how our frugal brains are willing to let a little bit of knowledge go a long way. Our brains thin-slice the available data in order to make that data manageable. Thin-slicing describes the ability of our brains to find patterns in situations and behaviors, based on *narrow slices* of experience or information:

We thin-slice other people and, correspondingly, they thin-slice us.

For peer group perceptions, this mental tendency has a lot of explanatory power.

One theory that lets us use blink and the Theory of Thin-Slicing when studying peer groups is Social Identity Theory (see above and Table 1.1), since this theoretical perspective focuses our attention specifically on ingroup versus outgroup thinking. Social Identity Theory was developed by social psychologists and offers a rich perspective from which to understand the social behaviors and thinking about peer groups.

From this perspective, group scholars might examine

- the speech styles of gangs,
- group processes and leadership on competitive sports teams,
- hostile groups of students on a campus,
- cliques in high schools,
- neighborhood racial tensions,
- elite military squads, or
- the sorority and fraternity "Rush Week," where outsiders stressfully compete for bids from desired groups to become insiders (even when the standard to become a peer is admittedly fuzzy).

*This book will make you see other people and yourself in a different way. Gladwell (2005) revolutionizes the way we understand our inner thinking worlds. How do our brains really work, when it comes to thinking about other people?

Peer group scholars taking an ingroup versus outgroup perspective, consequently, would be interested in the effects of sport team rivalries (both between teams and between avid fans of sport teams) on peer member and group identities, on the identity-creating-maintaining role of group rivalries, or on the use of symbolic communication to display ingroup status (clothing, colors, or language, for example).

Conquergood's intensely participative and engaged ethnographic study of Chicago street gangs and the complex ways cultural space is claimed through identity not only with a neighborhood gang but, furthermore, through allegiance to either the People or Folks nation is an excellent example of knowledge that would be important to peer group students and scholars taking a Social Identity Perspective.*

Prosocial Helping Behaviors: Distressed Strangers in Our Pathways

Why should group scholars be concerned with prosocial behavior in the first place?

This book urges the enduring theme that we all live in a forest of peer groups, yet only some of these group are considered by us to be "our" groups, that is, those we perceive to be "like us," and a few we think of as "them," "enemies," or "outsiders." Furthermore, throughout our life spans, there will be occasions when we either need help from—or, alternatively, have the opportunity to render help to—someone "not of our clan."

A prosocial behavior approach may help us recognize some common and enduring issues about how our peer group affiliations, perspectives, values, and experiences impact *who we help* (or ignore) and *who helps us* (or ignores our needs). Prosocial research is profoundly about people encountering other people. As a result, it can also provide a powerful framework for understanding the variances in prosocial behaviors *within* peer groups: peer to peer. Not every peer group member, as pointed out before, is always equal to every other member, even within a peer group.

Living in a forest of social peer groups, it is, nonetheless, sometimes difficult to find a Good Samaritan when we need one. Too often,

---

*See Conquergood's (1994) description of gang systems, in particular Table 2.1, "Chicago Street Gangs Aligned with Nation," as well as Figure 2.1, "The Gang System."

individuals find themselves a member of an *outgroup* who nonetheless needs immediate help from an unfamiliar or hostile group in the path. The Parable of the Good Samaritan was, historically, a tale of hostile peer groups, each of whom nurtured intense ingroup vs. outgroup thinking. *Not* well known is the fact that the Samaritan, in the tale, had been in reality the *least* likely person to show compassion toward the Jewish victim.* Here is the backstory:

> The importance of the fact that this act of compassion was performed by a Samaritan rests in the historical reality that Samaritans were looked down on by Jews. In the time of this tale, Israel existed as a double nation, with another nation in between (much like the geography of Pakistan and India today). In the case of Israel, between the Galilean portion to the north and the Judean portion to the south, the nation in between was Samaria. Samaritans were believed to have been the descendants of intermarriages between Jews and local Gentiles (Philistines, Edomites, Syrians, and Moabites). Their worship focused on a mountain in Samaria, rather than on the mountain in Jerusalem. Jews considered Samaritans to be better than Gentiles, but inferior to Jews. Jews permitted Samaritans to travel freely in the two parts of Israel (since the Israelites often needed to pass through Samaria on their way from one part to the other). However, Jews and

*And behold, a lawyer stood up to put him to the test, saying, "Teacher, what shall I do to inherit eternal life?" He said to him, "What is written in the Law? How do you read it?" He answered, "You shall love the Lord your God with all your heart and with all your soul and with all your strength and with all your mind, and your neighbor as yourself."

So he said to the lawyer, "You have answered correctly; do this, and you will live." But the lawyer (desiring to justify himself) said to Jesus, "And who is my neighbor?"

Jesus replied, "A man was going down from Jerusalem to Jericho when he fell among robbers, who stripped him and beat him and departed, leaving him half dead. Now by chance a priest was going down that road and when he saw him, he passed by on the other side. Likewise a Levite, when he came to the place and saw him, passed by on the other side. But a Samaritan, as he journeyed, came to where the man was, and when he saw him, he had compassion. He went to him and bound up his wounds, pouring on oil and wine. Then he set him on his own animal and brought him to an inn and took care of him. The next day the Samaritan took out two denarii and gave them to the innkeeper, saying, "Take care of him, and whatever more you spend, I will repay you when I come back."

Which of these three, do you think, proved to be a neighbor to the man who fell among the robbers?" The lawyer replied, "The one who showed him mercy." Jesus said to him, "Go, and do likewise." *Luke 10:25–37*

> Samaritans did not mix socially. Jews did not want to risk their social position by being associated with inferior persons, and the Samaritans wanted as little as possible to do with the "snobbish Jews." This contemptuous relationship with Samaritans continued into New Testament times "for the Jews have no dealings with the Samaritans." For the Jews, the term "Samaritan" became a term of derision. Once, when the Pharisees were upset with Jesus, they were said to have used a Samaritan insult: "You are a Samaritan and have a Devil!" (John 8:48). Jesus began teaching that a new attitude must be taken toward the Samaritans when he passed through their towns, which he started to do instead of crossing the Jordan River to avoid them (John 4:4–5) and when he spoke with a Samaritan woman, contrary to Jewish custom (John 4:9). When asked whom to regard as our neighbor, Jesus told the story of the Good Samaritan—precisely because Samaritans were despised.[55]

Among social scientists, the behavior of interest is known as *prosocial behavior,* and some of us have it in larger doses than do others; it may also be contagious in groups. Researchers who study prosocial behavior ask, *Why do people help?* They also want to know the situational determinants of prosocial behavior and ask, *When will people help?* Finally, moving forward from the findings of their studies, researchers began to ask, *How can helping behaviors be increased?*

Few group scholars have examined the dynamics of prosocial behaviors in peer groups. Here, for the first time, you are invited to consider the profound connections between research on prosocial behavior, the Social Identity Perspective, and peer group dynamics.

At the outset, Social Identity Perspective necessarily invites our scholarly attention to the issue of *compassion* for others and how that impacts various peer groups. In fact, when compassion for others collides (as it must) with a peer group's ingroup versus outgroup division of the world, a (social) *group dialectical tension* emerges (see the discussion of Group Dialectical Perspective, below):

COMPASSION AND COMPETITION

HELPING AND OBSTRUCTING

What do we know about *prosocial helping behavior* that impacts peer group behaviors and processes? The most famous study to investigate helping behavior took place at a location that appeared likely to find considerable amounts of prosocial helping behaviors: a seminary. John

Darley and Daniel Batson designed a study that mirrored the parable of the Good Samaritan, wherein many passersby had failed to stop to help a man lying unconscious on the side of the road.[56] Those participants might be considered more altruistic, in fact, than most of us. They were seminary students preparing to devote their lives to the ministry. In the study, the students were asked to walk to another building, where they were told they would be recorded making a brief speech; some students were told they were late and should hurry, others were told there was no rush. Furthermore, some students were specifically asked to *speak about* the parable of the Good Samaritan.

As the seminary students walked to the building where they would lecture, each passed a man who was slumped in a doorway, who coughed and groaned, and who appeared to be in distress. Ninety percent of the seminarian students in a hurry did not help. Even when seminary students were *not* told to hurry, only 63 percent of them stopped to help the man in distress. (Seminarian students on a college campus!) Findings also, surprisingly, revealed that helping behavior did *not* increase for those seminarian students who had *just prepared a speech about the parable of the Good Samaritan.*

What explains why religious individuals would not help a groaning man, on their way to giving a talk about the Good Samaritan? Individuals vary, it turns out, in the degree to which each is motivated by prosocial helping behaviors (compassion), yet all people experience compassion for others (compassion is not a dichotomy but a continuum). Compassion does not consistently translate into action, and may, furthermore, be affected by our perceptions about whether someone in distress is "us" or "them."

Compassion comes in two major flavors: compassionate love for *close others* and compassionate love for *strangers.* According to the Social Identity Perspective, peer group members generally experience one another as close others, while they experience outsiders as strangers.* (Recently, Susan Sprecher and Beverley Fehr developed a

---

*Susan Sprecher and Beverley Fehr developed a scale for measuring compassionate love across relationships, depending on whether people were more or less religious/spiritual. Their working definition of compassionate love is useful for trial lawyers and suggests, in itself, ways to talk to jurors about compassion in their lives: "*Compassionate love* is an attitude toward others, either close others or strangers or all of humanity; containing feelings, cognitions, and behaviors that are focusing on caring, concern, tenderness, and an orientation toward supporting, helping, and understanding the others, particularly when the others are perceived to be suffering or in need" (Sprecher & Fehr, 2005, p. 630).

scale for measuring compassionate love across relationships and depending on whether people were more or less religious or spiritual.)[57]

Here are some of the generally agreed on findings from social science about people and prosocial behavior:

- *The empathy-helping connection.* When people feel empathy for another person, they will attempt to help for altruistic reasons, regardless of what they may gain.
- *A social modeling prosocial childhood.* Developmental psychologists have discovered that prosocial behavior occurs early in life and that parents can increase prosocial behavior in their children by behaving prosocially themselves.[58]
- *Prosocial behavior norms can be different for men and women.* Men and women learn to value different behaviors. This varies, furthermore, by culture and situation. In a review of more than 170 studies on helping behavior, two researchers found that men were more likely to help in chivalrous, heroic ways,[59] while women were more likely to help on long-term nurturing tasks.[60]
- *Mood affects prosocial behavior.* Positive moods provoke do-good behaviors in most people. Two researchers found that when they boosted the moods of shoppers in a mall in San Francisco and Philadelphia (by leaving dimes in coin-return slots of telephones), they were more likely to help someone (a confederate) who dropped a pile of papers. The effect was dramatic: phone users who didn't find the dime helped pick up papers 4 percent of the time, while dime-finders helped 84 percent of the time.[61] The effect is robust and not limited to occasions when we find money. People are more likely to help others when they are in a good mood after doing well on a test, receiving a gift, listening to pleasant music, receiving a compliment, or landing a job. It turns out that good moods increase helping for several reasons: good moods help us look on the positive side of life and it allows us to prolong the good mood.
- *Guilt triggers helping.* While bad moods can diminish helping behavior, guilt about anything can trigger it. One researcher found that churchgoers were more likely to donate money to charities before attending confession than afterward (presumably because confessing to a priest reduced their guilt).[62]
- *Cognitive-overload reduces helping.* The effect of "information overload" is such that prosocial behavior motivation diminishes as cognitive tasks multiply. When someone is bombarded

with task stimulation or stress, that person may feel overloaded and, consequently, have little energy left to give to strangers or outsiders.

- *Idle bystanders reduce helping.* Remember the Kitty Genovese incident reported by the media? In March 1964, she was murdered in an alley in New York City although many people admitted that they heard her cries for help. In Fredericksburg, Virginia, a convenience store clerk was beaten in front of customers who did nothing to help, even after the attacker left and the clerk lay bleeding.[63] A Good Samaritan peer, for example, may be less likely to aid someone in distress while in the presence of a "bystander" member of the peer group who is also not helping.
- *In the presence of their peers, "diffusion of responsibility" may block some individuals from helping an outsider.* In one experiment, when people were led to believe that they were the only one listening to a student have a seizure, 100 percent helped within two and a half minutes, and most had helped within 60 seconds. When people were led to believe that there was even one other student listening, the helping dropped dramatically, and it dipped shockingly if people believed four other students were listening.[64] This has been described as a "diffusion of responsibility," whereby each bystander's sense of duty to help a stranger *decreases* as the number of others present *increases.* An individual does not feel a strong sense that it is his or her personal responsibility to take action when there are others present who could (but do not) help.

It becomes clear that the literature on prosocial helping behavior has powerful explanatory power for examining the values, choices, and processes in competitive peer groups, gangs, cliques, military troops, and, especially, peer groups embedded in complex hostile environments. As hostile ingroup vs. outgroup thinking increases, it might be predicted that individual peer member prosocial behaviors decrease.* Alternatively, a focus on prosocial behaviors and social identity (us vs. them) would be useful for understanding differences between prosocial peer groups, such as religious groups, community

*"The whole idea of compassion is based on a keen awareness of the interdependence of all these living beings, which are all part of one another, and are all involved in one another." (Thomas Merton 1915–1968, American monk, poet, and author)

social activist groups, relief agencies, specific Peace Corps task groups, Doctors Without Borders, and various task groups within charities. Finally, prosocial behaviors and social identity perspectives illuminate how groups may seek to survive and maintain a vital identity by limiting prosocial helping to within group members.

The Group Dialectical Perspective (discussed next) further illuminates these ingroup versus outgroup tensions and dynamics for peer groups.

Group Dialectical Perspective: Managing Unavoidable Social Tensions

> *In any free society, the conflict between social conformity and individual liberty is permanent, unresolvable, and necessary.*
>
> —Kathleen Norris,
> (American novelist, 1880–1960)[65]

Group Dialectical Perspective (or Dialectical Theory) initially developed to offer students and scholars an alternative view of relationship issues in *dyads* (two people), rather than groups (three or more people).[66] A Group Dialectical Perspective encouraged a focus on how people manage the normal tensions between *opposing desires and needs* in close relationships.[67] Three pairs of dialectical tensions that are consistently mentioned in the dyadic relationship literature concern competing needs for both:*

Connectedness and Independence

Predictability and Novelty

Openness and Privacy

In addition to identifying various reoccurring dialectical tensions in close relationships, scholars have described a number of interpersonal strategies that people use in an attempt to manage or balance these tensions.

---

*Excellent discussion of these basic dialectics, as well as an overview of Relational Dialectics Theory, can be found in West and Turner (2007).

Since we all spend significant parts of our lives in small groups, it follows that these same three sets of unavoidable opposing forces or needs would regularly emerge in our group relationships. As a result, scholars have moved toward Group Dialectical Theory, as evidenced by the work of Kramer, who offered a communication theory of group dialectics.[68] He suggested that four main issues that may trigger dialectical (with subcategories) tensions can usefully be applied to study group dialectics:

1. member commitment
2. group activities
3. group membership
4. behavioral norms[69]

Encouraging future group scholarship using a dialectical perspective, Kramer also suggested a number of strategic choices that members have for managing these tensions: talking about them, remaining silent, avoiding them (people or issues), minimizing them, segmenting them, or denying them. Kramer also pointed out that members of a group may combine or alternate between coping strategies.

As described above in the discussion of the application of Social Identity Perspective to group work, normal *prosocial* motivations may collide with group affiliation loyalties creating at least two dialectical group tensions:

COMPASSION AND COMPETITION

HELPING AND OBSTRUCTING

In addition, unwanted or unanticipated changes that occur within peer groups may trigger dialectical tensions. Changes in a group's membership, for example, are evidence of the inevitable dialectical tensions that occur between *inclusion* and *exclusion* of people, accompanied by a second dialectic: *tolerance* and *judgment* of others. A third dialectic triggered when peer membership changes involves choices between *emotional expression* and *emotional management* (both of which are necessary).* Hence, three more dialectics for peer group members are possible:

*As shown above, dialectical tensions are generally described in paired "ands," which gives expression to two unavoidable colliding tensions that coexist (requiring, as a result, relational management). Both tensions must be accommodated.

INCLUSION AND EXCLUSION

TOLERANCE AND JUDGMENT

EMOTIONAL EXPRESSION AND EMOTIONAL REPRESSION

University undergraduates are often assigned to task groups in their classes, which traditionally causes tension, frustration, and complaints from many. It may be that a dialectical perspective can help explain the distress peers feel when asked to work on a task with other peers:

1. Students have experienced few, if any, models for leadership by peers (their teams had coaches, their scout troops had leaders, for example).
2. Students have a high need to belong, as well as to receive approval from their peers, which may trump the class task and approval (grades) from the teacher, causing some peers to remain silent rather than prodding their peers to work harder. (See Appendix: social loafing, sucker effect, and free rider.)
3. Social fears may collide simultaneously with social needs. (See Appendix—inclusion fragility—wherein students simultaneously experience being in a peer group and being at risk for exclusion.)

Symbolic practices are used by peer groups to survive such changes. An exemplar of a study that illuminates peer group dialectical tensions in an unusual religious group was the study of a witches' coven.[70] A coven is, in fact, an excellent example of a group whose members consider themselves to be similar in a significant way that may not be obvious to an outsider. The coven of peers that was studied faced a complex transition after the loss of one of its members, which demonstrated the dialectical tensions that had to be solved and survived by the remaining members. Group meetings that followed the member who left included exhaustive *metacommunication* (communication about communication), with stories produced and shared about the group's history, founding vision, core group values, group structure, and members' hopes for the future. Performed *ritual imagined stories* engaged in by coven members during this period cast themselves as protagonists, with forces antagonistic to the group depicted as enemies, threatening the group's existence and stability. Coven members also engaged in symbolic strategies, such as a planned farewell ritual, to recognize the loss of the member, while simultaneously preserving the group's desired identity and continuity.

Another example of group research that takes a dialectical perspective with peer groups is Kramer's ethnographic study of a community theater group.[71] He described one member's frustration with the group that emerged from dialectical tensions between the need for precision and the need for flexibility. Describing the group members' frustration with the lack of planned leadership at rehearsal, one member described how she managed her need for planning with her need for flexibility:

> It was irritating me at first and then I just sort of changed perspective and decided this would be my free time and I was going to, you know, read a book or talk with people, because I was just so irritated by it that I—it wasn't helping the situation any, so I was just sort of like, well, change perspectives. Make the best of it.[72]

A study of children's peer groups[73] found that adolescents who were members of desired peer groups at school experienced tension between their need for group belongingness and their need for individual value autonomy. When describing incidents where they personally disagreed with their peer group's rejection of another child, many described choosing the strategy of remaining silent, which was painful for them. In fact, across 682 adolescents, fears of group reprisal and general social fears accounted for more than 60 percent of the reasons that adolescents perceived for feeling paralyzed to speak during peer group exclusion events they disagreed with at the time (findings were consistent across gender and ethnicity). Functionally, children may have fewer social strategies available to them for managing peer group dialectical tensions, even though the emergence of those tensions is inevitable and even though successfully managing them may be necessary to continued peer group inclusion.

Thinking forward, the application of a Group Dialectical Perspective to peer groups remains an underused and unexplored theoretical perspective, particularly as it applies to everyday peer groups. Which competing tensions emerge in cliques and professional teams, for example? Which strategies do peer group members use to manage their loyalty to the group with their desire for autonomy? How do faculty scholars, as a departmental group of peers, manage commitment to group and commitment to their personal lives? (Who, in fact, do professors consider to be members of their peer group at universities? Must others have tenure or even full professorship to be peers?) To what degree are people aware of dialectical tensions in their important peer groups, and are they aware of the dialectical tensions that their peers experience? Do competing dialectical tensions in peer groups prevent some members from leaving an unwanted group or from disavowing a group's norms without leaving?

To date, however, at least eight robust paired dialectical tensions have emerged from various scholarly programs that offer useful lenses for understanding and describing peer group processes. Each pair of opposite needs or desires could be expected to emerge during normal group life, and, as a result, could be expected to confront a peer group with the additional task of managing the following competing or unavoidable tensions:

Connectedness and Independence

Predictability and Novelty

Openness and Privacy

Compassion and Competition

Helping and Obstructing

Including and Excluding

Tolerance and Judgment

Emotional Expression and Emotional Repression

The Bona Fide Group Perspective: Walking the Peer Group's Neighborhood

> *I grew up playing war. We threw dirt and rocks at each other. We'd lead attacks. We'd break up into squads. It became a neighborhood thing for a while, our neighborhood against the other neighborhood. There was always a war breaking out somewhere.*
>
> —David James Elliott (Canadian actor, 1960–)*

Since real-world peer groups are naturally occurring (rather than artificially assembled). As a result, peer groups are *not* best understood when considered in isolation from their environments. Peer groups are richly embedded in communities, surrounded by other groups; each of their members has, in turn, multigroup loyalties and shifting group memberships. Each peer group is surrounded by other groups that have political, geographic, religious, social, familial, historic, or

*Elliott appeared regularly on the television program *JAG*.

economic power (to name a few) that can affect the peer group. Peer groups face religious and political environments, and economic stresses and influences from their neighborhoods. The Bona Fide Group Perspective (BFGP) attempts to account for the effects and outcomes of this embeddedness (Table 1.1).[74]

A Bona Fide Group Perspective (BFGP) encourages us to study naturally occurring groups and these complex contexts, hence this perspective is particularly important for understanding the dynamics of peer groups. The BFGP challenges a traditional view of small groups as "fixed containers," suggesting, instead, that groups exist in dynamic interrelationship with their environments.[75] One of the assets of BFGP lies in its specific recognition of two significant characteristics of real-world groups:

1. The "boundaries" of natural groups are both symbolic and penetrable.
2. Natural groups are embedded in a social context that creates dynamic interdependence with groups outside their boundaries.

As applied to peer groups, BFGP suggests that peer group boundaries change—hence these boundaries are both redefined and negotiated by peer members within the group. This boundary-defining-negotiation task is ongoing, yet it may be the source of intragroup conflict. Furthermore, peer membership in a group itself changes over time. Group boundaries are symbolic, socially constructed through interactions with others, penetrable, and continually redefined and negotiated—in part, as a function of group identity formation and reformation.[76] Stohl and Putnam have specifically issued a call to group scholars to address boundary issues as a problematic for group researchers, worthy of exploration.[77]

Are all peer groups *bona fide groups,* according to this perspective? A naturally occurring group does not necessarily mean the members are volunteers (jurors, military, and office task forces may all consist of some who were drafted). However, in general, scholars agree that university courses that artificially assign students to groups for a class task and grade have *not* created a naturally occurring group. Consequently, laboratory groups (typically assembled by researchers in order to manipulate variables of interest) and course-assigned groups are generally beyond the scope of a Bona Fide Group Perspective. Importantly, such groups are peers who perceive one or more significant points of similarity, rights, and responsibilities with one another. Many of the other theoretical perspectives would be useful for understanding their processes (see, for example, the above discussion of group process problems that emerge in assigned student groups per the Group Dialectical Perspective).

Using a BFGP, researchers have found that allegiances to outside groups (multiple peer group memberships) challenged the ability of helping groups of peers to be successful at work. Allegiances to other groups can have potentially disastrous consequences. This was discovered in a study of a hospice team, where allegiances to other groups prohibited effective role coordination among team members, undermined the team's effectiveness, led to information-dissemination problems, and resulted in dissatisfaction and alienation among team members.[78] Conquergood specifically claimed a BFGP for his ethnographic study of Chicago's Albany Park neighborhood, not only studying an embedded group, but also embedding himself within the group.* More recently, journalists are embedding themselves in military units (peer groups) in war zones.

Each of these seven theoretical perspectives illuminates some aspect of communication in groups: types of talk, effects of talk, symbolic talk, and contexts of talk.

In addition to these seven theoretical and perceptual tools for understanding peer groups and their communication processes, there are a number of social science concepts that describe, reveal, or explain specific behaviors or outcomes that may occur in peer groups.

❖ BEYOND THEORIES: CONCEPTUAL LIGHTS THAT REVEAL PEER GROUP DYNAMICS

While less encompassing in explanatory scope than a theory, a *concept* usefully draws our attention to and names an event that occurs with enough regularity to be noticeable and intriguing. Sometimes these

---

*In December 1987, Conquergood (1994) moved into the Big Red tenement in a notorious quarter of that neighborhood called Little Beirut. He lived in that area until June 1992, experiencing the severe state of deterioration and disrepair of the living conditions that impacted the groups he wanted to describe.

Table 1.2 Theory/Perspective and Examples of Communication Focus

Theory/Perspective	Examples of Communication Focus
Symbolic-Interpretive Perspective	Symbols, language, rituals, objects, music, humor, silences, stories, art, competitions, and clothing
Social Comparison Theory	Words of comparison from self or others, self-talk, put-downs, praise, scoring, grading, ranking, competitions, and contests
Structuration Theory	Rules, norms, turn-taking, methods of voting, selecting leaders, procedures for decisional talk, and creation and recreation of structures that facilitate group goals
Decisional Regret Theory	Stories, fantasies, what-if scenarios, if-only regrets, resolving unwanted outcomes with other people, and helping others reduce anxiety about deciding
Social Identity Perspective	Using language to construct us-them perceptions, competitions, acts of inclusion or exclusion, prosocial behaviors, constructing group boundaries, labeling others, and put-downs
Group Dialectical Perspective	Managing tensions by sharing competing needs or desires and negotiating conflicts or issues concerning these need-tensions with others: sharing, negotiating, and arguing
Bona Fide Group Perspective	Use of language and symbols to construct boundaries, penetrate boundaries, negotiate embeddedness, deal with other groups, and talk about competing group loyalties of members

concepts come from traditional group scholarship, whereas sometimes they are borrowed from related disciplines such as social psychology, cognitive sciences, or persuasion, to name a few.

Social science concepts (for example, anchor points, social loafing, or emotional contagion) that help explain communication events in peer groups are set out in a second visual tool (see Appendix, Social Science Theories and Concepts That Help Explain Events in Peer Groups). In addition, the Appendix table borrows a number of useful theories from the social sciences that are not traditional group theories, but that explain events and dynamics that occur in peer groups (for example, Attribution Theory, Expectancy Violations Theory, or Face/Politeness Theory). Using three columns, this table names each theory or concept, describes the assumptions, then offers specific applications of that concept or theory to the dynamic processes of peer groups.

The Appendix table has two functions: (1) as a current reference (concepts and theories will be used to explain specific exemplar behaviors or dynamics of peer groups in this book), and (2) as a future resource (concepts and theories may expand your independent thinking about what happens in various peer groups, and why).

❖ USING MULTIPLE THEORETICAL OR CONCEPTUAL LENSES

This book will draw on these theories and concepts throughout, examining some of the trees in the forest-of-peer-groups that claim us: cliques, crowds, circles, gangs, hoodies, homies, hot groups, and juries. These concepts and theories can help us understand, differently, the communication processes and products of peer groups, the effects we might have on other group members, and the impact others have on our own experiences in these groups.

It turns out that the social context of any peer group may alter an individual member's perception of the world. There is recent evidence from neurobiology that our perceptual and emotional *perceptions* change in the presence of relevant others. People in small groups are profoundly affected by the "rule of the majority," which assumes that the collective wisdom of many people overrides the judgment of a single person. The supposed superiority of the majority, however, can disappear *when peer pressure is placed on those who see things differently.*

In a 2005 study using magnetic resonance imaging (MRI) scanners* that painted pictures of brain activity of group members during social conflict,** results showed that even when a group member *realized that the majority was factually incorrect,* many individuals decided to agree with the known incorrect answer. The MRI scanner showed that when wrong information originated from other people, *conformity to that wrong information* showed up as activity in the regions of the brain that deal with perception—and not in the regions of the brain that deal with higher-order mental activities. Going against our peers may be so uncomfortable at times that our decision-making thinking is short-circuited. The implications for teams, military troops, juries, gangs, athletes, or cliques are far-reaching. When it comes to disagreeing with a majority of our peers, the unpleasantness of standing alone can make a wrong opinion seem more appealing than sticking to one's own conclusions.

Studying communication in peer groups casts light on puzzling aspects of our social worlds, while suggesting vulnerabilities (as well as potential solutions) for facilitating different outcomes.

What other people say may change what you see.

—Folk wisdom

Critical Thinking About Group Theories and Concepts

- Consider whether certain theories may be more appropriate to explain the processes, behaviors, or experiences of specific peer groups than other theories. Which of these seven theoretical perspectives do you believe might be more useful in understanding adolescent cliques, rescue teams, or deliberating juries, for example?
- Using Table 1.1 for comparisons, when you want to understand more about a *specific* peer group, think of specific examples that illustrate what some theoretical perspectives, compared to others, *might miss.*

---

*MRI scanners detect which brain regions are active when people are performing various mental tasks.

**Researchers found that when people went along with their group on wrong answers, activity increased in the right intraparietal sulcus (spatial awareness), with no activity in brain areas that make conscious decisions. People who made judgments that went against the group showed activation in the right amygdala and right caudate nucleus (emotional salience areas). On average, people went along with the group on *known* wrong answers 41 percent of the time (Berns et al., 2005).

- Select some of the concepts in the Appendix table that help us understand peer group behaviors. For each concept that interests you, list several peer groups you believe these concepts might help us understand. Why doesn't each concept help us understand every possible peer group?
- What *anchor points* (see Appendix) might members of a gang hold that would not be shared by members of a baseball team?
- What *attributions* (see Appendix) about outsiders do you believe family clans have that are not generally shared by church youth groups? Now, apply the fundamental attribution error to these same two groups. What errors in thinking about outsiders may be occurring? Generate your own examples.
- Think of a task group you have belonged to where you were not satisfied with the efforts of some of the members in that task group. How does the Collective Effort Model explain those differences in effort or motivation? Now, consider *social loafing* (see Appendix). Does this concept explain in a different way your frustration with the lack of effort of some members than the explanatory power of the Collective Effort Model? Does the concept of *nominal group member* explain differently the perceived slacking behavior? Finally, critically think about the concept Free Ride Effect. Does this concept give additional or different perspective to what you experienced in that task group of peers?
- Applying concepts to explain the *behaviors of others* can be easier than applying those same concepts to our own choices and behaviors. Apply the same three-part exercise (see above) to a time when you realize you did not give your full effort to a task group of peers. Which of the three concepts best helps you understand your own lack of effort at that time?
- Consider the concept *Groupregret* (see Appendix). Name two examples of peer groups that you believe may regularly encounter this jointly experienced anxiety about making the wrong decision. What are your thoughts about whether groupregret more often has value for a decision-making group of peers (that is, keeps a group from moving toward a bad decision) or waste (that is, blocks groups from moving forward).
- The Investment Model of Relationships suggests that we may stay in and remain members of peer groups that no longer satisfy us, or, furthermore, that we wish to leave. Consider groups of which you have been a member, and reflect on whether you realize that some members were no longer satisfied with the group. Think about whether you find it difficult to leave peer groups to which you have invested time, effort, or shared history. In what ways might this reluctance to leave peer groups be beneficial or ultimately costly to a specific peer group?
- *Peer-suasion* explains one method that peer groups use to achieve *conformity* by exerting pressure on all members to feel they must comply

in order to gain (or sustain) group acceptance. What examples have you experienced that illustrate this?

- Recall an experience you have had in a peer group that might be explained by the *peak-end rule* from the Science of Happiness (see Appendix). In what ways do you now believe you may have been cognitively averaging how good or bad your best moments or worst moments in that group were, compared to the ending? Do you have an example of how "recalling a bad event is sufficient to make people who thought they were happy reframe their happiness downward?" Do Olympic teams, Super Bowl competitors, or World Cup teams regularly experience a peak-end rule at the end of the season, rather than actually considering the total pleasure or pain of their group successes? Might this thinking for individuals on these teams be different for winners, losers, gold medal winners, or bronze medal winners, in your view? As you consider this elite team-member thinking process now, in what ways might athletic teams face this more often than some social peer groups?

2

Peer Groups in Childhood

Learning the Rules of Peer Play

"You can't play" suddenly seems too overbearing and harsh, resounding like a slap from wall to wall. How casually one child determines the fate of another.

—Vivian G. Paley (American psychologist and MacArthur Fellowship–winning educator, and author of *You Can't Say You Can't Play*)[1]

Ever been picked last? If your family moved (forcing a change of schools), you probably have. If your face sprouted freckles, moles, scars, acne, or asymmetry—if you were clumsy, spoke with an accent, coped with a physical challenge, or dressed differently—you probably have been picked last by your peers. Your height, weight, hair, or skin color may have been a convenient target for the performance of painful exclusion rules by other children in your social world, on a more or less regular basis. *Both scholars and students of group dynamics have been chosen last and we remember it happening.*

Teachers unwittingly institutionalize the stigma of social rejection with their dreaded command to a classroom (or playground) of students:

"Choose teams!"

I came to hate those words.* Skinny, clumsy, and the new kid (complete with braces and glasses), I would be sick with embarrassment, as the enthusiastic peer team-choosing gradually slowed down, the choices dwindled, and captains reluctantly pointed at the leftover children.**

Group communication scholars have overlooked the unexpressed pain inflicted on children and adolescents by peer group rejection, despite strong lines of research from educational and developmental psychology confirming the dysfunctional effects of repeated group rejection.[2] In 1994, group scholar Keyton specifically urged the communication discipline to take the lead in developing lines of research that examine communication in children's groups, yet few studies emerged from that call.[3]

❖ COMMUNICATION PROCESSES IN EARLY CHILDHOOD PEER GROUPS

Two communication scholars, Socha and Socha[4] investigated the kinds of children's behavior in formal task groups and the extent to which communication among members was encouraged. While utilizing an admittedly small sample (41 families, with 57 children, ages five to

---

*Fairness, at this point, requires that I disclose a regular ritual of my own grade school peer group—in which I was an enthusiastic participant. It would be recess (so many of them, it seemed) or lunch (one every day) and the friends I was sitting with would notice an unwanted girl walking toward us. Quickly, a group chant began, as our small hands linked fingers around our circle:

Tick-tock,
the game is locked
and nobody else
can pla-aaay!

The unwanted child would ask if she could play. One of us would regretfully reply, *"Sorry, the game is already locked."* That no further explanation was requested by the outsider (or, it seemed, needed) to allow enactment of the game-is-locked rule is a tribute to the power of the Rules of Play children freely create, enact, and agree to live by everyday.

**That this *peer un-choosing* happened to me every school day during eighth grade rendered it the least favorite year of my life for a long, long time. (The fact that I had experienced an earlier childhood full of *peer inclusion* did not provide me with noticeable solace at age 13.)

nine), these researchers coded the taped talk of children. The results revealed that those children spent the majority of their time engaged in group activities that were directed toward *individual* rather than toward *group* skill development, with talk sometimes being discouraged within the groups. Observable group processes included uneven turn-taking, simultaneous talking, shouting suggestions, whispering and planning in dyads, marginalizing some group members, difficulties handling conflict and dividing tasks, and inability to inefficiently use time. These findings, however, may not apply to children's play groups in which adults are not observing and children are free to display more antisocial group behaviors.

❖ COMMUNICATING VALUES ABOUT GROUP RULES IN EARLY CHILDHOOD PEER GROUPS

The behavior of children in response to peer rejection may not match those children's individual social values. For instance, in one investigation, when preschool children were individually interviewed about hypothetical exclusion and inclusion from a group, they evaluated exclusion based on gender as "wrong."[5] Other findings on the moral dimensions of peer rejection support these observations. It has been discovered, for example, that *preschool* children are already forming moral rules and social exclusion. In one study, children consistently rated gender exclusion as morally wrong.[6] In addition, during one of the rare studies to attempt observation of peer rejection acts, researchers videotaped 86 preschool children and determined that preschool children were likely to reject an outsider after aggressive acts by the outsider.[7]

MacArthur Fellowship–winning educator Vivian Paley conducted the seminal ethnographic study of children's exclusionary peer behaviors in both a kindergarten and fourth-grade class in 1992.[8] Relying on the active participation of students, Paley began by talking to her class about exclusion and friendships and asking their opinions about having a rule that said, "You can't say you can't play." She discovered that some children voiced strong opinions about the right to exclude others in their social play, resisted formal inclusion rules, but were ultimately moved by Paley's use of specific storytelling interventions that allowed rejected children to share their rejection experiences. Teacher-initiated inclusion rules were found most effective in promoting prosocial inclusion behaviors in peer groups when those rules were instituted early (kindergarten or first grade) after full discussion about inclusion and exclusion *with* children in the classroom.

Extending Paley's work, other educators studied four elementary classrooms (kindergarten to fourth grades), with students representing a range of socioeconomic, religious, ability, and ethnic backgrounds.[9] They attempted to determine whether teachers could alter peer group social patterns by enforcing Paley's "you can't say" rule that had been designed to promote supportive group inclusion of outsiders. Their results varied not only across classrooms, but also across grade levels. First, classrooms in which teachers invoked the rule of inclusion consistently demonstrated an increase in overall prosocial behavior of students, even though the rule was not a cure-all, as enactment of the rule emerged only over time and after classroom discussions concerning *how* to include others. Second, for the inclusionary group rule to work, students had to trigger it by attempting inclusion. Teachers emphasized two things: (1) for group outsiders, models for acceptable ways of requesting group inclusion, and (2) for group insiders, encouragement to notice that another child was on the periphery, perhaps hoping to be included.

The specific dynamics of rejection investigated to date have included the finding that, in early childhood, it is generally the child seeking inclusion who must initiate communication with the group, that the most successful group entry attempts at this age are characterized by a combination of looking at another child, parallel play, and talking to the group, and that successful sequencing of behaviors that gain entry include aggressive behaviors (boys) and accommodation (girls). Children demonstrate their social values during rejection events, including gender preferences, distribution of scarce resources, attitudes toward aggression, and the right to choose one's social friends. As a result, it is apparent that when researchers speak of rejected children as a type of child (such as artistic children or introverted children), the rich dynamics of rejection as an interpersonal communication event, performed by more than one person, may be obscured. Scholars still know little about the rejection event itself and how it is constructed and experienced through communication.

❖ GENDER DIFFERENCES IN CHILDHOOD GROUPS

Research relating to childhood groups and gender has emerged primarily from educational and developmental psychology and has generally involved observations of preschool or early elementary playgroups, sociometric nominations (a form of ranking that involves asking kids who their favorite kids are, or the kids they prefer to associate with), or hypothetical scenarios.

Gender differences may be more noticeable over developmental time in childhood, as evidenced by one study that examined task-group behavior in triads among children ranging in age from three to eight (the task for the group of three children was to create and operate a grocery store).[10] This study found no gender differences in verbal activities during the grocery store task at this age, which suggested to him that later differences may be related to gender socialization norms. Children of this age might be ready for group interaction and capable of group skill training, yet lack sufficient prosocial behavioral models.

Young children demonstrate early gender preferences for the gender for their playgroups. For instance, in studying 92 girls and 92 boys ranging in age from 41 to 82 months, researchers determined that children believed that their own behavior was more likely to be approved of when they played with same-sex peer groups; they reported strong same-sex play preferences.[11]

In fact, the Gender Socialization Perspective (see Appendix) argues that masculine and feminine ways of communicating and behaving with others are organized by rules and roles learned by children.[12] Young boys may be socialized to be aggressive, direct, self-reliant, and funny, while young girls may be socialized to be sensitive to others, to be caring, to tolerate negative treatment, and to play nicely with others. The first place this might be noticed in peer groups, then, is in early childhood groups.

❖ STRATEGIES CHILDREN USE TO GAIN ENTRY TO PLAYGROUPS

An early study of attempts at boundary penetration in laboratory-constructed childhood groups was conducted in 1951.[13] The researchers investigated childhood group assimilation as a strategic process and conceptualized the task of group entry for new children as one of reducing the discrepancy between the other group members and themselves. They studied group entry attempts of newcomer six- and seven-year-old girls into experimentally formed, preacquainted, three-member groups that met for six 30-minute sessions. They found that it was the newcomer who attempted to communicate with the other children, and it was not the group members who initiated or even reciprocated those efforts. Rarely did any group member solicit comments or concerns of the new child, or take the newcomer into account in their activities, which confirmed that physical inclusion in groups does not translate into real inclusion.

What happens, however, when the peer group is a familiar one to the new member? The earliest work examining communication strategies to gain entry into familiar peer groups was by Malley in 1935. He recorded social behavior culminating in *successful* entry into social groups in nursery school, by means of on-site observation. He suggested that entry success when the outsider maintained group contact. According to Malley, successful peer group behavior included vocalizations (statements or laughter), physical contact (direct or through the use of objects), parallel activity (independent side-by-side engagement in related activity), and cooperative activity (engagement in related interdependent or supplemental activity).[14] The patterns most successful for a child in gaining group entry consisted of a combination of *regard* (looking at another child), *regard and parallel play,* and *regard and vocalization.*

Importantly, childhood rejection histories for some children may actually trigger an ongoing *reputational bias* in available peer groups. Group members allegedly respond more favorably to popular children's entry overtures than they do to those of unpopular children, even when the outsider children use similar entry strategies.[15]

Child development scholars have explored developmental and gender differences in the ways children sequence their actions when attempting to join peer groups. One group of researchers employed a design in which 24 unfamiliar children (ages five or seven) formed six-member playgroups, homogeneous by age, meeting for 12 one-hour sessions over three weeks.[16] Videotaped records revealed a variety of group entry behavior. Boys, for instance, were more likely than girls to use forceful strategies (that is, by displaying their own qualities, asserting superiority over group members, or criticizing group members). Following negative feedback from the group, boys were also more likely than girls to engage in face-saving behavior or to appeal to playroom norms mandating acceptance. By age seven, girls were more apt to accommodate to the group following rejection (for example, by making neutral comments to the group about themselves, or by asking permission to join the group). Behaviors triggering peer group rejection may differ for boys and girls. One study reported that the most powerful predictor of peer rejection for boys in third through sixth grades was undercontrolled behaviors (such as aggression, hyperactivity, or inattention-immaturity).[17] Studies have consistently shown that, in addition, persisting and behaving in a manner consistent with the group members are likely to result in eventual group acceptance.[18]

❖ LEADERSHIP IN CHILDREN'S PLAYGROUPS

In early childhood, peer groups generally reject formal leaders. Consistent with this view are findings of French and Stright, who studied emergent leadership in task groups and noted that children favored leadership styles characterized as either that of *diplomacy* or *bullying* and frequently rejected formal leadership roles for members who dominated group discussions.[19]

More recently, group research has studied the emergence of leadership and group effectiveness in children's cooperative learning groups. Using a sample of 30 participants from fourth-, fifth-, and sixth-grade classrooms across five elementary school classes, one investigation created three-member learning groups in which a math task manipulated instructions either to "learn and improve" or to "see who was best."[20] The intragroup competitive condition affected the emergence of leadership: one member dominated or bullied and took over the group process. In the learning condition, *prosocial leadership* emerged, which tended to be shared and distributed throughout the performance of the task. Furthermore, the learning condition groups were more effective in completing the math task (as measured by their arithmetical strategies and positive communications). Competitive groups were less effective, possibly because the friction created dysfunctional communication and task strategies. The study does not offer direction, however, about how groups larger than three members manage these tasks, or whether the results would apply in naturally formed playgroups, as opposed to artificially constructed laboratory task groups.

❖ SILENT CHILDHOOD STRESSES: EARLY EXCLUSION EFFECTS

These cross-disciplinary studies demonstrate, in part, the lack of prosocial models for children in playgroups, the leadership preferences of preschoolers, and early gender preferences in group members. None of these studies, however, provides much insight into naturally occurring childhood peer group processes—in situations in which adults are *not* present and children are free to negotiate group membership with outsiders. When children in peer groups enforce boundaries, how are other children affected by peer group social exclusion?

Child development scholars agree that peer rejection is a significant factor in social and cognitive development, with outcomes that include poor school performance, delinquent behavior, depression, physical illnesses, and impaired adult relationships.[21] Prior studies of children's peer play have often focused on adult accounts of childhood traumas, sociograms that provoke forced-choice popularity poles among elementary school children,[22] or observer accounts of young children's playground behavior.[23] Peer-rejected children may become less talkative and more aggressive.[24] Rejected preschool children may be more noncompliant, hyperactive, and socially withdrawn than other children.[25] Similarly, developmental psychologists discovered that low peer group acceptance of fifth-grade children predicted higher self-ratings of loneliness, though how group rejection is experienced or explained by the rejected child was not examined.[26] At the same time, lower levels of preadolescent peer rejection appear to be predictive of overall life status adjustment, including general self-worth (though group scholars know little about the cause-and-effect dynamics of this relationship).[27] Prior research has largely focused on the left-out child rather than the peer group as the problem; this assumes that poor social skills or aggressive behavior trigger exclusion.[28]

Describing the experiences of three children in child-centered classrooms in elementary school, one study reported ineffective attempts by children at group inclusion, as well as their unique individual coping strategies (for example, persisting in attempts to be included, playing alone, or demonstrating aggressive behavior).[29] Effects of group exclusion on individuals in the classroom were found to be complex, with relevant variables including a child's independent desire for peer interaction, competence in critical learning abilities, and whether there exists at least one other child with whom the left-out child can interact. Hodges, Malone, and Perry studied 229 children in the third through seventh grades.[30] Childhood behavior problems related more strongly to peer group rejection when a child had fewer friends and was not well liked, from which the authors also concluded that the particular effects of individual rejection risk variables depend on a complex social context.

Peer rejection histories affect the expectations and strategies of children and adolescents as they face future attempts at group inclusion and alter their interpretations of ambiguous social events. Educational scholars studying children's groups, for example, focused on the sensitivity of children to rejection in a series of studies involving urban minority (Hispanic and African American) fifth- to seventh-grade students.[31] In hypothetical scenarios, children who angrily expected rejection demonstrated heightened distress following an ambiguously intentioned rejection by a peer. Furthermore, rejection-sensitive children were more aggressive (as reported by teachers), engaged in troubled interpersonal relationships, and declined in academic performance over time. Persistent peer group rejection of rejection-sensitive children may explain why some adults more readily attribute hostile intent to other people.

Recently, it was reported that peer group rejection in early elementary school was associated with later antisocial aggressive behavior (even when the researchers controlled for antisocial acts occurring before rejection experiences).[32] In a longitudinal four-study design involving 259 early elementary children, followed by another study with 585 children, group researchers reported that antisocial behavior subsequent to rejection was equally apparent among boys and girls and was partially accounted for by a child's tendency to develop biased patterns of processing social information as a result of peer group rejection. We do not know, however, whether preexisting aggressive behaviors were merely accelerated by group rejection, or whether any interventions might have altered a rejected child's biased processing of social exclusion. In a study investigating the relation between peer rejection and children's academic adjustment during kindergarten, researchers found that rejected children were more likely to report loneliness, express a desire to avoid school, and to decrease their classroom participation.[33]

Early peer rejection or inclusion seems to affect life adjustments, general impressions of self-worth, later aggressive behaviors, and academic achievement, including attitudes toward school and learning. Rejection histories affect a child's strategies in future attempts at inclusion, and alter the child's cognitive interpretations of ambiguous social events.

❖ TALES OF PEER GROUP REJECTION: A BONA FIDE GROUPS PERSPECTIVE

A focus on naturally occurring groups, boundary permeability, and the negotiation of group identity renders the *Bona Fide Groups Perspective* relevant for increasing our understanding of childhood group entry, inclusion rules, and group rejection events in childhood, for example.

For the first time, a recent study applied a Bona Fide Group Perspective to children's peer groups.

That study gathered narrative accounts of peer group experiences from 682 adolescents.* In one phase of this study, the teens in this study shared specific hurtful accounts of being excluded from peer groups, focusing on how peer group members communicated exclusion to them when they were attempting to join the group. The study "probe" to the adolescent participants asked,

> Think of a time when a group of people excluded you and it hurt your feelings. What did someone in that group say or do (behavior and/or words) that let you know you would not be included?

These adolescents were, for the most part, ninth graders, and, as a result, bridged the transition from childhood to high school years. Many of them chose to reflect on incidents from their early childhood, while a lesser number focused on more recent events (either middle school or high school). According to these data, peer groups used five primary communication tactics for refusing group entry to an outsider, as experienced by these adolescents: (a) ignoring, (b) disqualifying, (c) insulting, (d) blaming, and (e) creating new rules. Intriguingly, we found no significant differences between the rejection accounts of males and female, or between the accounts of Whites and non-Whites.

Below are exemplars that give deeper meaning to the adolescents' peer experiences.

How did demographics (gender or ethnicity) affect the *communication of rejection* by peers? Both White and non-White teens reported being told they were not wanted because of their race or skin color; both males and females reported being ridiculed or told they were not good enough to join a peer group; and males, females, Whites, and non-Whites all reported being silently ignored when they tried to gain entry to a group of children.

The Bona Fide Group Perspective invites us to examine peer group boundaries; this is particularly useful in thinking about children's

---

*The questionnaire (part of a larger investigation of social exclusion in childhood groups) consisted of sections containing both free-response and closed-ended items, as well as quantitative scales. To date, three studies have been published from the data, see: SunWolf & Leets (2003; 2004) and Leets & SunWolf (2005).

Table 2.1 Adolescents' Accounts of Communication Tactics That Peer Groups Used to Reject Them

Peer Rejection Tactics ➔	Responses: What did someone in that group say or do that let you know you would not be included?			
	Males		Females	
	White	Non-White	White	Non-White
Ignoring	• They pretty much ignored my presence.	• Walked away. • I was talking and they would make a comment like, "Is that the wind?"	• The group wouldn't look at me. They seemed to be avoiding looking at my face and they turned their backs to me.	• They all gave me an awkward look and continued to talk among themselves. • They pretended I wasn't there.
Disqualifying	• They needed an extra person, so I offered. The person making the team said I was not good enough, even though we played on the same school football team. • Just because my feet are crooked, I couldn't run fast.	• Because of some difficulty I have with my heart, they mocked me and made fun of my situation telling me that I'll die or have a heart attack.	• They said I couldn't play cuz I wasn't a good enough of a player. They were mean.	• Basically, that I wouldn't understand what they were talking about because I was scholastically far behind them. • They said, "Oh, you don't even speak English."

(Continued)

Table 2.1 Adolescents' Accounts of Communication Tactics That Peer Groups Used to Reject Them (Continued)

Peer Rejection Tactics ➜	**Responses: What did someone in that group say or do that let you know you would not be included?**			
	Males		**Females**	
	White	**Non-White**	**White**	**Non-White**
Insulting	• They told me to shut up and go away because I was stupid. • "Get out of here, stupid, you're gay." • They said I was fat and stupid, so they didn't want to include me in anything. I walked away crying.	• I was told no "Ghandhi's" were allowed. • They told me to leave and play with my Asian friends. • Someone was making fun of my head's shape. They were making fun of me by saying "E.T. phone home."	• The boys said I couldn't play with them because I was a girl and I had cooties.	• Other kids did not want to play with me because I had a mole on my nose. They would call me "mole face." • They said, "Hey, look at the ugly girl, how she dresses."
Blaming	• They said we have even teams and that I could not play very well. • Because no one knew me and because of all my freckles.	• They said that I sucked at [baseball] and they hurt [my feelings]. • Because I don't look good enough. I'm not a good dresser kind of person.	• People do it all the time because I'm not like them or I'm not <u>cool</u>!! • Back in grade school I was really [fat] and people would exclude me all the time. It hurt me a lot.	• I wasn't a fun or smart person to be with. • Once a group of girls didn't want me to hang around with them because I wasn't like a girly girl.

Peer Rejection Tactics ➔	Responses: What did someone in that group say or do that let you know you would not be included?			
	Males		Females	
	White	Non-White	White	Non-White
Creating New Rules	• They said I didn't get there in time and they already started. I would have to get another person in order to play. • They ignored me and left me for last pick. Then they told me I couldn't play because it was uneven.	• One time I ask to play football with some people and they said that I was too late, then "we have too many people," then "you're too small." Next time I got there early and asked if I could play and they act like they did not hear me."	• They said "Sorry no more room" but I knew that there was about five spaces left. I saw someone else go up there to ask if they could play and the kids let that person in. • They said that they had to go home because they were leaving. I thought it was cause they didn't like us.	• One time in eighth grade we were supposed to be getting into groups of four people and then I was going over to this one group to ask them if I could be in their group because they only had three. When I asked them, they were like, "No, because Amanda was going to be in our group."

Source: Sunwolf, & Leets, L. (2004). Being left out: Rejecting outsiders and communicating group boundaries in childhood and adolescent peer groups. *Journal of Applied Communication Research, 32(3)*, 195–223.

playgroups. While peer group boundaries are, of course, penetrable, the reality is that they are not capable of being penetrated by all outsiders at all times. Social cruelty may be woven into the enactment of symbolic boundaries. Evidence that rules were designed to exclude one person but not others emerged when rules changed a second time for a subsequent entry attempt by someone else:

> They said, "Sorry, no more room," but I knew that there was about 5 five spaces left. I saw someone else go up there to ask if they could play and the kids let that person in.

Students in this study told stories of being made to feel *invisible* when they tried to join groups, and one young student's personal pain hit at the core of her self-esteem:

> Everyone was invited right in front of me, except me. Being left out is one of the worst feelings there is. When someone is left out they feel they are not good enough and want to change themselves.

The communication of rejection without reasons or words was memorable to many of these students, even if it happened only once:

> When I was new to a junior high and we were in P.E. they had to pick teams and I of course was new so they didn't pick me. I felt like crying or even like—Well the thing is that I felt bad. I don't think I'll ever forget that.

When given the chance to quantity the frequency of being excluded by peer groups these participants wanted to join, a surprising 15 percent of them (100 children) reported being *continually left out.*

The Bona Fide Group Perspective suggests that boundaries may become ambiguous or unclear and alter group identity for both insiders and outsiders when membership in a peer group is threatened with change. This study advances our understanding, from a Bona Fide Group Perspective, about how adolescents and children interpret and experience boundary penetration attempts in peer groups. The narrative accounts in this study offer preliminary descriptions of boundary ambiguity, stress, and penetration failures in childhood peer groups.

When it comes to breaking into a desired peer group, some kids are enduring a lot of social pain. Penetrating peer group boundaries in childhood may be more painful to all children and adolescents than anyone has previously acknowledged. However, adolescents who reported being continually left out were almost twice as likely to report elevated levels of stress *when watching the exclusion of other children,* compared to reports by the children who claimed only moderate to low experiences with peer group rejection.

❖ CONCEPTUALIZING PEER GROUP INTERVENTIONS

Storytelling and Peer Modeling

Many children may lack knowledge about how to gain access to desired peer groups. What are the successful words a child can use to request peer group membership, even temporarily, in childhood? One 14-year-old female Hispanic student in the above study described her social ignorance:

> I have a problem with people. I don't know how to act in social situations. I get excluded all the time because I really don't know what to do, or where my place is.

One study of peer inclusion concluded that a child's strategy knowledge and frequency of peer acceptance were positively related, which suggests that interventions that provide students with inclusion or exclusion communication skills would be valuable.[34]

Paley's work initiating storytelling in the classroom to uncover and transform social injustices reveals an intervention that is easy to fold into an existing course or classroom day (subsequently applied in the classroom by other educators).[35] Using findings and accounts reported in peer group studies as exemplar-triggers, specific accounts, words, and themes relevant to peer rejection can be used to trigger student memories and discussion in peer classrooms. Teachers–coaches–youth leaders can generate dialogue with the children's groups they help by sharing the words of the adolescents who have described being left out, for example, and continuing with such questions: "Has that ever happened to you?" or "What do you think about what was said?" Most students—and not just a targeted few—have painful stories of rejection, not just a targeted few. Sharing stories helps students become "real" to one another, hence moral disengagement from one another becomes more difficult.

It turns out that *watchers* of peer rejection have important stories to tell, as well. Storytelling connects with peer modeling when students are encouraged to share tales of regrets after watching peer group rejection ("I wish instead that I had . . .") or tales of including others. Thus, the lived-life experience of one student becomes usable information for others. One team of researchers attempting to help children reclaim rejected peers reported that interventions allowed for constructive affiliations with previously rejected peers through new activities.[36] Storytelling is a fluid format for such reclaiming of acceptance. Stories model both successful and unsuccessful behavior by fellow students in rejection events. At the same time, teachers are resources for one another when they collaborate with neighboring schools in a storied exchange. When we have read the accounts from our data to teachers and students in elementary and middle schools those accounts have immediately provoked reciprocal tales. It may be less ego threatening to critique stories involving someone else than it is to receive a behavior adjustment critique concerning personal behavior.

Co-Constructing New Classroom Rules

One recurring robust theme in the accounts of adolescents is *being picked last* (or not at all) when teachers ask students to choose work groups or competitive teams. Whether or not that is an expedient choice for teachers, it is clear it is painful to those chosen last. Group facilitation manuals are replete with ice-breakers and group-formation tools that can be quickly adopted by teachers, including random methods (for example, counting off, drawing numbers), grouping by profile (such as cat lovers, hip-hop lovers, January-February birthdays, anyone who plays an instrument, favorite foods), scavenger hunts (for example, find someone who has a hamster, knows how to sew, has been to Canada), or rotating memberships (such as every day or every half hour the group rotates one member), which avoids permanent status markers and sets an expectation that everyone works with everyone. A climate of inclusion in classrooms requires that teachers abandon opportunities for children to select those with whom they want to work, play, or compete.

Once teachers examine traditional structures in their classrooms that allow social exclusion, the stage is set, especially in primary school, to invite students to collaborate on creating and adopting rules of inclusion. In addition to Paley's negative "You can't say you can't play" rule, positive rules can be engaged ("Everyone gets to play for at least five minutes" or "You have to find out something you have in common with someone before you decide"). Sharing peer rejection accounts from our study with children in classrooms, for example, can precede the teacher's probe, "What should the rule have been for those students?"

In a study utilizing classroom peer groups to address students' inclusion needs, researchers determined that a Circle of Friends intervention improved the social acceptance of mainstreamed special needs children.[37] As a further measure, rule-changing can be combined with the facilitation technique of "positive peer reporting" (or "positive tattling"), in which students report prosocial behaviors exhibited by their peers.[38] A climate of inclusion may involve rewards for the positive tattler, or for the target of the prosocial report, or it might take the form of accounts posted around the classroom. Although many classrooms encourage all prosocial reports, selected themes (inclusion, empathy, sharing) allow the entire classroom to focus on targeted behavior.

The creation and enforcement of group inclusionary rules for children or adolescents reportedly affects teachers as well as students in positive ways:

> Surprisingly, the effects of implementing the rule had at least as much influence on me as on the children. It challenged us all to work hard creating and maintaining a more idealistic world. . . . At the end of the year, I had to admit I'd never seen a group of kids change so dramatically. I had grown, too. (Second grade teacher)[39]

When prosocial inclusionary rules for children's peer groups are initially implemented by adults, benefits extend to others in the school's organizational culture. A Bona Fide Group Perspective reminds us that all groups are embedded in contexts that include both other groups and a larger organization:

> As the rule began to permeate the entire school (one of the most exciting results of the project), some of the upper-level teachers actually taught and implemented the rule with the help of students who had already been in "You can't say" classrooms at an earlier grade.[40]

All of us, as peer group members, teachers, and scholars, can become more intentionally thoughtful about changing how we have socialized students in our classrooms. The social behavior of any peer group member depends on an increased awareness of communication choices. Unfortunately, as evidenced by extreme recent school tragedies, few communication models exist in schools for facilitating group inclusion (yet while respecting unique group identities or values). Although teachers cannot eliminate the rejection of some children by their classmates, teachers may be able to increase peer group inclusion, as well as to reduce a student's exposure to damaging rejection processes.

❖ NEW THEORETICAL LENSES: CONCEPTUALIZING CHILDREN'S PEER GROUPS

Drawing on the discussion above, there is a wide variety of peer group dynamics for childhood groups that might be explained through each of the seven theoretical perspectives presented in this book. As examples of new theory thinking, consider Table 2.2.

Table 2.2 Theoretical Perspective and Application to Children's Peer Groups

Theoretical Perspective	Application to Children's Peer Groups
Symbolic-Interpretive Perspective	What symbols of peer inclusion do children create and at what age? How do children symbolically communicate exclusion to unwanted outsiders? Do younger children enact dress, music, or words to display peer group membership?
Social Comparison Theory	Who are the reference groups with which children's peer groups compare themselves? Do gender differences emerge in childhood in the social comparison process for those included in peer groups and those attempting to gain entry? Does Social Comparison Theory explain peer group rejection of unwanted outsiders? What social comparison processes do rejected children use to make sense of their own peer group rejection?
Structuration Theory	How do the structuring processes of children's peer play groups change as children grow older? Do boys' peer groups structure themselves in ways that are different from girls' peer groups? What rules emerge in play groups of peers and how are they enforced or communicated to members?
Decisional Regret Theory	How do children anticipate and think about the task of attempting entry to a new peer group? If children have previously had unsuccessful attempts at

Theoretical Perspective	Application to Children's Peer Groups
	peer group entry, does this cause some of them to anticipate regretting future attempts? (What stories are they imagining about what would happen if they asked to join?) Do children in peer groups who reject outsiders later regret those decisions? What are the effects of social regrets in childhood on future peer group behaviors and rules?
Social Identity Perspective	How do children reconstruct their individual identities when they are (a) included in a peer group, or (b) excluded by a peer group? How do children's groups compare themselves to other peer groups? Do children construct peer group identity by negation?
Group Dialectical Perspective	How (and at what age) do children balance their need to belong to peer groups with their emerging need for independence? How do children learn to both express and suppress their emotions—often simultaneously—during activities in peer groups? Do boys and girls experience different dialectical tensions as a result of gender socialization in their childhood peer groups?
Bona Fide Group Perspective	How do children perceive the boundaries of their peer groups? How do peer group members perceive the penetrability of their group's boundaries? To what degree do schools, neighborhoods, or families affect children's peer groups? How important is the presence of other peer groups in a school or neighborhood to the behaviors or identity of children in a specific peer group?

Childhood is embedded in peer groups: Children are born into a primary group (many with siblings or close cousins), learn in classroom groups, socialize in formal-informal playgroups, compete in teams, identify territorially with neighborhood groups, worship in groups, collaborate in scout troops, and reproduce social structures in cliques. This chapter illuminated the dynamics through which children learn the rules of group peer play, gender differences in group behaviors and leadership, the challenges of gaining inclusion, and the challenges facing young ingroup peer members in sustaining their peerness.

Critical Thinking About Children's Peer Group Experiences

- Reflect on events of social exclusion or inclusion that you experienced in elementary classrooms you were a part of. First, how did young children attempt to gain entry to playgroups? What do you remember about how some children created boundaries that did not allow certain children to play with their group? How was exclusion communicated?
- Paley's work with altering peer group social patterns at school (including at recess) revolved around instituting and explaining a, "You can't say you can't play" rule. What are your thoughts about how that would work across different schools, mixed ethnicities, or gender differences? If you have worked as a teacher or coach, what have you observed about childhood exclusion—and what processes of exclusion do you now believe may have been invisible to you?
- Interview an elementary school teacher about: (a) observed social exclusion events, (b) adult attempts to promote inclusion, and (c) that person's opinion about the "You can't say you can't play" rule. What, in that teacher's view, causes (attribution, see Appendix) some children to be excluded by their peers? What institutional/classroom *climate* (see Appendix) factors may be contributing to facilitating social exclusion in that school (Bona Fide Group Perspective)?
- *Temporality* invites us to consider *time* and peer groups; the duration of any peer group varies, especially in early childhood. How long do childhood peer groups last, and how often are they regularly reconstituted?
- If *scripts* and *schemas* are important cognitive structures that organize our expectations and interpretations of roles and events in groups, what role do childhood peer groups play in creating social scripts for members? How does an excluded child develop useful social schemas (behaviors expected between people) as an outsider?
- In an increasingly mobile society, some children are faced at an early age with the complex task of entering new schools and classrooms. What impact do you believe entering a new school without any peer group memberships might have on a child's in-class learning? What other learning challenges might a peerless child face during the transition when he or she is new to a classroom of already-organized peer groups?
- *Symbolic Interaction Theory* (see Appendix) argues that people interact with others by creating symbolic rituals, objects, and language. What examples can you give of how children's early peer groups create social interaction around rituals, objects, or special words?

3

Peer Groups in Adolescence

The Power of Rejection

"They ignored me and left me for last pick. Then they told me I couldn't play because it was uneven."

—White male teenager[1]

A hidden culture of social cruelty exists in childhood peer groups, as evidenced by the rich anecdotal narratives collected by one writer about the culture of aggression and exclusion among teenage girls.[2] Describing the social phenomenon of the "odd girl out," one researcher of female bullying talked to both rejected and rejecting teens and uncovered painful behaviors in girls' cliques that teachers rarely notice.[3] When young teenage girls appeared on the Oprah Winfrey television show to admit their ongoing roles in provoking painful group exclusion of others at their schools, the audience (and their parents) were shocked.[4] The manner in which social cruelty is regularly perpetuated by peer groups was poignantly described by middle school students on ABC's *20/20*. On that show, children described their desperate goal of gaining access to the "in" crowd, even at the cost of hurting others.[5]

❖ FREAKS, GEEKS, JOCKS, AND STARS: PEER GROUP TEASING AND BULLYING

Ask high school students how they fit into the hierarchy of peer groups in their school and they can tell you, since our social rankings are never invisible to us. Teasing and bullying, as well as ingroup and outgroup talk tells every adolescent what groups others assign them to. Most of us remember our adolescent peer assignment vividly, even as adults.

Every minute of every day, some child is being cut down by a peer group to which they do not happen to belong. Some students have only to log on to the Internet to be told whose nerd list, hit list, or revenge list they appear on. Researcher Charol Shakeshaft at Hofstra University asked 1,000 middle and high school students one open-ended question: *"What's it really like in school?"* The prevailing answer that Shakeshaft received was that "school was a miserable place, because of all the peer teasing and bullying."[6]

Drive by any school bus stop. Walk by any school playground, stop by any school cafeteria. Sounds of silence may be signs of peer group shunning and exclusion. Sneers and cutting remarks announce impenetrable peer group boundaries. Just when the need to belong is greatest, the difficulty of entering peer groups may seem overwhelming to some teens.

Every adolescent, it appears, feels the hurt and the additional anxiety of peer-exclusion. If it didn't happen today, it might happen tomorrow:

> Even mothers of the prettiest girls in the class have complained. A well-heeled Chicago mom confessed that her beautiful sixth-grade daughter cries in her room nightly, afraid she won't look *right* tomorrow and as a consequence she will lose her standing. A popular 14-year-old admitted that she slashed her arm with a wallpaper cutter to bleed out the shame she felt after hearing rumors accusing her of sleeping around. The smartest boy in a seventh-grade class in Ohio told us that his homework is his only refuge.[7]

Some children pursue popularity illegitimately, opting for control by knocking down the competition (Social Identity Perspective, Table 1.2). Some peer groups are simply fan clubs of bullies: the bystander effect blocks even compassionate intervention. There is a significant risk in defending on outcast or a victim (*inclusion-fragility, rejection contagion;* see Appendix). Someone's rejection, it is feared, might stick on you. Alternatively, your own treasured group inclusion might be one word away from disappearing.

Dr. Thompson describes an inevitable tendency of all children to torment and reject their peers.[8] Rejected children suffer terribly, however. Children who watch this rejection happen also become stressed. Few adults (parents, relatives, professionals, or teachers) fully understand the peer group dynamics that sustain this social cruelty.

❖ COMMUNICATING GROUP VALUES IN THE CULTURE OF ADOLESCENT PEER GROUPS

Adolescents may claim to hold social values that do not appear to match their peer group's behavior. One recent study investigated adolescents' reasoning with regard to issues that involve social exclusion on the basis of reference groups, and the factors that influence such reasoning. Using hypothetical vignettes, Horn surveyed high school students concerning a member of a high-status or low-status group being denied school resources (scholarship or a free school trip) or group membership (cheerleading squad, basketball team, or student council).[9] She reported that 9th and 11th graders viewed the exclusion from social groups on the basis of some other peer group membership (high status or low status) as wrong.

❖ STRATEGIES THAT ADOLESCENTS USE TO ATTEMPT TO GAIN ENTRY TO PEER GROUPS

Interventions for peer groups have generally been constructed with the rejected child or adolescent as the "target" of the "cure," and have focused on changing the behaviors of at-risk students by encouraging them to develop characteristics that might make them more acceptable to peer groups. What if we consider adopting *group*-targeted interventions for children's peer groups? Inclusion is a behavior that the included children must choose. Group-based interventions are *community*-based and facilitate attitude and expectation changes for peer group members toward outsiders. The urgency of initiating school-based interventions is clear: negative consequences associated with peer group rejection are linked to a child's adjustment immediately after entering grade school[10] and primary school children spend most of their task group activities at school.[11] Teachers increasingly rely on group activities, but learn that mere physical inclusion of children in a class group by teachers does not guarantee *social* inclusion.[12] One participant in our study shared an account that illustrates this situation:

> When we were picking teams to play basketball. Someone in there say "I don't like her, she is stupid and ugly." Well, the teacher came and solve it out. I have to be in their team and when we were playing, they didn't pass me the ball or anything.

During peer group play, children learn the strength of belonging to a group, but also the vulnerability that loners face outside the group. One researcher has taken his findings to the streets, making vivid both normal and painful rejections for parents on television shows. Dr. Thompson's book, *Best Friends, Worst Enemies: Understanding the Social Lives of Children,*[13] argues that one dynamic law that influences the peer group life of children is that children perceive that you *must* belong to a group. Thompson's work as a psychologist in schools described group inclusion as so critical that *rejected* children frequently create groups of their own. Peer group membership is emotionally fraught, characterized by both intense intimacy and bewildering cruelty. Further studies of bona fide childhood peer groups would be enriched by an acknowledgment of the embeddedness of these groups in complex social-academic-community contexts.

❖ BITTERSWEET PEER POWER: THE EFFECTS OF PEER GROUP REJECTION AND EXCLUSION

Research is increasingly revealing a hidden culture of social cruelty that is created and perpetuated in teen groups, both in middle school (or junior high school) and in high school.[14] Every peer rejection communicates a lack of worthiness. What, then, is the result of such a message being communicated repeatedly to unwanted outsiders? At its terrible extreme, the rage of a rejected adolescent has the potential to produce either other-directed violence (school shootings) or self-directed punishment (suicides). Furthermore, initiation rites of high school and college groups carry deadly consequences for adolescents who are attempting to gain inclusion.

In 2000, the National Institute of Mental Health reported that suicide continued to be the third leading cause of death among young people 15 to 24 years of age (following unintentional injuries and homicide), with a gender ratio of four males for every one female death.[15] This gender ratio continues in recent high profile school shootings, which are frequently accompanied by reports of peer exclusion.

Sadly, media reports indicate that this list goes on. Furthermore, research from educational and developmental psychology confirms that *repeatedly rejected children*

- spend more time isolated, with fewer opportunities for development of social skills,
- have an increased probability of future rejection and antisocial behaviors,
- become emotionally distracted and unable to listen or learn in the classroom,
- feel inner numbness, and a feeling of being empty, bored, or disconnected from their lives,
- experience an altered sense of time, such that they are immersed in the painful present, without meaningful thoughts about their past or future,
- engage in self-destructive behavior, making a higher proportion of unhealthy choices, procrastinating, and taking foolish risks, and
- give up sooner on frustrating tasks and are less motivated to control their own behaviors.

Children and adolescents who are repeatedly rejected from participation and membership in groups necessarily spend more time isolated, and consequently have fewer opportunities for social growth or the development of social skills,[16] increasing the probability of future rejection and antisocial behavior.[17] Within classrooms that increasingly rely on small peer learning groups, rejected children have fewer opportunities to develop either instructional or learning skills, or to have access to social resources (for example, the knowledge of other students).

There is new evidence that rejection hurts physically and impairs our brains. While the categories of "hard science" (such as biology, physics, neurology, or medicine) as opposed to "social science" (for example, sociology, psychology, anthropology, communication, or religion) have often provoked criticism between these disciplines, more

Table 3.1 High-Profile School Shootings by Children and Adolescents, 1997–2003[1]

Date	Location	Event
4-24-03	Pennsylvania	A male student (James Sheets), 14 years old, at Red Lion Area Junior High School, shot and killed principal, Eugene Segro with a handgun before killing himself.
4-14-03	Louisiana	Four gunmen ranging in age from 15 to 19 killed one 15-year-old male and wounded three females at John McDonogh High School. The shooting was apparently gang related and was in retaliation for a fight.
3-30-01	Indiana	A male (Donald Burt), 17 years old, who had withdrawn from Lew Wallace High School for nonattendance returned to the school to murder Neal Boyd, a student who had bullied him and others.
3-5-01	California	A male student (Charles "Andy" Williams), 15 years old, took his father's gun to Santana High School, killing two teenagers and wounding 13 other people. He was arrested on murder and other charges stemming from the shooting. According to many students, Andy had been bullied and was frequently a victim of taunting.
1-10-01	California	A male adolescent (Richard Lopez), 17 years old, fired shots at Hueneme High School, Oxnard, before taking a student hostage. The teenager apparently was not a student at the school and did not know the girl he held hostage. He was later shot and killed by police. No one else was injured.
5-26-00	Florida	A male honors student (Nathaniel Brazil), 13 years old, killed his teacher, Barry Grunow, on the last day of classes in Lake Worth. He was charged with first-degree murder.
2-29-99	Michigan	A boy, six years old, shot and killed a six-year-old classmate at Buell Elementary School in Mount Morris Township. Because of his age, the boy was not charged. A 19-year-old man was sentenced to 2 to 15 years in prison for allowing the boy access to the gun.
12-6-99	Oklahoma	A male student (Seth Trickey), 13 years old, fired at least 15 rounds at Fort Gibson Middle School in Fort Gibson, wounding four classmates. He was convicted on seven assault charges, but will not remain in jail past the age of 19.

Date	Location	Event
11-19-99	New Mexico	A girl, 13 years old, was shot in the head in school at Deming, and died the next day. A 12-year-old boy later pleaded guilty and was sentenced to at least two years in juvenile custody.
5-20-99	Georgia	A male student (T. J. Solomon), 15 years old, opened fire with a .357-caliber Magnum and a rifle at Heritage High School in Conyers, wounding six students. He pleaded guilty, but was diagnosed as mentally ill. He was sentenced to 40 years in prison and 65 years of probation.
4-20-99	Colorado	Two male students, a 17-year-old (Dylan Klebold) and an 18-year-old (Eric Harris), at Columbine High School in Littleton, killed 12 students and a teacher and wounded 23 before killing themselves.
5-21-98	Oregon	A male high school student (Kip Kinkel), 15 years old, in Springfield, killed his parents, then went to his school where he shot 24 students. Two of his victims died. Wrestled to the ground, he yelled, "Shoot me!"
3-24-98	Arkansas	Two boys, a 13-year-old (Mitchell Johnson) and an 11-year-old (Andrew Golden), in Jonesboro, set off a fire alarm to draw their schoolmates outside. They then started shooting, killing four students and one teacher.
12-1-97	Kentucky	A male student (Michael Cameal), 14 years old, in West Paducah, shot three students to death at an early morning high school prayer meeting. A student in the Bible group grabbed him when he stopped to reload.
10-1-97	Mississippi	A male student (Luke Woodham), 16 years old, in Pearl first shot and killed his mother, then went to his high school and opened fire, killing three and wounding seven.

[1]Adapted and extended from: Aratani, L. (2001, March 11). Violence highlights dilemma of "snitches." *San Jose Mercury News*, pp. 1A, 6A; and, The National School Safety Center (2003). *Report on school associated violent deaths*. Retrieved August 1, 2003 from http://www.nssc1.org.

recently they are borrowing from one another. One example of this intersection is a 2003 study of the effects of a social science issue (rejection) and a hard science issue (neuroimaging of the brain).

An fMRI (neuroimaging) study of social exclusion by psychologists at the University of California, Los Angeles, found that the brain bases of social pain are similar to those of physical pain.* Research has further demonstrated that rejection can dramatically reduce a person's IQ and ability to reason analytically, while at the same time, increasing aggression. Roy Baumeister (who has extensively investigated unrequited love) recently reported that when students were randomly assigned to rejection experiences, their IQ scores were lowered (some by as much as 25 percent), their analytical reasoning lowered (by as much as 30 percent), and their aggression scores increased. He theorized that social rejection interferes with the brain's self-control. People, therefore, become more impulsive and even more self-destructive when they are rejected.[18]

Ironically, the successful entry into childhood peer groups is a prerequisite for interpersonal interactions and constitutes a critical task of emotional and cognitive development.[19] Since a significant portion of any child or adolescent's life unfolds and develops in the context of small groups, adult attitudes toward group work are affected by their own childhood group experiences:[20] since individuals enter new groups carrying perceptual schemas shaped by their previous groups.[21] Group scholars have been challenged to utilize a wider lens to view the expansive array of groups across the life span.[22] In fact, dysfunctional group behavior scripts from childhood may resurface in adult groups.[23]

Antecedent experiences with groups can affect subsequent intragroup processes and member adjustments.[24] The *antecedent peer group effect* may be related, in part, to the fact that rejection during social play may be the forerunner of all the rejections to come, so rejection effects are individually compounded.[25] Some children and adolescents endure intense social pain but grow from the experience, whereas others report feeling socially paralyzed and crushed.[26]

---

*The anterior cingulated cortex was more active during exclusion than during inclusion. This correlated positively with self-reported distress during social exclusion. The right ventral prefrontal cortex was active during exclusion and correlated negatively with self-reported distress (Eisenberger, Lieberman, & Williams, 2003).

❖ ADOLESCENT GROUP BOUNDARIES

Several possible group dynamics may cast light on boundary ambiguity and penetration failures:

(a) Childhood group boundaries may at times be clear to members, but unclear to outsiders, since the structuring of group boundaries constitutes an intragroup symbolic process.

(b) Childhood group boundaries may be generally unclear to both members and outsiders (that is, may be unstructured) until a nonmember seeks entry, at which point the group begins to structure boundaries.

(c) Childhood social group boundaries may be highly permeable in general, but become impenetrable when an unwanted outsider attempts entry, at which point a single group member who communicates rejection functionally initiates restructuring of group boundaries.

(d) Some childhood groups may be unable to tolerate the ambiguity of fluid group boundaries (threatening group identity), and, as a result, communicate rigid impenetrable boundaries to outsiders, in order to reassure group members of their uniqueness.

(e) The structuring of "group" boundaries in some childhood groups may be the result of a single group member, who acts without consensus, enacting unshared social rules or values.

This last explanation, an individual-member-boundary-builder dynamic, might also account for watcher-stress findings of this study. Group rejection decisions that are not shared by a member may trigger unexpressed stress. One adolescent who had remained silent while his group rejected another adolescent reflected like this:

> I wish I would have left the group and made my own, in which everyone was welcome.

A neglected variable associated with peer group processes is *entry stress.* Although no robust line of research by communication scholars on emotion and group communication currently exists, one construct that is gaining attention is *grouphate,* a term first used to describe the negative attitudes some people have toward working in groups.[27] Little is known about what creates grouphate, but the stress children and adolescents experience when their group inclusion attempts are rejected is a likely contender.[28] An outsider's *anticipatory entry* into groups and the negative anxiety that may accompany an attempt to gain peer group inclusion may be one source of adult grouphate.

Orenstein reported such conclusions in her research with middle school girls.[29] One girl who was new to school remembered her desperate desire to gain social inclusion as she anticipated entry, when, instead, she was cruelly stigmatized on the first day for her weight. The stigma kept her from gaining group access:

> Nobody even gave me a chance. It was like they were afraid to talk to me because I was fat, like I had a disease. (p. 100)[30]

The perceived stigma of peer group rejection may enhance anticipated group entry stress, when children believe that their rejection may seem "contagious" to other potential friends. (See study describing the peer group "rejection contagion" belief among adolescents.)[31]

One group communication researcher, Dr. Oetzel, has called for a greater focus on cultural differences that affect group processes.[32] The data in the "Being Left Out" study revealed a counter-intuitive outcome: non-Whites were more likely to report *low* (33 percent) stress for personal experiences of group rejection than were Whites. In turn, Whites were more likely to express *elevated* (71 percent) stress relating to the same event. Future studies are needed to discover whether such an effect would hold across diverse populations of children or adolescent peer groups.

❖ CONCEPTUALIZING PEER GROUP INTERVENTIONS

Moving forward, what interventions (and by whom) might facilitate more frequent and fruitful peer group inclusion of outsiders for adolescents? It turns out, of course, that schools provide the major context for childhood rejection, that rejection messages are negatively structured, and that entry attempt stresses are not confined to rejected children, but that they also impact observers.

The concept of *peer group facilitation* at school addresses these findings and foregrounds aiding performance, rather than governing it; and of coaching successes, rather than punishing infractions. Although exclusion is inextricably woven into the fabric of childhood play or competitive group experiences, injustices and pain associated with some strategies of peer group rejection can be reduced.

Behavioral Journalism

Our data revealed high stress levels for both observers and receivers of group rejection and accounts of uncertainty concerning how to manage exclusion or gain inclusion. One communication technique used to facilitate healthy change in high schools is behavioral journalism, a technique that emphasizes peer modeling of relevant audience-produced stories in preexisting school media forums.[33] Recently, behavioral journalism was successfully employed in a large ethnically diverse high school to reduce intergroup verbal aggression and hostility.[34]

Although a variety of violence prevention curricula are available, some teachers do not use them, because of limited resources. But school-as-community interventions such as behavioral journalism do not require teacher training or the implementation of new curricula. McAlister and colleagues designed simple statements in surveys ("If someone hits you, you should hit them back," or "Carrying a weapon can make me safer") and used them to collect data about students' values and experiences.[35] In a five-month communication campaign, student newspapers, school-wide publicity, and classroom presentations served as vehicles for sharing audience-generated stories designed to overcome processes of moral disengagement from "outsider" groups. Each news story explicitly focused on data from the surveys and included key words in headlines and captions. The results revealed that receptivity to intergroup affiliation at school and perceptions of similarity between groups significantly increased, whereas beliefs about the acceptability of violence decreased.

Teachers can assess extant media resources in their schools and then use our data or our question-format to institute semester-long information campaigns about attitudes, values, and effects of peer exclusion. Theater is one form of media resource, in which student-generated stories of exclusion and inclusion can be performed in classrooms and used to involve student audiences. For instance, Reader's Theater allows students to take on the role of other students, reading for one another what happened (or what might have been, if student groups rewrite endings). When the pain of rejection or the dilemma of exclusion-inclusion is not personal or in the moment, thoughtful reflection is possible.

New Theoretical Lenses: Conceptualizing Adolescent Peer Groups

While many of the above theoretical questions posed for early children's groups apply to adolescent peer groups, there exist new dynamics that emerge for teenagers as their mental, emotional, social, and physical needs mature and change. Adding to the questions posed for children's playgroups, our knowledge about the processes and effects of peer groups can expand by thinking about these issues:

> The main consequence of saying no to negative peer pressure is not just withstanding "the heat of the moment," as most adults think. Rather, it is coping with a sense of exclusion as others engage in the behavior and leave the adolescent increasingly alone. It is the loss of the shared experience. Further, the sense of exclusion remains whenever the group later recounts what happened. This feeling of loneliness then becomes pervasive but carries an easy solution—go along with the crowd.
>
> —Michael Riera
> (American author; former school counselor, teacher, and dean of students)[36]

Table 3.2 Theoretical Perspective and Application to Adolescent Peer Groups

Theoretical Perspective	Application to Adolescent Peer Groups
Symbolic-Interpretive Perspective	How do adolescent peer groups use humor to transmit values, reduce tension, or socialize new members? Do male and female peer groups use or react to humor or teasing differently? What is the role of dress in symbolically constructing peer group allegiance or in evaluating future members? Do adolescent peer groups create rituals? How do these peer groups symbolically construct identity?
Social Comparison Theory	What processes of comparison occur at the group or individual level, and how do they function to maintain or create peer group identity and loyalty? What role does social comparison play for outsiders in deciding which peer groups they wish to attempt to enter? How do rejected adolescents revise their self-comparisons (same/different, better/worse) after peer group rejection? How often and with what function do peer group members compare themselves to others in their own group? To what degree do adolescents compare themselves to media peer groups (television, film)?
Structuration Theory	What processes do adolescents use to create and maintain processes in their peer groups? What rules are adopted within peer groups? Are processes or rules imported by adolescents from other peer groups to which they have

Theoretical Perspective	Application to Adolescent Peer Groups
	belonged, or to which they currently belong? How frequent is the changing of structure and rules in adolescent peer groups? Do male and female adolescent peer groups structure and restructure themselves differently?
Decisional Regret Theory	How do adolescent peer groups manage anxiety about social or task decisions? When does counterfactual thinking emerge within these peer groups when they are making choices? Does the decision to reject an outsider involve counterfactual predecisional thinking on the part of any of the members of an adolescent peer group? Do rejected or excluded adolescents engage in counterfactual thinking before or after attempting inclusion? What decisions are most salient for adolescent groups? Do the decisions (and anxieties about decisions) of adolescent teams, church groups, school groups, hobby groups, or social cliques significantly differ? What regrets are most prominent for adolescents who are members of peer groups, and how do they affect group behaviors?
Social Identity Perspective	Which adolescent peer groups are most affected by comparison to (or rivalries with) outside groups? How do adolescent peer groups determine which outside groups are significant for their groups' identity? What role does perceived competition with outside groups have for constructing positive or negative identities of adolescent peer groups? Do adolescent task groups (for example, sports teams) engage in more ingroup/outgroup processing than adolescent social groups (school cliques, for example)?
Group Dialectical Perspective	As adolescents mature, do dialectical tensions or management strategies increase or change for them in their peer group relationships? How do adolescents in peer groups manage complex demands of family, friendships, romances, work, and school versus those of their desired peer groups? Do adolescents exit peer groups because of unresolved dialectical tensions?
Bona Fide Group Perspective	What do adolescents believe are the greatest resources or challenges for their peer groups? Which outside organizations (church, work, school, community, among others) impact their peer groups, and with what effect? How do adolescent peer groups acknowledge or interact with other groups? In what ways are these peer groups impacted by ethnic, socioeconomic, environmental, political, or educational organizations and issues in which they are embedded? How do adolescent peer groups construct their boundaries? Do male and female adolescent peer groups use different standards and processes for creating boundary penetration? How are group boundaries displayed, performed, and maintained by members?

Critical Thinking About Adolescent Peer Group

- Since peer group "sameness" is evaluated by the peer members of a group, it may not be apparent to outsiders. What examples of this have you seen, either with your own peer group experiences, or in your observations of other peer groups?
- How does the *Theory of Thin-Slicing* (or *Blink*) explain some rejection decisions made by peer groups (see Appendix)?
- In what ways have you seen *inclusion-fragility* or *rejection contagion* (see Appendix) fears affect teens and their decisions about whether or not to support outsiders?
- In order to sustain their own group's unique identity, what examples of *Fundamental Attribution Theory* can you offer to show that peer group members may evaluate their own mistakes, losses, or failures differently from those of other groups? Do you believe it is typical for coaches to help their athletic teams engage in Fundamental Attribution Theory in postgame reconstructions?
- What examples of specific adolescent peer groups are there that provide useful examples of the *Collective Effort Model* (see Appendix)? What behaviors, norms, or decisions would this model offer to explain adolescent peer groups?
- How might *deindividuation* (see Appendix), the tendency to feel invisible and less concerned with the rightness or wrongness of their behaviors when surrounded by a group of peers explain peer group pranks, mischief, and dares that end up with tragic consequences?
- What examples do you have about how adolescent peer groups deal with *deviants* within their own groups (see Appendix)?
- In what specific ways are adolescent peer groups vulnerable to *emotional contagion* (where the emotions an individual feels are influenced by the perceived emotions of those around that person)? How can wise group leaders use that natural phenomenon?
- What are some examples of adolescent peer groups that might tolerate the *free ride effect,* versus examples of adolescent peer groups that would be unlikely to tolerate a member who seems to be trying to benefit from the efforts of other task group members?
- Adolescent peer groups socialize new members in various ways (teaching culture, history, norms, values, rituals, goals). Which peer groups are more formal about this process, and which are more casual? How does the degree of formality impact the success of socialization for those groups?

4

Peer Groups in Neighborhoods

Hoodies, Homies, and Gansta Girls

Kings is not only like a gang, it's a family. Everybody cares about one another. You can never leave one behind. Everywhere we go we watch each other's back. We never leave nobody running behind. . . . 'Cause, see, the same way we watch their back, they're watching our back. When he [gestures toward Shadow, his friend] walks in the street and I'm walking on the other side of the street, I'm watching his back and he's watching mine. That's how we watch our own. That's the way you gotta do it. You gotta watch each other's back. We're all family, we're all Latin Kings. And see right there on the wall [points toward graffiti on nearby wall] you can read over there by that crown over there with the LK—it says "Amor." And "amor" right there means love. Amor stands for a lot of things. It

stands for, uh, the A stands for Almighty, the M stands for Masters, the O stands for Of, the R, Revolution—'cause that stands for Almighty Masters Of Revolution. See, amor.

—Latino boy, talking to professor on a Chicago rooftop*

Instead of grist for moral self-congratulation, as if we were violence-pure, and they were violence-prone, we need to recognize street gangs as magnifying mirrors in which we can see starkly the violence, territoriality, and militarism within ourselves.

—Dwight Conquergood**

Urban street peer groups have been largely ignored by traditional group scholarship. This is surprising, in light of current estimates that at least 24,000 gangs flourish in the United States, in large cities and small.[1]

What is a gang? Struggles over definitions of what constitutes a gang are still debated in the scholarly literature. Can a loose-knit neighborhood group be considered a gang? If some members commit crimes, is it a gang? The *United States Attorneys' 2006 Bulletin* on gangs (May) reports that gang definitions have been debated for decades, even among law enforcement. The one criterion used in virtually every gang definition, however, is that the members are involved in *continuing criminal activity.*[2] Every urban street group is not continually involved in crime (though many are), and every member of such a group does not participate in criminal behaviors (though some do); as a result, the term *gang* is a demonizing label, not useful for understanding the dynamic processes, values, conflicts, and goals of these peer groups. These groups, embedded in urban neighborhoods, might be more usefully understood by group scholars through reconceptualizing them as complex peer groups.

---

*Conversation from June 1989 between Professor Conquergood (1994) and one of the young men he met in his powerful ethnographic study of Chicago's Albany Park neighborhood, a working-class community that saw the arrival of many immigrants.

**For more than three years, Dwight Conquergood (1994, p. 219), professor at Northwestern University, studied the cultural practices of street gangs in a multicultural Chicago neighborhood. He began his study by quietly moving into Big Red, a huge dilapidated tenement.

Street gangs, as peer groups, are always a way of life and death for their members, representing a struggle for survival in the city, while creating and sustaining an intricate culture of communication practices that sustain identity and protect invisible geographic boundaries.[3] The peers in these groups enact and perform values largely invisible to outsiders. Sociologist Padilla quoted a young gang member in Chicago:

> We call ourselves a family, but, you know, when you really think about it we're also a team. And if you want to lose, play alone. Myself, I have gotten busted by the police several times because I was alone. I couldn't see them coming. When you're with your boys you have more eyes to check out what's going on—you can see the cops; you can see the opposition. . . . In the Diamonds, we teach the young guys; we practice how to be together all the time. We think that's our strength. Other people have money. We have each other.[4]

Peers have each other and they are always aware of that fact. In important ways, all peer groups watch the backs of their members: medical teams, sports teams, cliques, sisterhoods, quality circles, or squadrons. The members of any *street gang* do perceive that they are like one another, in one or more significant ways, even when they draw on divergent metaphors (family, team, soldiers, brothers) to describe their peerness.

❖ HOMEBOYS AND HOODS

> ***home•boy****, n., slang.* **1.** *male friend from one's neighborhood or hometown* **2.** *a fellow gang member.*
> ***'hood****, n., slang.* **1.** *someone from the neighborhood, usually in an inner city,* **2.** *a hoodlum,* **3.** *a rowdy or violent young person.*

The language with which some groups are described makes it difficult to escape their demonization by outsiders (see discussion above). As Conquergood repeatedly points out, the need to heighten and stimulate group consciousness by creating a strong boundary against the outside world accounts for a densely coded (and deliberately opaque) world of gang language.[5] Outsiders are largely ignorant of gang language that nurtures, however:

> Most outsiders, whose image of gangs is shaped by media demonology, would be surprised to hear the preponderance of gang

> terms rooted in nurturance and domestic tenderness. The entire 'hood is symbolized as a homeplace filled with bros and bloods, with specific apartments and domiciles referred to as "cribs" and "cradles." The nicknames that gang members give themselves and one another alternate between menacing and affectionate epithets. For every Hit Man and Pit Bull nickname there is a long line of Spanky, Teddy Bear, Baby Face, Hush Puppie, Kool Aid, Little Man, Pee Wee, Pollo, and other diminutives. The 'hood is imagined as a space of warmth and well-being.[6]

The identification of rivals versus brothers is performed symbolically (peer behavior explained by both the Symbolic-Interpretive Perspective and Social Identity Theory). Rituals of greeting are created for suspected rivals versus friends: "What you be about?" for example, may be a verbal challenge the equivalent of throwing down the gauntlet, or a demand for the declaration of gang allegiance.[7] *Reppin'*, is short for representing, and refers to a repertoire of communication practices whereby the members enact their group's identity (symbolic communication and ingroup/outgroup enactments) and includes dress, colors, throwing up hand signs, and calling out code words. Special argot (see Appendix) are created peculiar to certain gangs, with terms and phrases that circulate and are known only within specific gangs.* Rites of initiation into gang membership include complex norms and structures of interest to Structuration theorists. The stylized rites of handshaking (beyond the middle-class versions, two and one-half pumps) enact a blood-brother peer bonding. Most gangs have created unique choreographed rites of handshaking. Conquergood describes, for example, "shaking on the crown," as a graceful series of co-performed hand gestures representing the Latin King crown:

> These rites culminate in both partners throwing their right fist on their "heart" (chest), kissing their fingertips, and then tapping their heart with tips of fingers extended in the shape of a crown.[8]

Poorly understood by outsiders, this symbolic communication between brothers can be repeated dozens of times in the course of

---

*An example would be that "Violation" is shortened to "V." "Take your V." refers to accepting intragang discipline, including the administering of corporal punishment for infractions of that group's cultural norms (Conquergood, 1994).

walking a single block, if many brothers are out on the streets. Not to do so would be a sign of disrespect. As a group embedded in a larger society that is socioeconomically privileged, these symbolic rites recreate the dignity and love members feel have been stripped from them. Hand gestures function to reestablish and claim affiliation, restore respect, repair the loss of face, and redress the daily humiliations of poverty and prejudice.[9]

Symbolic peer group boundaries, of interest to the Bona Fide Group Perspective, are perceived as necessary to survival even within neighborhoods. The need for silence, secrecy, and alertness is intensified because the line between insiders and outsiders is experienced as slippery and shifting (Social Identity Perspective).[10] The complex organizational structures of street gangs, their respective alliances with People Nation or Folk Nation, and their manifestos (rule books) are aspects of particular interest to Structuration theorists.

Every part of gang life and the peer members within the gang is embedded in a clearly, though symbolically constructed, neighborhood territory called the *'hood.* Within this territory, particularly near the boundaries, graffiti announces the group's world and shouts out the entitlement of the group that claims it.

Visual Peer Talk: Graffiti

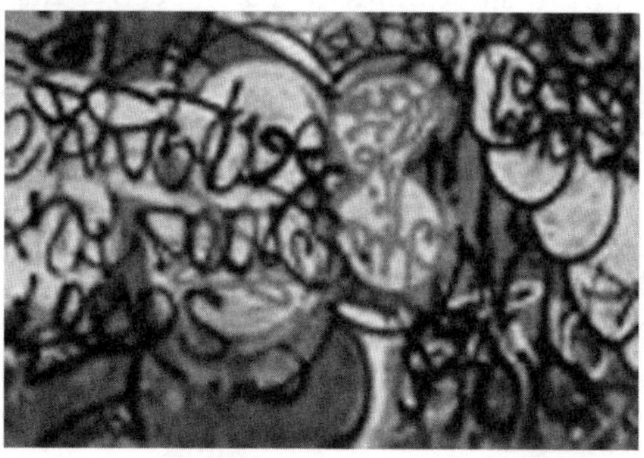

> *Middle-class citizens driving through the so-called "inner city" look at a graffiti-covered wall as meaningless gibberish and a sign of social disorder, whereas the local homeboys look at the same graffiti mural and appreciate the complex meanings and messages it artfully conveys.*
>
> —Dwight Conquergood[11]

"It is throwing up your love—it is all about love."

—Neighborhood youth,
explaining graffiti murals[12]

Derived from the Italian *sgraffio,* meaning "scratch," graffiti has always been with us (the carvings in the Lascaux Caves in France are often cited as early examples). Early man even appears to have anticipated the spray technique, holding his hand on the cave wall, then blowing colored powder through hollow bones to make a silhouette.[13] Over the years, the letter styles have morphed, with a wide range of forms: the legible blockletter, distorted or intertwined wild styles, bubble styles, and 3D.[14]

The word "graffiti" now conjures up vandalism and defacement, so street artists today have rejected the term, adopting "post-graffiti" or "neo-graffiti" to distinguish and legitimize their work. Peer group scholars are interested in the peer group's *designated* artists (functional group role), how the artist performs symbolic functions for the group, rather than in the talented independents who throw their art on the streets as visual gifts. Gang markings act to put down opposing groups, claim affiliation, designate safe areas, eulogize and honor deceased members, remember their history, and activate the cultural memory of that one peer group to insiders and outsiders.

Importantly, from a Social Identity Perspective that considers outside groups, graffiti frequently reflects tensions and conflicts among diverse groups in a single neighborhood.[15] One study, exploring graffiti at a predominantly African American university, found a focus on sex, sexual orientation, and racial identity, reflecting one avenue marginalized groups use to reclaim respect and identity.[16] Scholars of the rhetorical functions of graffiti between groups have argued that it functions to vent hostilities, express fantasies, communicate triumphs, declare rebellion, and promote propaganda.[17]

Playing the Dozens: Verbal Contests to Resolve Peer Conflict

Playing the Dozens is more than a game of fun—it is a battle for respect. It is an exhibition of emotional strength and verbal agility, a confrontation of wits instead of fists. The Dozens is a war of words—perhaps the best type of war there is.

—Dark Damian[18]

> ***snaps,*** n., slang [derived from "snappy comeback"] **1.** *artful insults traded between opponents in a contest judged by onlookers,* **2.** *public putdowns in consensual verbal street battles;* v. ***snapping***
>
> —Author's adaptation from Slang City[19]

The Dozens is an oral tradition, performed on urban streets, in which two people go head-to-head, taking turns insulting* one another, their opponent, or, most effectively, their adversary's mother**—until one of them has no powerful comeback. Playing the Dozens is an insult fight, full of rules and symbolic meaning that are important to the peer groups affiliated with the players. Each putdown (snap) ups the ante. Defeat is humiliating, though a skilled loser may gain some respect. Tips for play, including the "rules" are on many Web sites.***

Like playing chess, playing the Dozens requires a strategy. Unlike chess, the Dozens is an exhibition of poetry, where players strive to become a Dozens laureate.[20] The Dozens is a form of group conflict, performed verbally, with the necessity of onlookers, not only to inspire the competition, but also to reward the winner with a reputation of social strength. The Dozens is both a conflict and a form of entertainment, through which an understanding of self and others is created and recreated. Playing the Dozens functions to regulate relationships among neighborhood peer groups in places where the most pressing and recurring social problem for residents is "getting along."[21]

The Dozens game helps resolve social conflicts by encouraging and structuring communicative self-control in a public setting. The game does so through a two-part strategy that Garner has called "the strategy of cool":

> One aspect of cool means to be in control of the information one transmits. Players are expected to act aggressively and attempt to direct the

---

*Other words for insulting: burning, capping, cracking, heating, ranking, sparking, janking, frying, riding, cooking, owning, or snapping.

**"Yo' momma" is the widely recognized retort, also known as fighting words on the street, even when no explicit insult follows those two words.

***See examples on the Web of answers to ritual questions, such as: How do you get the audience on your side? Why is "your mother" so often the subject of snaps? Where is the dozens played? What is the distance that I should maintain between myself and my opponent? Do women play the dozens? What do you wear when playing the dozens? Do you need a loud voice to win a game? are found at Damian, D. (2005). Playing the dozens. Retrieved February 14, 2007, from http://darkdamian.blogspot.com/2005/04/playing-dozens.html

exchange of ideas. The second part of cool is based on projecting an image of composure by appearing detached or otherwise in possession of one's mental and emotional capabilities. To be effective the speaker must remain "poised."[22]

Using provocative "stingers," players attempt to demoralize or humiliate an opponent with insulting words. (See discussion of *face-threatening acts,* see Appendix.) The strategy is to verbally abuse an opponent until the opponent loses control, becomes angry, falls apart, gets rattled, or gets physical. These are signs that prove a player is weak. To "freeze" (by failing to respond to a powerful insult) is to demonstrate further weakness. Peer onlookers vigilantly evaluate nonverbal signs of weakness (facial expressions, postures, gestures, unnecessary movement). Playing the Dozens is a powerful intra- and extrapeer group tool for enacting identity and resolving conflict.

❖ GANGSTA GIRLS

Historically, female gangs were regarded as satellites of male gangs and there was little research undertaken to understand them, even among scholars of gang group processes. Some of the early work acknowledging female gangs trivialized them, concentrating their attention and theoretical analyses on male gangs. As a result, we have wide gaps in our knowledge about the girls and young women who are a part of these peer groups.[23] Consequently, a lot of the information available on female gangs comes from the reports of investigative journalists or social workers. (A 2001 summary of written scholarship was assembled by the Department of Justice.[24])

Every street gang, male or female, differs from the next, no matter where it is embedded geographically. A gang of girls may be autonomous or allied with a male gang. Female gang members may be part of a fully gender-integrated gang.[25] As with males, females joining a gang can be a statement of identity-claiming, or it can represent escape from an unwanted identity. Peer groups can represent alternative forms of femininity, or substitute for dysfunctional families, or, in immigrant neighborhoods, represent an expression of young women as independent Americans.

Both Latina and African American female gangs have been studied, though not from a group scholarship perspective. African American females in gangs were more likely than Latinas to feel they (not male gang members) controlled their gangs. By the time they were in their twenties, however, most had ceased to participate in their gangs. Latina gangs have been studied in New York (Puerto Ricans), the Southwest (Mexican Americans), and Los Angeles (where they have been continuously present since the 1930s). In terms of cross-peer-group dynamics, a study of Mexican American gangs in Los Angeles reported that even when female gangs were auxiliaries to male gangs, they often acted independently; within female gangs peers held more firmly to an egalitarian norm than males.[26] A scholar of New York City's Chinese gangs observed that females were an essential part of Chinese gangs, even when they were not allowed to become members: females were often the source of gang conflict.[27]

Young women in gangs must resolve their social role conflicts, such as being mother figures, tomboys, loose girls, good girls, or sisters. Dialectical tensions and role strains occur when gang norms conflict with outside family expectations and needs. One researcher found that motherhood was always an important role to female gang members, such that they sought to maintain a reputation within the gang as a "good mother."[28] White female gangs have rarely been studied.

❖ NEW THEORETICAL LENSES: CONCEPTUALIZING NEIGHBORHOOD STREET GROUPS

In this chapter, as a vivid exemplar of peer groups that are often marginalized but are embedded in our community, we have described neighborhood street gangs. It is important to acknowledge, however, that our neighborhoods are also richly populated with other urban peer groups. Consider, for example, scout troups, religious youth groups, homeless clans that adopt various street "homes" and care for one another, organized groups of con artists, activist tree-sitters, environmental protectors, crime watchers trained to protect their neighborhoods from crime, roving troupes of musicians, and many more. Specificity is a blessing and a curse, as it allows us to give attention to a specific group and develop our understanding but, at the same time, casts other important groups into the shadows. Our neighborhoods are, in fact, rich with peer groups at all economic levels: stable, transient, lawful, rebellious, and intriguing.

As alluded to above, there is a wide variety of peer group dynamics that might be explained through the seven theoretical perspectives presented in this book. As examples of these possibilities, consider the following table.

Table 4.1 Theoretical Perspective and Application to Street Gangs

Theoretical Perspective	Application to Street Gangs
Symbolic-Interpretive Perspective	What do we know about symbolic communication and behavior in these peer groups, including dress, humor, rituals, nonverbal street performances, graffiti, intragroup narratives, symbols of rivals, and meaning-making in a world in which these groups are largely demonized? How do members of these peer groups symbolically communicate their peer group affiliations? How do outsiders who wish to become members symbolize the value of membership?
Social Comparison Theory	How can we learn more about the types of comparisons that peers make with group members, as well as with nonmembers and those who are wanna-be members of street gangs? Who are the anchor points for comparison, who are the heroes or demons with which gang members compare themselves? Does this change after a member exits a gang? How do peer members deal with negative social comparisons (same/different, better/worse) both within their group and between their group and outside peer groups? Which social comparisons culminate in constructing an enemy peer group?
Structuration Theory	What structures are used to create brotherhood, community, intense loyalty, safety, protection against outsiders, and control of member behaviors? How are rules communicated to new members? What triggers restructuration of group processes within gangs? What resources do new members bring to a gang? Do existing members choose members based on perceived contributory resources?
Decisional Regret Theory	When faced with decisions about new members, what regrets from past decisions are resurrected? When requesting dangerous behaviors from members, how do gangs thwart anxiety about outcomes? What decisional thinking impacts relationships with enemies and outside groups? How do gangs deal with anticipated unwanted outcomes of their decisions? Does the death of any member trigger decisional regret and future changes in decisions about behavior of the group? To what degree does the criminal justice system and the arrest of members trigger anticipatory regret among gangs? What do members of these peer groups most regret?

Theoretical Perspective	Application to Street Gangs
Social Identity Perspective	How can we learn more about how these peer groups construct group identity or self-identity through group membership, disrespect rival group identity, perform rituals that claim, restore, or destroy face? What identity does a member lose by exiting a gang?
Group Dialectical Perspective	What strategies are used by members to balance the tensions between self and group, family and group membership, and independence and belongingness? In what ways might normal dialectical tensions impact intragroup conflict in gangs?
Bona Fide Group Perspective	What methods can be used for these hard-to-gain-entry groups to learn about neighborhood and community embeddedness, both in respect to rival gangs, nongang members in the neighborhood, law enforcement, the criminal justice system, social welfare resources, ethnic communities, and religious organizations and peer group climate? From the members' perspective, which outside groups and conditions most impact their lives and choices? How do they perform and construct symbolic group boundaries? What structures are created for the penetration of group boundaries or, alternatively, for the solidarity of these boundaries? Are there examples of some gangs that seem to have weak group boundaries that are more easily penetrated by outsiders?

Critical Thinking About Neighborhood Peer Groups

- How does *argot,* language unique to a group, explain communication and group-identity in a street gang (see Appendix)?
- In what ways might members of a street gang engage in the *Fundamental Attribution Error* when judging the behaviors of ingroup and outgroup members that appear to observers to be comparable?
- Gather specific media examples that represent demonization of gangs, as described by Conquergood. Could the headlines, for example, be written differently, yet still accurately describe the story?
- Using the concepts in Figure 1.1 (Chapter 1), diagram some of the symbolic practices and processes that you believe street and neighborhood groups rely on to communitcate to members and outsiders.

(Continued)

(Continued)

- Consider the climate in which specific street gangs around you are embedded (group climate includes the enduring qualities of the situation that arises from and influences member interactions, see Appendix). How do you believe the members of a gang experience the neighborhood climate, compared to how other citizens experience it?
- While gangs may be considered by mainstream society as "deviants," gangs may themselves be faced with *deviant* behaviors of their own members. How do you believe these groups manage nonconforming group members who regularly violate the significant norms of these neighborhood groups? (See Appendix.)
- Under what circumstances do you believe members of these groups are vulnerable to emotional contagion (see Appendix)? With what effects (on the group, the community, the members)?
- Notwithstanding how a gang might be viewed by mainstream outsiders, how do you believe ingroup members use Face and Politeness Theory (see Appendix) to sustain the desire of their own members to be liked and admired by relevant others (positive face) or to be autonomous and unconstrained (negative face)?
- If *reference groups* are any group that is admired and has the power to influence an individual through the process of identification, what explanatory power does this concept have for membership in gangs?
- In your view, do members of neighborhood gangs face the task of *impression management* (see Appendix)? Who do group members rely on to help them determine the success or failure of their contributions?
- What other neighborhood peer groups exist in your current neighborhood? To what degree are each of these groups prosocial, rebellious, marginalized, ethnically diverse, and to what degree do the groups impact your daily life or choices? Are there any concepts (see Appendix) that you believe apply both to neighborhood street gangs and some of the other peer groups that are embedded in your neighborhood?

5

Peer Groups That Super-Task

Hot Groups

The hot group state of mind is task-obsessed and full of passion. It is always coupled with a distinctive way of behaving, a style that is intense, sharply focused, and full-bore.[1]

Groups that super-task are not an exclusive phenomenon of modern organizations, nor are they the property of Americans, white males, adults, or prodigies. Rather, these tightly knit peer groups are task-obsessed and full of passion, with a self-sacrificing dedication to doing something together that each member believes is important. More task-focused than social, these peer groups nonetheless thrive, in part, because of their relationships with one another. As a group, they are "able to leap tall buildings in a single bound" (and do so regularly).

New to the study of peer group processes are specific small groups that are often invisible to the media or mainstream society, yet these peer groups accomplish together with passion more than is logically possible. This chapter introduces powerful examples and research on *super-groups:*

groups of peers whose members are task-obsessed, sharply focused, deeply loyal, and who generate within each group a contagious single-mindedness. Theoretical perspectives are offered to explain the dynamics of these small groups and to offer critical thinking about how we might stimulate *hot group dynamics* in our own peer task groups.

❖ HOT GROUPS: FLAMING AND FOCUSED—FULL-SPEED AHEAD

> *We even walked differently than anybody else. We felt we were way out there, ahead of the whole world.*
>
> —Aerospace executive, on his 1990s project team[2]

> *We didn't even obey a 24-hour clock. We'd come in and program for a couple days straight, we'd—you know four or five of us—when it was time to eat, we'd get in our cars and kind of race over to the restaurant and sit and talk about what we were doing. Sometimes I'd get so excited about things, I'd forget to eat. Those were the fun days.*
>
> —Bill Gates*

Maybe you called yourselves a team, a task force, a squadron, a band, a study group, or, maybe your group never had a specific name. You might have been at war or at play, in a hospital or a university, on the playing field or at a church. If that group was a *hot group,* though, you remember it as one of the most productive experiences of your life. Members of hot groups are overachievers. While these groups last (which may not be long), hot groups completely captivate their individual members.

❖ THE HOT GROUP STATE OF MIND: HOW HOT GROUPS THINK

HANDS OFF!! **HOT GROUP AT WORK**

Sign seen in hallway

---

*Bill Gates is the well-known American entrepreneur and chairman of Microsoft (1955–).

Fast, Focused, and Wide Open: How Hot Groups Task

Hot groups are not necessarily groups of peers. Hot groups may call themselves peer groups, some members may believe all members of the group are peers, yet, it turns out, that not all hot groups are groups of peers. The task itself is not sufficient to create a peer group, if the membership privileges and duties are significantly divergent.

Studying peer groups of health-care teams, Dr. Ellingson,[3] drawing on a Bona Fide Group Perspective, pointed out the fluidity of backstage settings that form the context for an interdisciplinary geriatric oncology team at a cancer center. However, when doctors, nurses, and social workers (to name only a few possible medical team members) work in a small group, the hierarchy, status, and responsibilities of each member are so diverse that they are not a peer group. These medical teams, however, may be *hot groups,* operating full speed ahead with passion.

One significant difference between the modern organizational "team" and the elite hot groups is that peers in hot groups (and the scholars who study them) agree that people's feelings about one another do not always matter in organizational groups, which, for example, tolerate gossip, backstabbing, or complaints. In hot groups mutual loyalty submerges personal irritations, as Lipman-Blumen and Leavitt explain in their foundational book, *Hot Groups.*

> In hot groups, it is not mutual loyalty and trust that generate effective performance. Neither is it friendship, nor understanding of one another's idiosyncrasies. Hot groups work the other way around. It is their task, not one another, that hot groups love, along with the *process* of working on that task together. When each person is being pulled by the magnetic power of the task, mutual trust can follow, albeit ineffably. Mutual understanding, loyalty, and friendship often occur in hot groups, but when they do, they are a result, not a cause, of commitment to their task.[4]

A peer group develops its sense of *peerness* (see Appendix) and community from its task. Furthermore, an emotional spillover may occur, when peer members become infatuated with everything associated with their mission; sacrifice resources, time, and relationships for that task; and only come up for air when the task nears completion.* For better or worse for the individual members and their outside lives, hot

---

*Peer irritation is, it appears, a final-phase event: "Later, as the task nears completion, the warts may become more noticeable, either to be tolerated or perhaps eventually to cause enough irritation to fracture the group" (Lipman-Blumen & Leavitt, 1999).

group peers' passionate commitment to task makes their group less vulnerable to interpersonal distractions and conflict than other groups (thereby avoiding the *sucker effect* and *free riders*; see Appendix). What may be needed, however, is the presence of peer members who share the vision and the same achieving style for getting things done.

Consistent with a Symbolic-Interpretive Perspective, scholars find that hot groups use unique mottoes, logos, language, t-shirts, hats, flags, or markers of identity* (one early Macintosh group created a skull and crossbones flag with an apple in its eye). It is characteristic of these groups that the peer members believe they are hot, believe they are elite, and strut their stuff to outgroups.

Conductors, Patrons, and Keepers of the Flame: Hot Group Leadership

As with most peer groups, hot groups do not value rank and authority. Rather, they embrace democratic or functional leadership. Communication flows in all directions. Traditional status markers lacking, a cultural of mutual respect emerges rather than titles among the members.

Decisional Regret Theory invites us to focus on examining how these groups, without traditional top-down leadership, make decisions that are, by nature, risky. Scholars of hot groups find that the communication patterns during decision making are egalitarian, in that all voices are heard and listened to, with wide-open interaction (though at high speed).

Task, rather than leadership, pushes performance. One example is a study by Roberts and King, who investigated a hot group of educational policy entrepreneurs who successfully changed the Minnesota school system.[5]

> Many declared [the policy entrepreneurs] to be effective because they outworked everyone else, putting in as much as eighty hours a week. One entrepreneur's dedication was so renowned . . . that an observer described him as a "policy junkie" who never stopped working because "it's his cause."[6]

Lipman-Blumen and Leavitt described a "connective leadership" that emerges in hot groups (which may be what emerges in adolescent

*Lippman-Blumen & Leavitt (1999).

peer groups). Connective leaders are divided into three subsets: conductors, patrons, and keepers of the flame. Conductors are hands-on leaders; patrons are nonparticipating resource providers; and keepers of the flame build bridges between one task and the next, one idea and the next, one stage to another, and keep the passion fired.

Standing in the Fire: Structures, Rules, and Processes in Hot Groups

Compelling examples of hot groups are in the media everyday. These peers share elite status, task-obsession, and passion for their work, as exemplified by this recent headline:

Elite Team Rescues Troops Behind Enemy Lines[7]

AVON PARK AIR FORCE RANGE, FLORIDA (CNN)—As a member of the U.S. Air Force's elite Combat Search and Rescue team, "Dan," a pararescueman, or PJ, is used to saving the lives of fellow U.S. and coalition troops in battlefield situations. But last month, he was the one in need of rescue . . . We originally met "Dan," a PJ, which is short for parajumper, right before he volunteered for that mission in Afghanistan. "We'll live up to our motto, 'That Others May Live,' " he said to us during covert night-operations training in Florida swamplands. "If you're out there, we'll go get you." The PJs are special operators within the Air Force, a kind of cross between a Green Beret and an emergency trauma paramedic . . . Their job is considered one of the military's toughest, and they are in constant demand. Lately, headline after headline about aircraft that have gone down in Iraq and Afghanistan have reinforced that fact.

For every helicopter that goes down, an Air Force Combat Search and Rescue team, which includes the PJs, must go into that same hostile territory to rescue and medically treat the downed crew. The PJs are part of what is called the Guardian Angel Weapon System, which includes combat rescue officers and survival, evasion, resistance and escape specialists. Pilots and aircrews of high-tech rescue helicopters, A-10 Warthog attack jets, fighter jets, reconnaissance aircraft and special refuelers round out the team. The PJs are the only unit designated by the Department of Defense primarily to rescue and recover U.S. personnel trapped behind enemy lines. These units take on other special duties that they do not talk about, but their main mission is to save and bring people home from hostile territory.*

Hot groups are also characterized by deep beliefs that their work is important and they bring to it a style that is intense, sharply focused,

*Air Force officials credit their Combat Search and Rescue teams with more than 750 saves in Iraq and Afghanistan since 9/11. They also credit these units with saving more than 4,000 lives during and after Hurricane Katrina. Hollywood has dramatized some of their exploits in movies such as *The Perfect Storm,* which showed rescues off the New England coast, and *Black Hawk Down,* which showed them helping bring back Army Rangers and others wounded or killed in helicopter crashes during the Battle of Mogadishu, Somalia, in 1993.

and full-bore ahead ("That others may live!"), as these same elite rescuers personify:

> The most comforting thing that was said to us was, "Because of you guys, a warrior was brought back," rescue helicopter pilot "TC" said.[8]

Furthermore, *danger* is often a component that keeps the fire burning in the eyes of the peer members of elite task groups. The reporter talked to members of the rescue team about the danger:

> The work has always been dangerous, but it is getting more so, according to one PJ: Insurgents have laid ambushes, or placed bombs or other "secondary devices," that specifically target the rescue teams. They call these "SAR traps," short for Search and Rescue traps. Six PJs have been killed since the beginning of both operations Iraqi Freedom and Enduring Freedom.
>
> Dan, the PJ injured in Afghanistan, said before he left for that special mission that his teammates know they can face hostilities every time they respond to a call "For the families of those soldiers and civilians, they should know we'll go out there and do what we can; we'll put our lives on the line to bring that person home," he said.[9]

As with those parajumpers, elite hot groups regularly overachieve with passion, but that effort carries with it the corresponding threat of peer member burnout.

When the Flame Fizzles

One temporal rule for hot groups is that they cannot stay hot for long. These peer groups cannot maintain that extraordinary level of effort, and they are never intended to exist forever. They are, by mutual agreement, temporary peer groups.

Some once-flaming task peer groups enter into a premature demise. Bona Fide Group Perspective offers insight here, reminding us of the importance of embeddedness for every group. In fact, hot group scholars point out that fizzled groups often failed to monitor their environment: members burn out or are lured away, companies are bought out, resources dry up, or new (and possibly difficult) members enter the group and capsize the boat before it reaches the shore.

Embeddedness: Where Hot Groups Grow

Just as hot group peer members thrive on passionate attachment to task, they wilt in cultures that are based on permanence. They have this in common with adolescent cliques, but for different reasons. Hot groups often emerge because of crisis, so it follows that they were never intended to survive the resolution of that crisis. Hot groups may emerge in response to perceived enemies, who, when vanquished, leave the group without purpose. They thrive on threat, attack, and retreat.

While studies to date of hot groups have examined adult groups with organizational challenges, these groups could emerge in high schools, in communities in response to disasters, among strangers building homes for other strangers, and, clearly, in survivors of disasters—horrific events creating impermanent but intense peer groups.

❖ WORKIN' FROM CAN'T TO CAN'T: AFRICAN AMERICAN COWBOYS

Like when we were on the ranch, everybody was knit close. Everybody was cousin.

—Willie Brown, 88
(African American cowboy)

We got up and worked from can't to can't. You know what can't to can't is? Can't see when you get up and can't see when you lay down. [Laughs.]

—Reverend Mack Williams, 90
(African American cowboy)

Everybody out there was kin to me, runnin' that ranch. Everybody out there was kin to me. I guess that's what made me love cowboying.

—Nathaniel Youngblood, 93
(African American cowboy)*

Imagine a western novel or film opening with a scene showing black cowboys hard at work on the Texas plains. This scene does not square with a traditional picture of the West—and you have never seen it. Yet thousands upon thousands of blacks labored on the broad plains of Texas before, during, and decades after the Civil War. Thousands of those people became cowhands.[10] They were groups of cowboys who super-tasked.

"They Just Wouldn't Take Our Picture!" Race and the Invisible Peer Groups that Were Always There

> An observer standing on a rise and watching a herd of cattle being driven up a trail could not differentiate one cowboy from another. He saw only a group of men doing a job in a cloud of dust.[11]

Eight thousand black cowpunchers helped shape a tradition as American as Thanksgiving and apple pie. Katz describes how, for the usual $30 a month and grub, these African American cowboys rode the wilderness trails and took their chances with flooding rivers, wild animals, and sudden storms. They just never had a chance to gallop across the pages of history books, Hollywood, movies of the Old West, or television.[12]

In their 1965 book, *The Negro Cowboys,* Durham and Jones pointed out that there had always been "Negro" ranchers and cowboys in the West.[13] The Negro cowboys rode with white Texans, Mexicans, and Indians. They hunched in their saddles during blizzards and thunderstorms, turned stampedes, and rode wild mustangs. In short, their lives were like those of all other cowboys (hard and dangerous), but later,

*Willie Brown, the Reverend Mack Williams, and Nathaniel Youngblood are three of six African American cowhands who describe their cowboy peers in the early 1900s on an Institute of Texan Cultures documentary videotape, "Workin' from Can't to Can't: African-American Cowboys in Texas," and available at store.the-museum-store.org/wofrcatocaaf.html

when cowboys became historical folk heroes, these Negroes were fenced out.* The black cowboy virtually vanished:

> John Wayne wouldn't be nothin' beside of us. They just didn't take our picture. No, uh-uh, John Wayne and Tim Holt, Durango Kid and, uh, that other one—Gene Autry, oh, no. they ain't nothin'. We had horses that do just what they do. So what, they just didn't put it in the paper. Yeah, didn't put it in the paper. . . . None of 'em could stick with us. We'd make a monkey out of 'em. On them picture shows back there when Durango and Roy Rogers and Tim Holt, all them were playing, you never seen a black cowboy there. I don't know if whether they just didn't work them or what, but there was always black cowboys.[14]

The point of their history is not that they were different from their companions, but that they were similar.[15]

Many of the early western cowboys were Black Indians, as an ethnic peer group, even more invisible than any other group of American cowboys. It has been estimated that a third of African Americans have Native American ("Indian") blood, though in the preface to the 1996 edition of his book, *Black Indians,* Katz indicated that today just about every African American family tree may have an Indian branch:

> Black Indians? The very words make most people shake their heads in disbelief or smile at what appears to be a joke, a play on words. No one remembers any such person in a school text, history book, or western novel. None ever appeared. Yet they lived and roamed all over the Americas.[16]

Beginning in the mid-19th century, the ranches of the Texas Gulf Coast nurtured close-knit communities of Mexicans, Native Americans, and African Americans, all focused on working cattle. These men claimed both African and Native American heritage,

---

*The first running of the Kentucky Derby (Churchill Downs, 1875) was, in fact, won by a Negro jockey. Not surprising, because of the 14 horses entered, 13 were ridden by Negroes. From the first running until 1902, Negroes won 11 of the Derbies and a Negro jockey (Isaac Murphy) was the first rider to win three Derbies. In the South, Negroes had been working as stableboys, trainers, and jockeys; they were good horsemen. Horses were critical when Texans began driving their longhorns to market (up to 100 horses needed for each cattle drive).

displayed in their names and on their faces. Awarding-winning documentary film producer Steven R. Heape and his Native American-owned film group (another task peer group!) have recovered much of the history of the early peer groups that shared a unique ancestry, African Americans and Native Americans, in his film, "Black Indians: An American Story."[17] In this documentary, the cultural and racial fusion explores how two ethnic peer groups were brought together and their continuing influence many generations later. One of the most powerful graphics on this film foregrounds the neglect of Black Indians, while posing the question: "To build the future you must know the past. But what if that past has been hidden, lost or denied?"

These early African American cowboys were peers in groups that were both *task* and *social* in orientation and challenges. Here, we harvest from historical documentary fieldwork to understand how group concepts are embedded and enacted in the 1800 and 1900 peer groups of African American cowboys—not to illuminate how different they were, but rather to show how similar to peer groups familiar to us they were. Drawing on the documentary data, an invisible peer-task-social group with a passionate obsession for their work together is described. The story of the peer group values, dynamics, roles, rules, and behaviors for these early cowboys of color is told through the lenses of group constructs and theories.

Symbolic Communication: Objects, Rituals, and Symbols That Sustain Cowboy Peers

The Institute of Texan Cultures created a powerful 30-minute documentary that captures the unique peer group culture of African American cowboys in the late 1800s and early 1900s: "Workin' from Can't to Can't".[18] The words of these cowboys offer a rich harvest of intimate group culture and sense of peerness. A Symbolic-Interpretive Perspective invites us to consider, at the outset, the symbolic objects, rituals, or symbols that sustained their peer culture.

Each cowboy who was interviewed, many well into their nineties ("Ain't many of us left"), wore his best western garb to the filming, then explained the importance of each piece. There was clothing, all of it functional, to fight the dust, protect their legs, spur the horses, or store medicine for treating ill cattle on the drive. As with many peer groups, however, what was functional for the task created identity and offered to the world a statement of who they were and what they cared about. In addition to dress, ropes were displayed as symbols of former task skills that were also entertaining and a source of skill-pride. You were a peer member because you could use these objects and because you valued them.

The ritual of meals, for example, as well as the role of the cook, is described in detail; food on a drive played into ritual meals of community and accomplishment:

K. J. OLIVER: We got a cook. And don't make him mad, 'cause you do, you come in, it won't be no dinner cooked. [Laughs] Everybody can't cook on a camp.

REV. MACK WILLIAMS: Our main dish was pinto beans—well, it wasn't pinto beans in those days; they were red beans. And it would take you half a day to cook a red bean, but they'd put 'em on so early in the mornin' until—my Lord![19]

"Workin' from can't to can't," for example, meant to these cowboys a work ethic in which you got up when you couldn't see anything but darkness and you stopped working when it was just as dark. There were routines and rituals, constructing meaning each day for each peer. Hours worked were symbols of the difficulty of the job and the kind of man it took to do it well.

Horses, necessary for the cattle drive, became objects that sustained identity, as the cowboys described how they loved riding so much they would do it for free. The cows herded became metaphors used by several of these cowboys to explain their vision of their task. One described, with obvious pride, how the owner of the cattle would come to him and say, "How your cattle gettin' along?"

K. J. OLIVER: I do everything I can to improve the cattle that I'm taking care of. And one guy told me, said, "You show more interest in the cattle than the man who owns the cattle." [Laughs] Well, he—whenever I ride the pasture and come in in the evening he [the owner] wouldn't say, "How's my cattle gettin' along?" He'd always say, "K., how your cattle gettin' along?" That's what he used to say, "K., how are your cattle gettin' along?" Yeah, that's the way it was, see?[20]

Oliver was explaining, with delight, that both he and the owner knew he loved those cattle and cared for them more than the owner.

"I Gotta Nickel, You Gotta Nickel": The Collectivistic Culture of the Cowboy-Task Group

One of the most powerful segments in this film for those who see it for the first time is always when the cowboys describe the relationship the cowboys had with each other. Nat Love describes a male social order in which the most significant rule of decorum was loyalty to those on whom one's safety and livelihood was reciprocally dependent. At one point, a cowboy looks into the camera and explains, "It was, just, 'I gotta nickel, you gotta nickel.'"[21]

This collectivistic culture of property and resources is foreign to most of us today. My students are quickly able to compare this to "borrowing" $5.00 from a friend. "You are expected to pay it back. If you don't, I get irritated." For this cowboy peer group, another cowboy was never borrowing money from someone who had it. If one had it, anyone who needed it had it. Social rules were firm and understood. There are robust examples of this collectivistic culture:

WILLIE BROWN:	Like when we were on the ranch—everybody was knit close; everybody was cousin.
REV. MACK WILLIAMS:	And everybody loved each other's family, and they'd take care of 'em. And then you, you'd get a family that didn't have, uh, food or somethin' like that—don't worry about it. They gonna get what they had in the garden or whatnot, and everybody—we used common food and they'd bring it and share.
E. J. GARZA:	If you saw me, you saw them; if you saw them, you saw me. That's the way we were. We were just like brothers.[22]

A second vivid example of the collectivistic culture of this social-task peer group involved task. One cowboy described an owner out looking for another hand named Bill. This cowboy (who was *not* Bill) said, "You lookin' for Bill, you found him." Both the owner and the cowboy knew he meant simply, "Whatever work Bill was supposed to do for you, I'm now Bill, I'll do it." Task was never one man's job. What task groups today have that culture? Super-task groups cannot afford chronic enduring conflict, and are passionate about their work; a collectivistic culture creates solidarity that avoids ownership of objects, resources, or duties.

"Today's Cowboy, Yesterday's Cowboy, Day-Before-Yesterday's Cowboy": The Role of Sustaining Historic Group Identity by Putting Down Modern Cowboys

Social Identity Perspective suggests that some form of us-them thinking is not only inevitable, but also that it functions to sustain healthy peer group identity. In this documentary, there are three robust examples. Intriguingly, the outgroup that is the target for the social comparison is "today's cowboy." Three groups are used: the African American cowboy (Yesterday's Cowboy), his father (Day-Before-Yesterday's Cowboy), and the modern Texas cowboy (Today's Cowboy).

Same/different comparisons and better/worse weave together (Social Comparison Theory, Table 1.1). Today's Cowboy has a truck (said with disdain), and doesn't have to round up the cattle: they all come running to the truck for the hay. Yesterday's Cowboy had it tougher. Today's Cowboy has breakfast in the daylight and, worse, has orange juice (speaker rejects the idea of orange juice and a cowboy)! In a third comparison, these cowboys make fun of work "breaks" that modern cowboys want ("We didn't know what a break was!"). One robust example of this same/different or better/worse comparison used by these peer group members was the following description of the task of chemically treating cattle for ticks, then and now:

REV. MACK WILLIAMS: That dippin' vat is a long shoot made I guess, about five feet wide because you get some cattles in there that's pretty hefty. And, uh, it's deep, right in there, see? When you slide here, the cow can't turn around. And so, you get there and hollerin' at 'em and all the confusion, they hit that water, and some of them trying to jump, "WHACHO!" down in the water they go. And the water gets all over 'em. And then they start swimmin' out. And they had the ticks on 'em, or lice, or whatever you wanted to get for that. That killed the ticks. . . . What today's

> cowboy do, they got the electric pump. And they go out there, and they won't even have a gasoline pump like they used to have. They'll put electric lights all over that pen and get that, and sprrrrrrr—spray 'em. Well, what kind of a cowboy is that?[23]

Throughout (consistent with a Symbolic-Interpretive Perspective), humor is used to make the comparisons as the delight in how hard the tasks were is used to sustain their concept that it will never be that way again: "We're the last." A super-task group with passion, even in the remembering.

A robust example of a super-tasking group with deep social bonds, these cowboy peer groups had a lot in common with today's rare elite hot groups that task with technology. A peer group member of these African American cowboys had to adopt the unique group culture and profound passion, just as with the hot groups studied today:

NATHANIEL YOUNGBLOOD: If you wadn't solid, you couldn't stay at that ranch—that's one thing for sure. There's been many one there. You look up, and they headed to the highway—couldn't take it. You've got to make up your mind to be one, I guess. 'Cause if you ain't solid, you just can't stay. Yeah, you've got to be solid.

❖ NEW THEORETICAL LENSES: CONCEPTUALIZING SUPER-TASKING PEER GROUPS

The primary peer group questions that emerge for groups that are more social than task (childhood and adolescent peer groups, or street gangs, for example), are different in some ways from those that emerge for groups where self-identity/group-identity keeps the peer group more task than social.

What peer group scholarship could be effectively explored by applying our seven perspectives specifically to super-tasking groups, who are both social and task, but exemplify a passionate commitment to task?

Super-task groups are tightly knit peer groups that are consistently task-obsessed and full of passion, with a self-sacrificing dedication to doing something *together* that each member believes is important. As pointed out at the outset of this chapter, these groups are typically more task-focused than social-focused, yet they nonetheless thrive, in part, because of their relationships with one another. As a group, the members perceive that they passionately accomplish together more than appears to be logically possible.

Table 5.1 Theoretical Perspective and Application to Super-Task Groups

Theoretical Perspective	**Application to Super-Task Groups**
Symbolic-Interpretive Perspective	What symbols, humor, stories, rituals are used by super-task peer groups and with what purpose? How do the peer members of these groups symbolically think about their missions? How is the culture of these groups and their perceived mission symbolically communicated between members? How are new members socialized? Are colors, music, signage, logos, or clothing important in this group's display of itself?
Social Comparison Theory	What level of comparison do members of these peer groups use (same/different or better/worse) when (a) comparing peers within the group, or (b) comparing their group to outside groups? What is the effect of having been a member of a super-task group on subsequent social comparisons that former members make about themselves and other people? What role does social comparison play in triggering the passionate commitment to task? What language or metaphors are used to create or maintain functional comparisons to outside groups?
Structuration Theory	Since task is a dominant concern, how do peer members judge the resources each member brings to super-task groups? What structuring processes within group dynamics occur to maintain or sustain a passionate task attitude? In what ways do the rules and norms of super-task groups differ from other peer groups that these members belong to? Why might members of super-task groups import the rules, norms, or culture of their super-task groups to other peer groups they later join?

(Continued)

Table 5.1 (Continued)

Theoretical Perspective	Application to Super-Task Groups
Decisional Regret Theory	In a group that is based on fast-paced confidence, what role does anticipated decisional regret play? How many decisions do super-task groups consistently face? How do peers in super-task groups cope with or react to expressed anticipated decisional regrets of peers? What decisional rules are used and how does such a peer group cope with apparent decisional deadlock? To what degree is it functional for these groups to ignore member anxiety about task decisions?
Social Identity Perspective	What symbols and metaphors are used to distinguish their peer groups from outside groups? How do peer members of super-task groups create and maintain their unique identities? What is the effect of membership in a super-task group on individual identity (both during and after the group's life)?
Group Dialectical Perspective	For a group that demands 24/7 loyalty and passion, what dialectical challenges arise for members who also have commitments outside this group? What strategies do super-task group peers use to balance an extraordinary group commitment with competing social needs outside that group? To what degree do these groups openly acknowledge and help members cope with dialectical tensions that will inevitably arise in these groups?
Bona Fide Group Perspective	What environments do these super-task peer groups thrive in? What environments challenge them or destroy them? How do super-task groups construct their symbolic group boundaries to outsiders? How penetrable are the boundaries of super-task groups?

Critical Thinking About Peer Groups That Super-Task

- In what ways does *synergy* (see Appendix)—the result that occurs when a group's performance seems to surpass the apparent capabilities of any single member—explain the process, member satisfaction, and outcome produced by peer groups that super-task?
- In your view, could a successful super-task group be composed of adolescents, or do you believe such tasks and results require adult peers?

- How do the cognitive neurological brain processes described by the *Science of Happiness* (see Appendix) explain the passion experienced by hot group members? Do these members use a *peak-end rule* to evaluate their group experiences?
- What explains the passionate commitment of super-task members to their groups and tasks, to the degree that considerable self-sacrifice is willingly made?
- Since some super-task groups operate in the midst of crisis, how does the *Theory of Thin-Slicing* (see Appendix) explain the ability of these groups to produce rapid accurate evaluations and snap judgments about the group task?
- Does the anxiety and awkwardness of a *zero-history* moment (see Appendix) affect, in your view, a super-task group?
- What *anchor points* might super-task group members hold in common that allow these groups necessary mental shortcuts? In what ways could anchor points held by super-task groups that are grounded in previously successful or unsuccessful peer group experiences block the perceived success of a specific super-task group?
- Is a *task leader* relevant, threatening, or unimportant to super-task groups? Is a task leader a social leader?
- How are super-task groups, such as the African American cowboys, successful in managing *dialectical tensions?* Which specific dialectical group tensions (Chapter 1) do you believe most frequently need to be successfully managed by super-task groups? To what degree are members aware of these tensions, in your experience?
- How do super-task groups manage to avoid or manage *social loafing,* the *free ride effect,* the *sucker effect, deindividuation,* or the effects of the *Collective Effort Model* (see Appendix)?
- Do you belong to any peer groups where "If I gotta nickel, you gotta nickel" is truly a group value and norm? How might a particular peer group be different if a norm like this one was shared by the group members?

6

Peer Groups as Decision Makers

Juries

jury•o•lo•gy, n. *1. the study of behaviors of people who serve as jurors in the culture of the courtroom. 2. the sum of the structures, culture, social rules, laws, communication, and dilemmas of trial jurors. 3. the legal-psycho-sociological study of jury deliberations and verdicts.*[1]

Art: Vanna Rocchi

Twelve men of the average of the community, comprising men of education and men of little education, men of learning and men whose learning consists only in what they have themselves seen and heard, the merchant, the mechanic, the farmer, the laborer; these sit together, consult, apply their separate experience of the affairs of life to the facts proven, and draw a unanimous conclusion.

—*Sioux City & Pacific R.R.* v. *Stout,*
84 U.S. (17b Wall.) 657 (1873)

There is at first the sense of buzzing, booming, confusion. After a while, we become accustomed to the quick fluid movement of jury discussion and realize that the talk moves in small bursts of coherence, shifting from topic to topic with remarkable flexibility. It touches an issue, leaves it, and returns again.

—Unnamed juror[2]

SCENE: Courthouse Jury Assembly Room.

Dozens of restless citizens who were summoned for jury duty wait in dusty theater chairs, on their third day of service.
They are peers.

JUROR A: [low gravelly voice, musing out loud to no one in particular]: You know—there are so many factors in a homicide case.

JUROR B: [sitting nearby and turning]: What do you mean?

JUROR A: It's not humanly possible to do everything or remember everything.

JUROR B: I suppose.

JUROR A: Then there's the money problem. It's expensive.

JUROR B: Umm.

JUROR A: Then you have F. Lee Bailey trying to pull a rabbit out of the hat! The defense is trying to do that. Everyone's on trial, except the defendant! If you're a witness, *you're* accused.

JUROR B: They blame everyone else.

JUROR A: The poor jury. They haven't been in court all week long.

JUROR B: I saw a TV show once. They had this trial in Germany and some new evidence was found, you know. I can't remember all the details, but you know the defense, the prosecution, and the judge got together to discuss this. They talked about the effect it had on the case.

JUROR A: What does it mean?

JUROR B: They seemed to be getting together to find out what the *truth* was! Of course, it was very brief in the movie. But it made me wonder if there was another way to the adversary way of doing things.

JUROR A: Just get to the facts! I call attorney-words, "smoke screens." I wonder: Does it go to protect the client? Does it go to help citizens?

JUROR B: Are you in law enforcement?

JUROR A: I was a sergeant for 31 years in the police department.

WIDESHOT: All nearby jurors lean forward, obviously listening.

JUROR B: I have been wondering about something. It is so interesting. [*No response.*]

JUROR B: [*resuming, anyway*]: I've been writing a book, you see, and I always wanted to ask a police officer some questions. Would you mind? It's about the Mafia. Sort of.

JUROR A: What kind of questions?

JUROR B: Well, in my story, these people from the Mafia have $10 million. Now, how would they get that? Would it be drugs? Is that too much money? It's $10 million in a chunk. Maybe I should make it $2 million?

JUROR A: You could come up with that much money, conceivably. Usually it would be the upper echelon, though. Not the lower Mafia. Middle or upper.

JUROR B: I would think upper.

JUROR A: Of course, I am no expert.

JUROR B: There is Mafia in Los Angeles, isn't there? Of course, they have gone legitimate and mostly underground.

JUROR A: They are involved in white-collar crime. Computers and stuff, you know. There's no limit to what they can do now. From drugs and prostitution to all crimes affecting all of society. They're on the Internet. [*Pause, hesitating.*] Do you do any kind of investigation for these books?

JUROR B: No, not really. I am trying to deal with it, without getting too deep. I am concerned with the relationships between two people who get drawn into a relationship. Well, we'll just see what happens. Now, when there is a murder, that's clearly, well, would law enforcement treat it differently?

JUROR A: Yes and no.

JUROR B: Huh?

JUROR A: Originally, it would be treated as a crime. But if there was information that the Mafia was involved, the FBI would be called. If we had a suspect, you know. It depends on the circumstances of the case. Investigators might even go to Interpol. All depends on each case. Other sources also assist—[*interruption*]

SCENE: ENTER, staff person from jury commissioner's office.

Clerk: Your names have been selected as a panel of possible jurors for a criminal trial in Courtroom A.

Book writer, police officer, and eavesdroppers rise from dusty seats
and walk down the long Halls of Justice.
Some of them became jurors.*

❖ HISTORICAL JURIES

Juries are a relatively modern tradition. In earlier times, defendants were expected to round up friends to vouch for him or her; it had not occurred to anyone that these 12 people should have been strangers to the parties. More alarming were trials by ordeal, dunkings,

*Shorthand notes from Dr. SunWolf (who was present) from conversations overheard between citizens who were sitting in a jury assembly room—the place where *juries of peers* actually begin forming—long before they are called to a courtroom.

or fire.* It was not until the Magna Carta that the concept of community peers as decision-making jurors to adjudicate disputes was created:

> *39. No freeman shall be taken, or imprisoned, or disseized [dispossessed], or outlawed, or exiled, or in any way harmed—nor will we [the king] go on or send on him—save by the lawful judgment of his peers or by the law of the land.*
>
> —*Magna Carta*
> ["Great Paper," 1215; translated from the Latin][3]

Peers who have served in these small decision-making groups of their equals, however, report mixed experiences. When the summons came to serve as a juror on a murder trial, a professor of science described being shocked at the reality of his actual courtroom peer group "**decision-making**" experience.[4] That professor shared the painful side of his jury's deliberative arguments, describing a clutch of strangers who yelled, cursed, rolled on the floor, vomited, whispered, embraced, sobbed, and invoked both God and necromancy. His jury experience was not, unfortunately, unique.

Describing their jury as a dysfunctional family, some jurors in a police corruption trial that ended in deadlock complained that fellow

---

*Before there were juries, there were three popular methods of "trial" in England: (1) *wager of law,* required the accused person to take an oath, swearing to a fact (in those days, a person's oath carried great weight); "jury" derives from the word "jurare" which means to take an oath. Those who were accused of a crime had only to swear that they were innocent to be acquitted—if others swore against the accused, however, a *compurgation* was assembled. The accused had to bring in 11 supporters called *compurgators,* making 12 people in all who would be willing to take an oath on behalf of the accused, as character witnesses, swearing that the accused was credible. No one wanted that role, however. If the accused was found guilty, compurgators might also be punished.

An accused who was unable to find enough compurgators willing to swear to good character, could be subjected to a trial by ordeal: (2) *trial by hot water,* a ring might be suspended by a string in a cauldron of boiling water, either wrist deep or elbow-deep (depending upon the severity of the crime). The accused reached into the boiling water to grab the ring and if the hand and arm were burned, that was a sign of guilt. If not burned, the miracle was a sign of innocence. There was also *trial by cold water* (used in the Salem witch trials), in which the accused was bound and placed in a body of water. The accused who sank was adjudged "pure" enough to have been accepted by the previously sanctified water (innocent, though dead), whereas those who floated were considered polluted by sin and adjudged guilty (therefore, punished). Finally, there was (3) *trial by fire,* in which an accused was subjected to hot coals or white-hot iron; only the failure to be burned resulted in a judgment of innocence. See for more complete history, from which this excerpt was adapted: http://en.wikipedia.org/wiki/Trial_by_ordeal

jurors laughed at them, made fun of them, and refused to listen to their arguments.[5] Tempers grow short during jury arguments, as evidenced by another juror's note to the trial judge, complaining about the emotional climate in the jury room:

> "Tension is high, nerves are frayed, and all minds are not sound."[6]

Jurors create unexpected procedures during deliberations that the legal system does not sanction—consider the modern dates of these events: Behind closed doors, juries of peers have admitted that they agreed to flip a coin to decide between murder and manslaughter (2001), consulted a Ouija board to ask the victim who the murderer was (1995),* allowed some of the jurors to deliberate in Spanish rather than English with the other jurors (1993), and complained that one of their peers was misbehaving by pressing her hands over her ears in the jury room to avoid hearing them (1933).[7] Recent high publicity trials have made much of "stealth jurors" who, it later turns out, lie to get on certain juries, then enact their own form of justice.**

Juries are particularly relevant to consider in our study of peer groups because many of us will (without volunteering) have a chance to serve on a jury with our community peers; many of us will have that opportunity more than once. Peer juries are unique in the United States in that the members of these groups make decisions *with and for* complete strangers.*** Furthermore, they do not self-select, unlike many peer groups. In fact, a jury is dependent on group outsiders

---

*Four of these jurors were feeling anxious about whether the defendant was actually guilty, so they decided to consult a Ouija board, communicating their questions to the deceased victim, who then "responded" with facts about who had killed him, with what weapon, and with what motive—all of which was then shared with their peers.

**On March 10, 2004, the judge in the Oklahoma murder trial of Terry Nichols was faced with allegations by one prospective juror that other citizens were willing to lie to get on the jury. One potential juror heard another juror brag, "I'll do whatever it takes to get up there. I'm going to say what I can to get on the jury. My decision is already made." Associated Press, March 10, 2004, Law Center, "Prospective Nichols Juror: Some Would Lie to Be on Jury." Retrieved on July 4, 2007 from http://www.cnn.com/2004/LAW/10/nichols.trial.ap

***For an excellent historical teaching guide to the jury system, see http://trustee.montanabar.org/groups/lrecenter/lawdaywethejury.pdf, which produced a document from the American Bar Association, "We the Jury." A complete curriculum guide is offered, including the history of the jury in the United States from medieval times, juror oaths, voir dire of jurors, questionnaires, instructions, and steps of the jury trial.

(judges and lawyers) to decide who will and who will not be a "peer" on a particular jury.

Every year in the United States, thousands of citizens are involuntarily summoned from private lives to courthouses across the country. Most of them actually respond to that summons; some of those are further asked to join with strangers who are peers to form powerful decision-making groups that we call juries. Verdicts result from their peer work. The possible incompetence of groups of peer-citizens to decide court cases was publicly raised in the 1966 Harvard Law School Dean's Report:[8]

> The jury trial is the apotheosis of the amateur. Why should anyone think that 12 persons brought in from the street, selected in various ways for their lack of general ability, should have any special capacity for deciding controversies between persons?

Juries are also criticized by their communities when their peer-work verdicts shock us. Ask anyone if they have heard of a jury award they felt was outrageous and they will tell you about the millions of dollars that were awarded to some woman *who spilled coffee on herself* at a McDonald's restaurant. The McDonald's coffee case involved an elderly woman who scalded herself on coffee and was initially awarded $2.7 million. People tend to remember that verdict. (The facts of the case are included here in an endnote, in case you are curious.)*

Real-world jury deliberations remain a tantalizing puzzle for lawyers, judges, consultants, and group researchers. After 253 days and more than 100 witnesses, the jury in the O. J. Simpson murder trial delivered a verdict in less than four hours;[9] much of the public criticized this swiftness as superficial—but the jurors defended their careful consideration of the evidence.[10] A sampling of federal trials coping with unexpected communication during deliberations of juries illustrates the burden of the task we ask of this particular peer group.

In an excellent review, however, Professor Marder describes how the media ridicule of jury verdicts, both civil and criminal, detracts

---

*What few people realize is that McDonald's coffee was consistently hotter than coffee at other restaurants, that there had been prior complaints about the hot temperature, and that the elderly woman required painful skin grafts for her burns—though she initially only requested medical expenses, which McDonald's refused. Only then did she take the incident to trial. After the jury's $2.7 million verdict was reduced by the trial judge, the parties settled.

See Liebeck v. McDonald's Restaurants, P.T.S., Inc., No. CV 93–02419, 1995 WL 360309, at *1 (D.N.M. Aug. 18, 1994). McDonald's Makes Out-of-Court Settlement in Hot-Coffee Case, Chicago Tribune, December 2, 1994, p. 1.

- Jurors sent a note to the judge, detailing their belief that one of them was incompetent to deliberate.[11]
- Since there was no requirement that federal jurors deliberate in English, a subgroup decided to deliberate in Spanish, thereby excluding the others.[12]
- A juror's note to the judge complained that a fellow juror was obnoxious.[13]
- Two jurors complained *after* their verdict had been accepted by the court that they had been coerced during deliberations into altering their votes.[14]
- A juror admitted that during deliberations she had talked with her sister-in-law, who was an attorney, because she wanted the sister-in-law's advice, which she shared with other jurors.[15]

significantly from a rational consideration of what these involuntarily assembled peer groups may be doing well.[16]

Juries offer vivid examples of concepts that concern scholars of group processes. Juries are challenged by a need to structure communication in their deliberative processes, enact effective leadership, and balance both task and social needs among their peer members. While their deliberative processes are protected behind closed doors, their end products (verdicts) are not only public, but also are certain to disappoint either one party or the other. Increasingly, today, the courts (in the midst of national jury reform movements by court administrators) are offering rare filming of real deliberations.*

❖ ENACTING GROUP LEADERSHIP

While much of the existing research about the communication behaviors of jury leaders has been based on simulated trials, findings have reported that (a) the formal selection of the foreperson is typically

*Since the federal ban on recording deliberations in the 1950s, three valuable examples of real-world deliberations have emerged: (a) a one-hour television documentary aired by the Public Broadcasting Service involving a single trial that resulted from special court permission to place two cameras and cameramen in the jury room during deliberations (Levine & Herzberg, *Frontline,* 1986); (b) 10 years later, the televised excerpts from the CBS special (1996), based on four trials used as data by SunWolf (*Practical jury dynamics: From one juror's trial perceptions to the group's decision-making processes.* Charlottesville, VA: LexisNexis); and (c) ABC television offered a reality series (2004), "In the Jury Room," in which cameras were allowed to film a number of real-world criminal trials across the country, including the deliberations. The first trial was a death penalty case and transcripts were posted on ABC's news Web site. These now represent excellent sources of data for group scholars for theory-building.

related to nonleadership factors, (b) once selected, forepersons seize a disproportionate share of the conversational turns, and (c) the communication acts of forepersons affect verdict outcomes.

The jurors' first act impacting their future communication may be nonverbal. A jury's first structuring challenge occurs at the point when jurors walk into a deliberation room after closing arguments. Those at the front of the line will have a wider choice of seats, leaving those at the end to fill the vacancies. This task is performed nonverbally, though not necessarily unconsciously (for example, one study found that leaders have a preference for the end positions).[17] The jurors' first verbal task, however, (election of the foreperson) can be impacted by the seating positions. Researchers find that although the selection of the foreperson may appear casual, it is by no means a random process.[18] The foreperson is frequently selected from one of the two persons seated at the ends of the table, in such a way that a move to select someone *other* than a person at the end of the table could be perceived by other jurors as a rejection of the end-seated-juror (social stress), while selecting an end-person carried a benign presumption that would not offend the others (avoiding early conflict). Studies have further demonstrated that these peer groups may attempt to quickly resolve the leadership issue, rather than consider what their group might need for the task. The three types most likely to be elected forepersons were (a) the first person to mention the issue of choosing a leader, (b) someone sitting at the head of the table, or (c) a volunteer, with the entire process taking less than a minute.[19] Jury leaders have tended to be selected quickly (only one or two minutes spent in the selection process).[20] When citizens assembled for jury duty were asked how they would approach selecting a group leader in deliberations, almost half suggested selecting a foreperson on a voluntary or random basis, ignoring traits or experience.[21]

Once selected, how does this leader of peers differ from his or her equals? The jury's foreperson has been found to be responsible for one-fourth of the total communication acts in 12-person juries.[22] Furthermore, the leadership style of a foreperson affects peer persuasion, with high-prestige autocratic leaders most influential and making the greatest number of statements, and with low-prestige democratic forepersons ranking last and making the fewest number of statements during deliberation.[23] Communication researchers Boster, Hunter, and Hale noted the influential role of the foreperson and reported that the larger the size of the jury, the stronger the impact of the foreperson: in six-person juries the foreperson's influence was stronger than the sum of the influence of all other jurors, and almost eight times as powerful as the average (mean) juror.[24] Using a mock trial, psychologists reported that the average foreperson spoke three times more frequently than other jurors, but made fewer comments about his or her own preferences.[25]

Does the communication behavior of a jury foreperson reflect competent leadership? Scholars of small group processes have focused attention on whether or not a formal group leader's acts of leadership are functional for the group's task or needs and whether or not nonleaders perform communicative acts of competent leadership. Some people are leaders because of their formal position within a group. Nevertheless, the person assigned a leadership position does not always become the functional leader. Others may be leaders because of the way group members respond to them (emergent leaders). The Communication Competency Model[26] to leadership assumes that an effective group leader's communication will be occupied, in large part, with mediating and organizing the decision-making group. This leadership ideally includes applying criteria, creating operating procedures, managing conversational turns, and displaying concern for member feelings. Two communication scholars, Barge and Hirokawa, have anchored their approach using three assumptions about the nature of effective group leadership:

- leadership helps a group overcome goal barriers,
- leadership occurs through the process of interaction, and
- leadership is principally exercised through specific communication skills.[27]

Perhaps the disproportionate participation rate of group decision-making leaders in a jury of peers could be attributed to their (perceived) procedural and social duties.

The "competent group leadership acts" described by top group scholars are not necessarily being enacted by forepersons, who are, in fact, untrained in the challenges of leading or facilitating communication in a jury. The following excerpt of a conversation that occurred immediately after the selection of a foreperson in a trial that involved drug charges illustrates this point:

JUROR E: [Foreperson—whose name was randomly selected by jurors from a name-draw] I think we should discuss how we want to go about doing this.

JUROR H: Maybe we should start with the lower crime to see if we get agreement and then, you know, build on that.

JUROR E: The lower crime was just theft. Does everybody, you know, what are people's thoughts and issues, say, on the theft? We could just go around the room and see whether—[interrupted by another juror, conversation diverts][28]

Judges typically offer juries no guidance as to *how* to select a foreperson,[29] yet the act of making such a selection immediately distinguishes one member of a presumably democratic (peer) group. One communication challenge to a jury, then, is to create equal opportunities to influence one's jury peers, while simultaneously surrendering limited power to a leader who functions to assist the group toward completing its task.

The Functional Theory of small group leadership argues that leadership happens when *any* group member performs an act that moves the group toward accomplishing its task.[30] The functional approach, consequently, offers a useful perspective on the behaviors that diverse members of the community bring to jury service. The functional perspective represents one of the dominant theoretical influences on the study of communication behaviors in decision-making groups. Although it has not been applied by researchers to the study of juries, it remains available to illuminate a focus on the task of jury leadership, and helps us determine what new variables to look at.

❖ STRUCTURING MEMBER COMMUNICATION

Only one (or at most a few) people can talk at any given instant and be understood by the group, so the structuring of who talks and for how long must be resolved by the jurors. It appears that, in decision-making groups, those who speak are themselves more likely to be spoken to by other group members. It comes as no surprise, then, that jury researchers have found similar reciprocity frequencies,[31] leaders have been noted not only to initiate, but also to receive more comments than other jurors,[32] and men were both initiators and targets of more messages than were women.[33]

A jury of peers probably does not showcase equal turn-taking, which is of interest for group scholars. The average participation per juror has been found to decrease as faction size grows. Once a deliberating jury splits into factions, the smaller the size of the faction, the higher the participation.[34] The communication task among jurors must deal, in addition, with issues of frequency (how often speaking turns occur), target (who is spoken to), and receiver (who listens). Within particular deliberations, there may be a steep differentiation between the most- and least-speaking jurors; one early jury researcher found the top three participators accounted for one-half or more of the total speech acts.[35] One finding is obvious from prior research: all jurors do not contribute equally to the discussion, and research with simulated juries reveals that most juries include several people who virtually never participate in the deliberation, and have little impact on the decision-making process.[36] Leaders of task-oriented groups participate at a higher rate than other members and both formal and emergent leaders have been found to participate more often than other members.[37] High-status members frequently take a greater proportion of speaking turns and, consequently, garner more opportunities to influence outcomes.[38] It may be that some jurors are only *nominal peers,* while others seize (or are allowed) more communication opportunities.

What is the effect of variable juror participation on the verdict? Historically, the view that deliberation played a minor role in determining jury verdicts predominated: jury researchers believed that the first ballot generally decided the verdict. Verdict-focused studies have been criticized for failing to take into account or describe individual opinion shifts that occur as a result of jury deliberation, but before a first vote.[39] Discussion, however, does appear to influence a jury's outcome, beyond first ballot preferences. There is a group "leniency" shift associated with criminal cases, in particular, in which a defendant prevails if jurors conclude a "reasonable doubt" exists with regard to guilt, as well as juror shiftings of initial "guilty" votes, after group discussion, to "not guilty" votes.[40]

Furthermore, as discussion time increases, individual participation by jurors tends to silence some of the "peers"—with a small fraction of the group's members accounting for most of the participation.[41] At the same time, one judge pointed out that the right of each juror-peer to equal and responsible participation in the group's deliberation is an institutional expectation; therefore, when a jury of peers participates in significantly unequal ways, judicial expectations may be thwarted.[42] Are attorneys' assumptions that the jurors they pick will actually get equal opportunities to influence one another and communicate in these peer groups naïve?

❖ THE *WORK* OF JURY WORK: WHEN INDIVIDUALS BECOME A JURY OF PEERS

> *The great mystery of all conduct is social conduct. I have had to study it all my life, but I cannot pretend to understand it. I may seem to know a man through and through, and still I would not want to say the first thing about what he will do in a group.*
>
> —Anonymous British statesman

> *The discussion now tended to wander from one point to another, depending on which juror managed to command our attention. The deliberation turned into a process of "thinking out loud," with one or another juror giving voice to something that bothered him, or that he thought particularly significant, or that was simply irrelevant. His statement often induced a comment from another juror on the same point or it simply served as a stimulus for a series of unrelated statements from other jurors.*
>
> —Juror[43]

The *unspoken* communication rules that dynamically control deliberations may be, in some trials, ineffective for the task. Many group norms that emerge during deliberations, in reality, may function in some juries to restrict inappropriately the decision-making responsibilities of individual jurors. *Norms* are informal rules a group has about how things are done. While norms describe typical group behavior, two caveats are important: (a) not every member has to agree with any particular group norm, and (b) a norm does not occur all the time. Nonetheless, a norm represents the way things are generally done in that group for that task. (For example, with regard to juries, the foreperson has more opportunities to speak than other jurors. Not all jurors have to contribute for a discussion to be effective.)

When discussions are uneven or when some jurors rarely speak, a *group climate* is created in which peer-equality disappears. In any peer group, there may be *nominal* members (a peer in name only); juries are an excellent example of how that can happen. Some jurors may be members of the jury *in name only.*

Among scholars who study group dynamics, these group members are referred to as *social* or *task loafers.* A group discussion loafer is a group member who makes a minimal contribution to the group, assuming that other members will take up the slack or that their own contribution would merely be a duplication, and not needed by the group. A juror who is a *discussion loafer* will watch and listen, but contribute little, satisfied to let the rest of the jurors carry the argument task. While there are several obvious causes for discussion loafing (lack of understanding of group processes, lack of confidence, mixed emotions about jury duty, resentment of other jurors, cultural differences, personal distractions, and social anxiety, to name a few), social loafing damages groups of peers and evidences a lack of investment in the group's task.

When discussion loafing occurs in a jury, whatever the reasons, that jury is not playing with a full deck. An excellent example from the jury deliberation videos I analyzed is one in which the only juror of color, a young African American man who appeared to be in his twenties, was only spoken to once by the other jurors during hours of deliberations. He made, as a result, one speaking contribution, although he listened intently and was available. He was erased from the *message-sending part of deliberations*, participating only in the message-receiving part of the discussion task.[44] A juror may, in effect, "disappear" during the deliberative task for a variety of reasons—quiet jurors, elderly jurors, young jurors, jurors who have speech impairments, and jurors who are not socially attractive are ignored by a majority. This dynamic is evidence that not all the jurors in such a jury consider the others to be, in fact, their peers.

In part, juror loafing may occur when jurors bring into group deliberations the *group rules* they are already familiar with from other group tasks outside the judicial system (such as meetings, teams, or committees); jurors have been described as surprisingly ignorant of their task.[45]Another reason ineffective rules emerge and are enacted in deliberations, however, may be that jurors typically devote *no* discussion to procedure—that is, *how* they should go about organizing their deliberations. Scholars who study problem-solving groups have long agreed that a functional discussion group determines, at the outset, what communication structures, agendas, and discussion formats will best serve their new task.

❖ WHEN PEERS DISAGREE: DEADLOCK

> *I screamed that I couldn't believe this was happening, that we were possibly going to be a hung jury when in my mind the case was so obvious. Everything was there, DNA evidence, witness testimony. There was no room for interpretation. I was angry. There were words of profanity that came out of my mouth.*
>
> —Juror on the fifth day of deliberations*

---

*One holdout on a 12-member jury was reluctant to find the defendant guilty on murder charges. After the explosion by a juror who was in the majority and feared deadlock, a note was sent about the foul language to the judge from another juror. The judge "calmed her down," deliberations continued, and the foreperson "worked one-on-one" with the holdout juror to explain the legal terminology. Within an hour, the jury returned guilty verdicts, then quickly imposed a life sentence with no possibility of parole. Retrieved March 3, 2004, from *the Oregonian* newspaper Web site, www.oregonlive.com.

It is stressful for some jurors when they cannot agree. Some jurors may suffer from "deadlock phobia": they are anxious about becoming deadlocked, announcing that they are deadlocked, or allowing themselves to remain deadlocked. Deadlocked juries represent an appropriate jury outcome by law that is, paradoxically, consistently viewed as a jury failure by the trial judge, the jurors, and by at least one of the litigating parties. A deadlocked jury may symbolically represent to jurors a failure on the part of the jurors to achieve their shared goal. In one trial, one juror expressed this sentiment when he shared with the other jurors that he felt a deadlocked jury meant that *his job was not done.*[46]

Jurors are embedded (as argued by the Bona Fide Group Perspective) in a complex judicial system. During deliberations, the secrecy of the jury can be penetrated whenever a jury sends out a note to the judge (communication attempt). What happens when a jury sends out a note, "What if we can't agree?" While a hung jury is legally acceptable and not uncommon, judges generally send back the following instruction* to deadlocked jurors in an attempt to trigger a verdict:

> Members of the jury, you have advised that you have been unable to agree upon a verdict in this case. I have decided to suggest a few thoughts to you. As jurors, you have a duty to discuss the case with one another and to deliberate in an effort to reach a unanimous verdict, if each of you can do so without violating your individual judgment and conscience. Each of you must decide the case for yourself, but only after you consider the evidence impartially with your fellow jurors. During your deliberations, you should not hesitate to reexamine your own views and change your opinion if you become persuaded that it is wrong. However, you should not change an honest belief as to the weight or effect of the evidence solely because of the opinions of your fellow jurors or for the mere purpose of returning a verdict. All of you share an equal desire to arrive at a verdict. Each of you should ask yourself whether you should question the correctness of your present position. (Ninth Circuit Jury Instruction 4.04, Deadlocked Jury, 1993)

If you serve on a jury that cannot reach a shared verdict, you will likely hear an instruction very like the above federal instruction.

---

*The giving of a further instruction to a struggling jury has historically been so effective in triggering a unanimous verdict that it was nicknamed the "dynamite charge" (a reference to the practice of loggers, who used an explosion to break a log jam in the river to get the logs moving smoothly down the river toward their intended destination).

Since hung juries may help us understand other peer groups that cannot agree on a decision, it is worth looking at their processes.* Researchers have struggled in the laboratory to create situations that may usefully replicate factors influencing whether a jury hangs or reaches a verdict. One team, using three-, six-, or 12-person mock juries found that as the size of the jury increased, the probability of a hung jury increased significantly.** At the same time, this study found that voting procedures influence the likelihood of a deadlocked jury, with open/public polling increasing the likelihood of a hung jury, compared to using secret ballots.[47]

❖ REGRET AMONG PEERS: JUROR FLIPPING

> *The air reeked of hatred and people were angry and I had never been in an atmosphere like that before.*
>
> —79-year-old juror***

Any decision-making group may reach a decision only through pushy persuasion by the majority of a reluctant group member. When jurors later describe their reluctance to agree to a verdict, however, we often hear about it as reported in the media—especially in celebrated trials. Hence juror flipping (rethinking) is more often in the public eye than the flipping of other decision-making peers.

Most jurors rethink their intended votes *during* deliberations; such rethinking is one of the valued opportunities that shared deliberative time is designed to provide. Some jurors, however, rethink their actual votes *after* deliberations have concluded—a situation that our legal system is not designed to accommodate. Some trials are more likely to produce jury flipping than others. Peer pressure, as well as community and institutional embeddedness, can produce juror flipping. Three

---

*When juries hang, there is an unwanted impact on the judicial system. Juries whose members are unable to return a unanimous verdict are discharged by the court, necessitating a retrial. As a result, judges are faced with the task of crowding their dockets with a second (or third or fourth) retrial of the same case. The key problem with a hung jury from the point of view of the judicial system is that it may represent an interim rather than a final disposition of a case. Concerns are traditionally expressed about the monetary costs associated with retrying cases, as well as emotional effects on alleged victims and witnesses.

**Note, however, that these mock jurors were given only 10 minutes to deliberate, an ongoing issue with mock jury research designs.

***Describing, in August 2005, her regretted verdict in the Michael Jackson trial, which took place in June of that year.

principles of juror rethinking among peers (and, as noted, for any peer rethinking of a group choice) are worth noting here:

- A verdict is more likely to be regretted by a juror when the verdict's consequences are perceived as being both highly *salient* and highly *public.*
- Individual juror verdicts (votes) are more likely to be surrendered during deliberations when the trial has been *lengthy* and a juror thinks that a *hung jury* would result without a vote change.
- A surrendered juror vote during deliberations (in a trial that is both highly salient and public) is likely to be regretted by the surrendering juror(s) later.

The process of consciously rethinking personal votes during deliberative discussion is never an easy task for a juror. Furthermore, the group's deliberative *culture* that helped produce a vote-surrender will dissolve after the jury is discharged, leaving some jurors confused about why they did not stick to their initial vote. Any jury's communication culture may have included unspoken talking "rules" and styles to which some jurors were either sensitive or unfamiliar: yelling, rapid talk, simultaneous talk, interruptions, tears, teasing, bullying, name-calling, or threats, to name a few.

A vivid example of juror-verdict-regret emerged in the Michael Jackson trial. After more than 130 witnesses and almost five months of trial, a jury of eight women and four men in California found entertainer defendant Michael Jackson not guilty of all criminal charges. Their deliberations had lasted more than seven days (32 hours). Two months later, on August 8, 2005, two of those jurors (one man and one woman) claimed on national television that they personally believed Michael Jackson to have been guilty and, furthermore, that they regretted their "not guilty" verdicts.* While one juror explained that he could not tolerate the idea of a hung jury (necessitating a retrial), after all the time he had put into the trial, the second juror tearfully blamed group dynamics and a threat she received from the foreperson:

> He said if I could not change my mind or go with the group or be more understanding, that he would have to notify the bailiff, the bailiff would notify the judge, and the judge would have me removed.[48]

*The two jurors were Eleanor Cook (age 79) and Ray Hultman (62). They acknowledged that they first thought Jackson was guilty but claimed to have been railroaded into a not-guilty verdict (MSNBC's *Rita Cosby*, 2005).

The physical anxiety produced by group argument after a lengthy trial was real for this juror, as she then described her heart palpitating and the "gut-wrenching" position she felt she was in with other jurors. She began mentally to *reframe* her position for herself as perhaps "ambivalent," in order, she explained, "to stop the pain." Peer pressure.

There is another compelling explanation for the recent Michael Jackson trial juror-regret phenomenon, which points out that this sort of thing can be anticipated as a normal part of juror thinking. One line of research describing mental processes *after* a decision has been made has pointed out that people often experience *post*decisional dissonance.[49] Further complicating the decision-making challenge, immediately after making a decision people have a tendency to focus on the negative aspects about the choice made, as well as the positive aspects of the choice rejected. To reduce dissonance and feel better about a decision, people may enhance the attractiveness of the chosen alternative, while devaluing the rejected alternatives. As a result, a juror who was ambivalent before the verdict decision can be expected to experience post-verdict thinking that enhances the reasons the verdict was wrong and that the other verdict would have been wiser.

There exists a compelling intuition that the anticipation of regret is a significant factor in decision making.[50] A juror may wonder how a verdict choice might affect the parties, the attorneys, the judge, their community, the press, outsiders, and, perhaps, their families. Other jurors may "catch" the anxiety. Regret contagion, in which one group member's regret anxiety may be transferred to other group members, can be triggered by the communication of counterfactual narratives during decisional talk.

So common is decisional regret in juries that it can be anticipated in all trials that are lengthy, that have highly salient outcomes or significant publicity—and, by extension, to other decision-making peer groups coping with highly salient public decisions (for example, awards, war strategies, or medical decisions). Decisional Regret Theory explains the manner in which regret arises, touching first an individual juror's *thinking* as that juror approaches choosing a personal vote. One of the most interesting understandings about jury thinking to emerge from Decisional Regret Theory is the fact that when the verdict decision is painful, some jurors will engage in a type of thinking involving restorying the trial.

Jurors begin to imagine what *could have happened* so that there would not even *be* a trial! This is counterfactual thinking. One effect of such restorying ("If only he'd called someone first!") during decisional talk may involve simply delaying the decisional task. Group members may think about an outcome that would have been *better* than what actually occurred *if only someone had behaved differently* (such as no child abuse, no breach of contract, no surgery, no contract, no shooting). Counterfactual thinking is common in dog mauling and medical malpractice cases, for example, since often jurors prefer to imagine the tragedies being avoided. *Such stories offer a fantasized reality in which decision makers imagine that they would never have to be faced with the current decision at all.* If the story of how someone should have behaved differently than they did is joined or restoried by others, the jury may be diverted from its painful decisional task. As a result, this form of jury thinking must be anticipated by trial lawyers. Decisional regret and a juror's inclination to restory the trial in a way that would have avoided the trauma, injuries, or lawsuit can usefully be anticipated.

❖ CONCEPTUALIZING PEER GROUP INTERVENTIONS: FUTURE JURY PEERING

The judicial system's view of the ideal "equally participating" juror and the "competent" foreperson may be based on unsupported assumptions or wishful thinking about the nature of group dynamics. Yet some of us will serve as jurors, many of us will be called, and a few of us will be selected to lead those groups of peers.

Jurors are sent into the jury room to deliberate in most courtrooms with an inadequate model of how power should be distributed, speaking turns shared, and conflict resolved. Peer groups are left with little guidance about how to accomplish their verdict task. Trial attorneys or judges devote little (if any) attention to the issues that jurors confront during their decision-making phase—yet the quality of justice reflected in verdicts is affected by the processes that precede them. Typically, courts and lawyers slip into a "passive" phase while jurors deliberate, confronting the profound challenges of deliberative work only when forced to do so (that is, on the occasions when jurors send out notes expressing their frustration).

Theory and research on small group behavior has rarely examined "democracy" in group decision making.[51] One communication scholar, Professor Gastil, offers specific suggestions for fostering democratic participation in group decision making that would be useful for jurors: affirmation of competence, agenda setting, reformulation, new approaches to persuasion, voting, and listening. Future research might examine variables or leadership moves that might increase peer participation. Judge Dann argued persuasively that procedures such as juror note taking and asking questions of witnesses produce more educated and democratic juries.[52]

Jurors have a difficult task participating in a peer group to which they did not ask to belong, with people they do not know, and that will have consequences for other people. Conscripted to serve and formed as a heterogeneous zero-history group, with different backgrounds, interests, experiences, values, stresses, and biases, jurors must nonetheless coordinate and make sense of the complex cases presented, under courtroom situations that impose numerous restrictions on the type of communication citizens engage in everyday. If the judicial system offered information, training, or guidance on group decision-making challenges and competent group leadership skills to citizens summoned for jury duty, there is reason to believe that democratic, inclusive, cohesive, and trustworthy deliberations might increase.

❖ NEW THEORETICAL LENSES: CONCEPTUALIZING JURIES AS PEER GROUPS

It has been said that citizens are called on to serve their country in three ways: voting, military service, and jury service. Since we all face the possibility of being summoned more than once to serve with our community peers as jurors, understanding more about this peer group's processes and communication challenges is useful. (At the same time, some of us will one day be injured, betrayed, or accused, and may ourselves be asking for our jury peers to decide the matter.)

Again, however, remember that any group of peers that is making a group decision about which many outsiders care, faces similar challenges and constraints. The jury is not only a specific group that we may need or on which we may serve, but is also a rich exemplar of a peer decision-making entity.

We consider here groups that are primarily task groups (decision-making groups), adding the dimension that the members did not self-select, may resent the task, and may bring to the group vastly different values, skills, and experiences, nothwithstanding that they are considered to be community representatives in court (and, therefore, peers). When a group is assigned a task, however, it does not mean that the group does not have social needs, norms, perceived violations, or tensions. Task and social relationships continue to intersect throughout the decision-making process.

What peer group scholarship might be effectively explored by applying our seven perspectives specifically to these *involuntary* decision-making peer groups, whose members are strangers to one another, but whose decisions will impact the lives of people they do not know in their communities (that is, juries)?

Table 6.1 Theoretical Perspective and Application to Juries

Theoretical Perspective	Application to Juries
Symbolic-Interpretive Perspective	What is the effect of courtroom symbolic icons and practices on jurors and on constructing meaningful task definition for juries? How do jurors use humor, metaphor, and language to enact their new decision-making role? What are the differences in the ways peers who are members of the same jury nonetheless differently make sense of their purpose, role, and task?
Social Comparison Theory	With *Court TV*, film, and books available on how other juries interpret and construct their task, do jurors compare their trials, judges, or attorneys (same/different, better/worse) to the media models they have been exposed to? In what ways do diverse jurors compare the peers within their jury (education, income, gender, occupation, ethnicity, to name a few)? What effect do those comparisons have on their subsequent group discussions? Do jurors use social comparisons during deliberations to evaluate witnesses and the behaviors of the parties? In what ways do jurors compare their values, opinion, and votes to those of other jurors?
Structuration Theory	How do jurors choose their foreperson, organize their deliberations, seize speaking turns, structure voting, or restructure processes during their deliberations? What rules to jurors bring with them to their deliberative task from prior decision-making groups (committees, meetings, clubs)?

(Continued)

Table 6.1 (Continued)

Theoretical Perspective	Application to Juries
Decisional Regret Theory	How do jurors begin anticipating the consequences of their verdict choices? When jurors become anxious about a verdict with unwanted outcomes, do they share those anticipated regrets with other jurors? When one or more jurors have shared anticipated regrets for one or more possible verdicts, what effect is there on other jurors? How does a jury that disagrees on a verdict communicate in order to avoid or deal with deadlock? Do jurors bring outside experiences in and share them in order to cope with unwanted anxiety about possible verdict outcomes? Do jury cultures that consider deadlock to be a problem increase the chances that individual jurors will leave the group's task with task regret?
Social Identity Perspective	How do jurors perceive outsiders? Do they construct meaning about other juries, the court system, or other groups? What factors influence a jury developing an ingroup sense of belongingness? Are trial time, deliberative time, or issue intensity factors in creating a sense of ingroup with a jury?
Group Dialectical Perspective	Since jurors necessarily have lives, jobs, and commitments facing them during jury duty, how do they cope with the resulting dialectical tensions? How is a juror's group task impacted by competing needs from those outside the jury? Does group deliberation create new dialectical tensions? Do jurors face dialectical tensions after reaching a verdict, as they anticipate the end of their peer group and begin making sense of the value of their decision?
Bona Fide Group Perspective	When juries have alternate jurors, who may or may not actually serve on the jury, are there boundaries drawn around who is or is not a *real* juror? Are alternatives considered peers? How do jurors, who are instructed not to talk about the trial to outsiders, symbolically construct boundaries that block friends, family, and coworkers from their new identity as a juror? How do jurors manage the environment in which they are embedded when it includes media attention, perceived political interests, and community interests in their potential verdict?

Art: Author

In courtrooms
lawyers and witnesses tell the stories,
but juries of peers write the endings.

Critical Thinking About Juries and Decision-Making Peer Groups

- How would a decision-making jury benefit from enacting the structure and role of *devil's advocate* in its deliberative task (see Appendix)?
- To what degree might a jury's deliberative task be impeded by the positive and negative face needs of individual jurors, according to *Face and Politeness Theory* (see Appendix)? Must an effective jury of peers engage in some form of "facework" during its task? If so, how?
- How might a jury verdict be impaired by the *free ride effect, deindividuation, social loafing,* or the *sucker effect* during deliberations, especially with 12 members? Could a jury foreperson avoid those effects through appropriate leadership, in your opinion?
- Using *Gender Socialization Perspective,* how might turn-taking and leadership be enacted differently and understood differently by male or female deliberating jurors?
- When a jury of peers begins experiencing anxiety about making the wrong decision, how might the concept *groupregret* explain a resulting deadlock (rather than an agreed-on verdict)?
- Which *social allergies* (see Appendix) might some citizens bring to their jury experience that might adversely impact the deliberative process? Do other decision-making groups face the same concerns?
- How do you believe the *Social Facilitation Effect* might explain jury deliberations in some trials?
- If members of a particular jury have extremely different levels of education, income, employment, family lives, sexual preferences, and religions, how can that jury develop a since of *peerness* or enact *peer-suasion* (see Appendix)?

Epilogue

Ever-Aftering

Living in a Forest of Peer Groups

The honor of one is the honor of all. The hurt of one is the hurt of all.

—*Creek Indian Creed*

Un pour tous, tous pour un.

—*D'Artagnan (1625)**

Workin' together—white, black, Spanish—work together. If anything happened to one, it happened to all.

—Rev. Mack Williams[1]

The only tragedy is never-aftering. Never fully participating in our peer groups, never expanding our experiences with seemingly diverse others, never examining the effects our communication choices have on other group members, never knocking on the doors of new groups, never allowing outsiders to penetrate the membership boundaries of our own treasured peer groups.

The purpose in this book has been to alter your consciousness about what is possible concerning the communication dynamics of peer groups that impact your life, to stimulate new thinking about your own behaviors and reactions in these groups, and to suggest new avenues for group research. This book has attempted to function as both a window and a door: to let you see group processes and consequences that may have been invisible to you, and, at the same time, to allow you to enter future peer groups and behave differently, when you hope for different results. (At times, these pages may have served as a useful *mirror* for you, as well.)

There are undoubtedly more delightful peers around us than we realize. Swarms of them; droves, routes, packs, paddlings, pods, bevies, and clowders.

---

*"One for all, all for one." In 1844, the French author Alexandre Dumas wrote a serialized novel, *Les Trois Mousquetaires* ("The Three Musketeers") set in 17th-century France. They are comrades who together perform many daring deeds. In fact, there were not three, but four Musketeers. The young d'Artagnan, a teenager, arrives in Paris and almost immediately offends three musketeers (Porthos, Aramis, and Athos). Before they can fight one another, the four are attacked by the Cardinal's guards and their courage is tested, leading them to a fast friendship of inseparable peers. Along the way, of course, they encounter demons, treachery, a beautiful young spy, and surprising enemies. Intriguingly, the familiar phrase, "All for one, one for all," appears only *once* in the entire book.

We live in the midst of people like us, who share our beliefs, values, goals, abilities, inclinations, experiences, gripes, or responsibilities. More to the point, we are living in a social forest, surrounded by people who—if we managed to herd them into a small peer group—would share our interests, applaud our dreams, bemoan our losses, crew our ships, rebuild our neighborhoods, join our revolutions, jump to our defense, stretch our compassion, pull us from fires, join us in crafting good decisions, or inspire us regularly to exceed our personal bests.

We do not study peer groups simply because we think *other people* need to know about them. The core, heart, sticky-gooey center of peer group studies involves *us*. We need to understand the dynamics and processes of these groups, because we will be embedded in them for the rest of our lives. We are less alone than we might be without them.

You will have opportunities throughout your life span to belong to more peer groups: We need peers to watch our backs. We need more eyes looking out for us, because we can't always see what's coming. Peer groups give us practice on how to be together.

May you achieve successes
(in your careers and in your relationships)
one conversation
and one peer group
at a time.

a pallor of night students • a drowse of underachievers • a leap of overachievers • a platitude of sophomores • a gratitude of juniors • an attitude of seniors • a fortitude of graduate students • a clamber of assistant professors • a tenure of associate professors • an entrophy of full professors • an oversight of deans • a conjunction of grammarians • a shelf of classicists • a shush of librarians • a brood of researchers • a discord of experts • a tribe of group scholars • a browse of readers • a tedium of footnotes • a providence of publishers*

---

*Harvested from Lipton, J. (1968/1991). *An exaltation of larks* (the ultimate edition). New York: Penguin. James Lipton is the son of a prominent American poet and was publishing his own poetry by the age of 12. He is an author, director, choreographer, and producer who has written screenplays for eight motion pictures, written and produced hundreds of hours of award-winning television drama and entertainment specials, and who wrote the book and lyrics for two Broadway musicals. Lipton is a *Delight of Writers,* even alone (which he apparently never is).

There's one advantage to being 102. There's no peer pressure.

—Dennis Wolfberg

Gratitudes

This book stands on the shoulders of many gifted, insightful, and patient scholars, colleagues, and friends.

Any author of a book about human behavior must offer both profound gratitudes and apologies:

Gratitudes: This book is a product of my own peer group memberships, in a variety of contexts. My valued peers read, prodded, extended, questioned, applied, and applauded these ideas and, therefore, helped *Peer Groups* grow. They raised their hands in classes, challenged me at conferences, stopped me in hallways, shared their stories, emailed me, and, consequently, continually prodded my thinking with conversations that began, "What about?" *So, the best parts are their fault.*

At the outset, I am grateful to the many group communication students I've taught, starting with my first classes at the University of California–Santa Barbara and Santa Barbara City College. These students shared the complex delights and struggles they faced in their own peer groups and got me thinking. I remain in happy debt to Dr. Laura Leets, scholarly partner in my quest to understand what it means to be left out by our peers, and, ultimately, my treasured friend. From the field of group dynamics, I first benefited from the brilliant mentoring of my dissertation director, Dr. David Seibold, who always made me feel I had something useful to say about groups. Dr. Lawrence Frey, Professor at the University of Colorado–Boulder, mentored my scholarly writing and profoundly influenced my thinking about symbolic processes in groups of diverse human beings. The cutting-edge scholarship of Dr. Renée Meyers, at the University of Wisconsin–Milwaukee, challenged my thinking about gendered differences during group argument and cheered me on as I began applying new theories to understand more about the multilayered talk of jury deliberations. Decisional Regret Theory owes a happy debt to the editorial talents of Dr. Jim Query, applied scholar extraordinaire.

I could not have been gifted with a better book team than those at SAGE; shepherding this book into existence was Todd Armstrong, Senior Acquisitions Editor, who consistently listened, was quietly insightful, and, later, usefully pushy. Finally, a most welcome debt is owed to this book's thoughtful reviewers, who pored through the first drafts with wise challenges and generous enthusiasms:

Carolyn M. Anderson (University of Akron)

Gloria J. Galanes (Missouri State University)

Audrey E. Kali (Framingham State College)

Paul Kang (University of California–Santa Barbara)

Scott A. Myers (West Virginia University)

James W. Neuliep (St. Norbert College)

Jim L. Query, Jr. (University of Houston)

David Seibold (University of California–Santa Barbara)

Apologies are owed by me to all readers who may find themselves thinking at some point in this book, "Yes, that may be true, but what about when . . . ?" Whatever you thought of, I wish I had thought of that, too. (Special gratitudes, however, to those who go on to send me their Intriguing Questions and Spot-On Ideas; you will improve a future edition of this book enormously.)

A low bow of respect
to all of our peers [past and future],
who increase our strength, listen to our gripes, and stretch our compassion,
who alter our awareness about the possibilities of togetherness,
and who watch our backs when Bad Things creep up behind us.

If you want to go quickly, go alone.
If you want to go far, go with others.

—African proverb

Appendix

Appendix Social Science Theories and Concepts That Help Explain

Theory/Concept	Assumptions
Anchor Points	Anchor points are mental shortcuts the brain uses as a starting point when it makes a judgment about experiences in the world. People decide whether a new event or message is positive or negative based on (anchored in) past experiences or future expectation—which then become their anchor points for judging what actually happens. Anchor points are used in social thinking and are normal, often highly adaptive, yet are error-laden.[1] Anchor points explain why people are frustrated when they miss reaching a goal (the goal had become the expected outcome), or delighted when imagined bad news never happens (even the status quo becomes positively elevated if a bad event that had been anticipated does not take place). The level of confidence a person has in an anchor point affects the subsequent level of positive/negative judgment about the real-world event (or nonevent).
Argot	Language unique to a group, intended to be understood by the ingroup members, but not to be understood by outsiders. Argot may consist of words commonly used by many, but which now have a unique meaning agreed on by insiders. On the other hand, argot may be created words that are not familiar to outsiders.
Attribution Theory	Explains how people interpret events in their social worlds; specifically, how people decide whether a behavior is caused by someone's personality (ongoing) or the situation (single event).[2] Typically, people assume that another person's norm-breaking acts are a reflection of their personality (typical of that person), while their own norm-breaking actions/mistakes are circumstantially caused (a self-serving bias). People are less likely to blame people they are close to for failures, thus are more likely to attribute that person's mistakes to situation (unless they are unsatisfied with a situational cause). Furthermore, causal judgments people make about their romantic partners seem to depend, in part, on how satisfied they are with the relationship.[3]

Communication Events in Peer Groups

Application to Peer Groups
• Group insiders or outsiders judge group events by anchor points from similar personal or observed experiences. They remember past successes and stresses, or imagine scenarios for anticipated peer group events. When their anchor point is *exceeded*, they experience a stronger positive judgment, whereas when their anchor point is *not met*, they experience a stronger negative judgment. • Past reactions (positive or negative) to behaviors experienced in groups influence future decisions of members who are entering or exiting a peer group—even when the peer group has changed. • When receivers self-generate desired imagined behavior or words from others, the actual behaviors or words of a group member will be judged by comparison to those imagined.
• Expands our understanding of peer groups to which we do not belong. • Invites attention to the power of a group to symbolically enact identity through words and language, as well as to symbolically exclude others. • Commonly used by various peer groups in schools, in prisons, by street gangs, by ethnic youth groups, by task groups in medical or technology settings, among others.
• When people feel a peer's behavior was inappropriate, they are likely to assume the social failure was caused by that person's personality (that it is *typical* of that *person*), rather than a temporary product of the *situation*. • People are more likely to make negative attributions about a peer's behaviors or words when they are unsatisfied with the relationship or the group. • In retrospect, people are likely to attribute the cause of their group missteps to the situation or circumstances (temporary) rather than to their own character (stable and ongoing).

(Continued)

Appendix (Continued)

Theory/Concept	Assumptions
Balance Theory (Cognitive Dissonance)	When newly acquired information is inconsistent with a person's prior beliefs, the person feels uncomfortable and uses strategies to reduce the inconsistency (dissonance), such as misinterpreting information about others or revising opinions about others.[4]
Climate	Group climate has been defined as the enduring qualities of any group's situation that arises from and influences member interactions and that all group members experience.[5] Group climate, however, is not static, but, rather, situationally dynamic. Group climates may include such elements as flexibility, participation, effort, warmth, support, cohesiveness, openness, and trust. On the other hand, it might include rigidity, defensiveness, anger, distrust, secrecy, exclusion, or authoritarianism.
Collective Effort Model	This model argues that group members become lazy when they do not expect their individual efforts to lead to personally valued outcomes, or if they do not believe their effort will be instrumental in obtaining those outcomes. As a result, social loafing occurs.[6]
Deindividuation	The tendency to feel invisible when surrounded by a group of other people causes people to be less concerned with how others will evaluate their behaviors. The "lost in a crowd" perception triggers behaviors that may be contrary to an individual's personal values; people do things in a group they might never do when alone.[7]
Deviants	Nonconforming group members who regularly violate significant group norms.

Application to Peer Groups
• A group member experiences cognitive dissonance when a peer's behavior or group outcome is not what was expected or wanted, and will then use mental strategies to revise his or her previous opinion about self, the peer, or the group. • A group or peer member behavior or event that triggers uncomfortable dissonance for another peer member will mandate a perceptual change about the relationship and the group.
• Offers a perspective for longitudinal study of peer groups, focusing on the emergence and changes in a group's emotional/cultural climate over time. • Suggests a connection with another group construct— socialization— which may enhance understanding of how group climate is experienced by new members. • Useful for a structurational perspective in studying peer group processes, since peer group climate both will emerge from and will be sustained by communication. • Invites attention to both positive and negative climates within peer groups.
• Suggests a focus in studying peer groups on the norms and rules that emerge about individual effort. • Suggests one reason for dissatisfaction and conflict in some peer groups. • Highlights the value inherent in having all peer members buy into the perceived outcome of effort.
• Explains violent, criminal, antisocial behavior of some individuals when they are with their peer groups. • Draws attention to the way in which a peer group may cause members to become less aware of themselves, their values, and the consequences of their choices. • Suggests that a peer group may operate to make some members feel both more aroused and more anonymous, hence causing them to behave impulsively.
• Suggests dialectical tensions that peer group members may feel when a peer implies, by ignoring group norms, that his or her own needs and wishes are more important than the needs of the group.[8] • Focuses attention on the structures and rules that peer groups adopt to deal with deviants who are peers. • Points toward emotional effects of deviants on other peer members who may become uncomfortable, angry, or anxious when a peer consistently violates important group norms.

(Continued)

Appendix (Continued)

Theory/Concept	Assumptions
Devil's Advocate	A role a group member in a decision-making group may take, in which that member attempts to help the group avoid a mistake by actively advocating reasons why the emerging decision might not be correct. The "devil's advocate" is not offering his or her own opinion, but rather is adopting a contrary position in order to help avoid a group mistake.[9]
Emotional Contagion	The emotions people experience are influenced by the emotions of those around them. Emotional contagion describes the process by which emotions are transferred from one person to another, as if they were "infectious."[10] The longer the contact between people in a group, the more contagious emotions appear to be.
Equity Theory	People evaluate their satisfaction in relationships by comparing their outcomes in the relationship to those of their relational partner, such that fairness is a central issue. Relationships perceived as inequitable result in distress; when people are overbenefited they feel guilt and when they feel underbenefited they feel anger.[11]
Expectancy Violations Theory	People hold expectations about the nonverbal behavior of others, such that unexpected changes are arousing, often ambiguous, and require an interpretation by the message receiver. Expectations are learned and the reaction to an expectancy violation will be positive or negative, depending on the reward value of the communicator to the receiver.[12]
Face and Politeness Theory	People have a desire to be liked and admired by relevant others (positive face) and to be autonomous and unconstrained (negative face). When perceiving a threat to social face, people will use a strategy that will restore their or their partner's face (that strategy is known as facework), including minimizing differences and highlighting commonalities, or minimizing blame and maximizing praise of others.[13] Consequently, facework involves a set of practices in which people build, maintain, protect, or threaten their dignity and honor, making it a vital aspect of all interpersonal communication.[14]

Application to Peer Groups
• In peer groups with a high conformity norm the role of devil's advocate might not be rewarded, might not emerge, and the group might be more vulnerable to making poorer decisions. • Explains asocial behavior by peer groups when the individual values of some members disapprove the behavior (no devil's advocate). • Suggests that unwanted complaints or objections by some peer members may actually have a healthy effect on group decision-making processes.
• Peer groups are vulnerable to groupthink, groupregret, group fantasies, grouphate, and group highs, as members catch the doubts, despair, imaginings, excitement, confidence, compassion, or joy of their peers. • The longer peers have been in a group, the more contagious positive or negative emotions may be.
• Group satisfaction or dissatisfaction for peers results, in part, from social comparison processes. Groups, group members, and group events will be compared to behaviors or outcomes expected, previous behaviors of the same people or previous groups, and behaviors, effort, contributions of peers compared to those of the perceiving peer member. • Feelings of guilt (overbenefited) or frustration (underbenefited) will result when group members compare their behaviors and benefits to those of others in the group.
• Peer groups create and enact nonverbal behaviors and rituals that can result in message ambiguity and require interpretation tasks. • Group expectations are socially learned, so early peer group experiences affect subsequent group behaviors, satisfactions, and perceptions. • Group member behaviors that are unexpected will be positively or negatively perceived, depending on the relational reward value of the group or peer member to each of the other members.
• Membership in any peer group always involves a potential threat to the face of one or more members. • Any group behavior (or the absence of a behavior) may be perceived as threatening or enhancing the private or public face of a peer group member. • The number of other people present during any peer group event (insiders or outsiders) will increase the perceived face threat to peer group members. • People develop strategies as peer group members to minimize negative face threat and to maximize positive face outcomes, including reframing, blaming, praising, and ignoring perceived effects on face.

(Continued)

Appendix (Continued)

Theory/Concept	Assumptions
Free Ride Effect	When some people think they can get away with it, they try to benefit from the efforts of other task group members, while expending less effort themselves. They slack off when they see other members of the group working, if they think they will not be blamed. They enjoy the reward of the group, while giving less effort.[15]
Fundamental Attribution Error	Fundamental attribution error is a strong but normal bias in social perception in which people tend to attribute the causes of another person's negative behaviors or mistakes to that person's disposition (internal-stable), without taking into account situational factors (external-unstable).[16] At the same time, there is a tendency to explain one's own behavioral mistakes as due to situational (temporary) factors, rather than dispositional (ongoing) factors. These error-laden attributions are then used for judging future behaviors of others or self.[17]
Gender Socialization Perspective	Masculine and feminine ways of communicating and behaving with others are organized by rules and roles learned as children.[18] While men are socialized around themes of success, aggressiveness, sexuality, self-reliance, and not-femaleness, women are socialized around themes of the importance of appearance, sensitivity and caring, tolerating negative treatment by others, and super-femaleness (successfully enacting multiple roles).[19]
Groupaha!	The creative discovery experience that occurs *during group activities* in which innovation or problem solving results in new ideas or solutions for that group.[20]

Application to Peer Groups
• Dissatisfaction with some peer groups may be the result of some group members perceiving that they are able to do less when others do more. • When peers in a group are silent about the lack of effort of others, group cohesion suffers. • Task success suffers when peers do less, even though it may be difficult for a peer to raise the issue for discussion.
• Peer group events are highly vulnerable to the fundamental attribution error, since peers will attempt to make sense of any disappointing behaviors of the peers. • Peers will tend to attribute disappointing or unwanted words or behaviors to a peer's disposition (thoughtless, selfish, uncaring), rather than to situational factors (presence of others, illness, distraction, ambivalent cues). • Peers will tend to attribute their own behavioral mistakes within the group to situational factors, rather than to dispositional factors. These error-laden social attributions may be used by other peers to judge the future behaviors of peers in that peer group relationship. • Peer group members will judge or evaluate the behaviors of outsiders with the fundamental attribution error bias (disposition), while allowing for situational explanations for the mistakes of their own members.
• Men and women are socialized differently regarding their roles in groups. Women are socialized around *process tasks* of taking turns, listening, connecting, and reaching consensus, among others. Men are socialized around *outcome tasks* of success, competition, scoring, and finishing, among others. • Suggests attention be paid to how women are socialized to the tasks of displaying emotions in peer groups, as well as maintaining or enhancing the social face of their peers during public events. Women may also devote cognitive time to thinking about hurt feelings, what people meant by comments, whether or not they are liked by peers, and whether others are being included. Suggests men in peer groups may contain emotions, judge the utility of a suggestion or behavior, as well as focus on the outcome of peer tasks, such as winning, scoring, displaying competence, protecting, creating, or building. Men may devote cognitive time to ruminating about perceived failures, unmet deadlines, incomplete tasks, or peers who are not directly contributing to task outcomes.
• Focuses on understanding how (and with what effects) peer groups experience creativity within group processes. • Suggests that some peer group members may have to balance the dialectic of *self versus group* during successful group processes in order to cope with frustration during group discussions.

(Continued)

Appendix (Continued)

Theory/Concept	Assumptions
Group Dialectical Perspective	Personal change takes place as the result of the attempt that people make to resolve the inevitable tensions of relationship life, such as the need for both novelty or sameness, belongingness or independence, and openness or privacy.[29]
Groupregret	A jointly experienced anxiety about making the wrong decision that occurs within groups who are anticipating various consequences for more than one possible decision choice. Groupregret keeps a group from moving toward a decision until the perceived unwanted outcomes of the emerging preferred choice have been resolved through counterfactual talk (what-if).[21]
Group Socialization	The process by which any group (as an entity) teaches its culture, history, stories, norms, values, and goals to its members (as individuals), particularly when new members are added to that group. How a group member should behave, what attitudes the member should hold, and what beliefs the member should adopt are communicated during group socialization processes.

<table>
<tr><th>Application to Peer Groups</th></tr>
<tr><td>• Offers a focus on how various peer groups structure themselves to spark creative thinking processes in individuals.
• Highlights the need for peer group members to be willing to communicate with one another in ways that provoke the generation of new ideas and novel ways of combining the ideas of other peers.</td></tr>
<tr><td>Relationships among peer group members inevitably involve unavoidable tensions between normal dialectical needs:
• The desire for both novelty and predictability from other members
• The desire for both belongingness and independence (conformity and individuality)
• The desire for both openness and privacy (wanting peers to know you and your life challenges, but wanting to keep some parts of your life private)
Successful peer group relationships require flexibility and resilience, each peer continually balancing these tensions. Conflict arises when one or more peer group members do not successfully balance or acknowledge normal dialectical tensions of themselves or others.</td></tr>
<tr><td>• Suggests that peer group decisions, whether task or social, are more difficult for members when they are anxious about unwanted outcomes.
• Casts light on the value and effects of group discussions about peer group choices, as well as the negative effects that may occur when peer groups do not encourage the sharing of anxieties about decisional outcomes.
• Offers one variable in a peer group's history (previous unwanted outcomes from group decisions) that may impair or affect future social or task decisions by that group.
• Suggests a variable on which peer group members may have important individual differences: their tolerance for possible decisional mistakes.</td></tr>
<tr><td>• Offers a dimension of peer group scholarship that examines intense initiations, forms of indoctrination, group persuasion, rituals, storytelling, and the outcomes of those forms of socialization.
• Points to scholarship that suggests that people value groups more if their indoctrination into that group was severe and intense (cliques, military, sororities, secret societies, cults, athletic teams, street gangs), which may explain why peer group members continue to support hazing.
• Suggests points at which interventions by peer group leaders or members might occur in ways that impact the commitment of future peer members.</td></tr>
</table>

(Continued)

Appendix (Continued)

Theory/Concept	Assumptions
Hot Groups	A task-obsessed group in which the members are passionately committed to the group's goals. The hot group's mentality is characterized by sharp focus, single-mindedness, and an all-out dedication to accomplishing something important. Hot groups might not endure beyond a singular task, but during that task the members are operating at full speed with a sense of zealousness beyond that typical of most teams.[22]
Impression Management	Impression management involves the activities people engage in to look good to themselves and others. People make conclusions about their own attitudes by noticing their behaviors ("I am generous"). People attempt to manage the impression they make on others through nonverbal behaviors, words, appearance, objects, and manipulation of physical settings.[23]
Inclusion-Fragility	The social perception some people have that being included in a group is fragile and that a group of which that person is a member may reject him or her at any time.
Investment Model of Relationships	Relational commitment can be predicted by three variables: satisfaction, a comparison to other perceived available alternative relationships,[24] and actual investments in the relationship. Investments include time, emotional energy, shared possessions, memories, or relationships. These increase commitment by making it more costly to end a relationship.[25]

Application to Peer Groups
• Opens up new language for describing the hallmarks of small peer groups that demonstrate a passionate, productive mentality toward their goals. • Term applies across a wide variety of peer groups whose members find meaning and ennoblement through their group's work. • Concept pairs well with "emotional contagion," suggesting that some groups uniquely catch fire, as members extend themselves beyond their personal best. • Allows a scholarly focus on both the group and individual levels, investigating group processes, leadership, products or outcomes, and the commitment and mentality of individual members. • Raises an important structurational question about what rules, resources, and structures are needed by these groups. • Useful for a Bona Fide Group Perspective, examining the way some hot groups fizzle and others flame (in organizations, neighborhoods, or communities): What environments help small hot groups thrive?
• Peer group communication always involves the task of impression management. • Peers will rely on the perceived reactions of other people to help draw conclusions about the success or failure of their contributions, including both nonverbal and verbal behaviors. • Peers who attempt to manage both their own impression and the impressions of others in the group will be dually burdened and stressed. • Social deceptions can result from the attempt by peer members to manage social impressions of other peers and outsiders (for example, pretending satisfaction, masking disappointment, or minimizing divergent values or opinions).
• Highlights a group-oriented social fear that is common to peer group members. • Offers one explanation for why some peer group members go along with or ignore behaviors that are contrary to their personal value systems. • Suggests that under some circumstances peer groups have power over their members: when members believe (a) that their peer group membership cannot be counted on, or (b) that they may be rejected at any time.
• Peers will compare the efforts they make and the rewards they are given within a group to the perceived available alternative rewards they imagine they should have received and the way they imagine they would be treated by available alternative peer groups. Consistently satisfactory rewards received in a peer group will enhance a member's group commitment, whereas consistently unsatisfactory gift exchanges lessen a member's group commitment. • The history of a peer group involves the various investments of time, emotional energy, shared possessions, and creation of memories of the

(Continued)

Appendix (Continued)

Theory/Concept	Assumptions
Nominal Group Member	A nominal group member is one in name only and does not participate in the group in any meaningful way.
Peerness	The sense any member of a peer group has of that group's identity, solidarity, and vitality, along a continuum that may vary over time, from a sense of strong to weak peerness.
Peer-suasion	Group conformity that is a product of the pressure group members feel to comply in order to gain or sustain group acceptance.[26]
Reference Group	Any group that is admired and that has the power to influence an individual through the process of identification. When individuals want to be similar to members of a group, that group may influence the thoughts, goals, or behaviors of members or nonmembers. The influence power of a reference group may be mindful ("we are aware of this

Application to Peer Groups
members, which are all variables in predicting a person's relational commitment to the group. • It will be more difficult to exit a peer group when someone has consistently been receiving rewards from others in the group. • Group members will use the perceived time, energy, and resources devoted to the group by any one member as a measure of the imagined relational commitment of that person to the peer group.
• Focuses attention on peer group members who do not participate in groups of which they claim to be members. • Suggests that others might not consider all group members to be "real" members of a peer group. • Helps account for member frustration, group ineffectiveness, and weakening peer group vitality, to name a few. • Draws attention to actual member contributions to a peer group, rather than to claimed membership.
• Offers a conceptual basis for thinking about peer group commitment, satisfaction or dissatisfaction, or the ability of a group to influence its peer members, to name a few. • Suggests a focus on identity both at the peer group and individual member levels. • Offers a basis to compare various peer groups, and suggests that each peer member may bring an inner comparison of a new peer group's peerness to the peerness that member experienced in prior peer groups. • Suggests that one of the covert goals of peer groups is to create then sustain a sense of peerness among its members.
• Suggests that a peer may have greater persuasive power over another peer in a group than outsiders, or even peers who do not share group membership. • Places a focus on intragroup persuasion, conformity pressures, and social coercion. • Peer group behaviors may be a product of perceived group pressure. • Peer group acceptance (and membership) may be a condition of behavioral compliance.
• Highlights the power of many peer groups to influence both members and nonmembers when that peer group is perceived as a "reference group." • Suggests that peers who are members of a group or who are outsiders who wish to be members of a peer group might adopt manners of dress, speech, and behaviors from the desired peer reference group. • Focuses attention on the manner in which an individual may have more than one reference peer group, which may create dialectical tensions for

(Continued)

Appendix (Continued)

Theory/Concept	Assumptions
	group may be mindful ("we are aware of this influence") or mindless ("we are influenced, but unaware of that influence"). Influence will be a matter of degree. That is, the more a person identifies with a reference group, the more influence power the group has on that person.
Reinforcement Theory	People like and are attracted to other people who reward them, through compliments, praise, resources, or gifts; people dislike and avoid people who punish them through criticism, hurtful comments, or by ignoring them.[27]
Rejection Contagion	The perception that one person's social rejection is capable of being transferred to other people.[28]
Science of Happiness	Happiness is experienced at a cognitive level (thinking), as well as a bioneurological level (body). At the cognitive level, happy people make positive perceptual judgments about their emotional states. People use the *peak-end rule* (an average of how good or bad the peak *moment* was plus how good or bad the *end* was), neglecting total pleasure or pain. Recalling a bad event is sufficient to make people who thought they were happy reframe their happiness downward.[30] Biologically, happiness occurs when the brain releases the neurotransmitter dopamine, a pleasure chemical.[31] Dopamine stimulates pleasure and dampens pain,[32] controlling not only behavior, but also motivation and commitment. The brain's experience of happiness is highly unstable.

Application to Peer Groups
that person. Social peer groups or professional peer groups may cause member role conflict for members. • Highlights the importance of understanding influence power of reference groups by examining the embeddedness of groups within communities and cultures.
• People like and are attracted to others who reward them through imaginative, thoughtful, desired gift objects. This helps predict or explain how peer groups form and maintain membership and cohesion. • Peers like and are attracted to people who reward them by praising their efforts and contributions and by displaying social gratitude. • Peers dislike and avoid group members or groups who punish them by ignoring them or by giving hurtful messages. This predicts why some peers leave or are shunned by the group: this is peer group membership fragility.
• Explains why some group members are reluctant to express disapproval of their peer group's rejection of an outsider. • Explains a group-oriented social fear common among children and adolescents. • Suggests that social labeling has consequences beyond the target of any label.
• People use both peak (best) and end (recency) group experiences to determine their own peer-happiness levels within groups. • Happy people are more likely to make positive perceptual judgments about their own emotional states when participating in peer groups. Peers who make positive perceptual judgments about their emotional states in peer groups are more loyal and committed to that group. • Ruminating on previous bad group experiences contaminates the perception peers may have of being happy in their peer group. • The body releases dopamine when people receive benefits from peer group membership, physically enhancing their perception of their own happiness. When dopamine is released for someone, it will also dampen the pain they would otherwise experience in that situation from other events. This explains the commitment of some peer members to their group during stress, including war, losing streaks, or attack. • The physical effects on an individual of a highly successful peer group is temporary and unstable. Peer groups need to act and communicate in a way to sustain those effects. • Members who have experienced peak group moments (and the release of dopamine during those moments) will seek to replicate that chemical pleasure in future group events and challenges, whether with this peer group or a future one.

(Continued)

Appendix (Continued)

Theory/Concept	Assumptions
Scripts and Schemas	Scripts and schemas are cognitive structures that organize both expectations and interpretations of roles and events, based on previous experiences. A social *script* is the expectation a person holds for the rules and sequence for a specific social event. A social *schema* is the set of behaviors expected of other people that influence memory, interpretation, or inferences about relational behaviors. Our prior knowledge influences how we experience a current social event.[33]
Social Allergies	Social allergies are common experiences. Negative symptoms similar to those produced by physical toxins occur when people come into repeated contact with a social toxin. Social behaviors that grate on people's emotions are "social allergens," defined as emotion-arousing behaviors or situations created by another person that are unpleasant (though not unbearable).[34] Prolonged exposure at periodic intervals to social allergens may produce a reaction of hypersensitive annoyance or disgust ("social allergy"). Social allergies occur in a variety of relationships and are described as people or behaviors that "get under your skin" or "drive you crazy," without necessarily intending to do so. They develop in involuntary relationships (coworkers, step-parents, in-laws, roommates),[35] as well as in voluntary friendships and romances.[36]
Social Exchange Theory	In relationships, people are continually exchanging resources that they then evaluate as being either rewarding or not rewarding, or as being valuable or costly.[37]
Social Facilitation Effect	When people in a peer group believe their performance will be evaluated by other members of the group, they are likely to work harder than they would when working alone.[38]

Application to Peer Groups
• People make sense of their present peer group experiences based on scripts and schemas they hold from previous peer group experiences. • People hold scripts (expectations for how their peers should communicate or behave). They compare actual conversations and messages to the scripts they hold of how others should communicate in their groups even when membership has changed. • People hold schemas (expectations for group behaviors from other people) based on their memory of past peer group behaviors, both negative and positive. • The perceived success and value of membership in a peer group is based, in part, on the scripts and schemas that form from memories of past peer groups.
• When peers are repeatedly annoyed by the behaviors of others, negative emotions increase over time. • The negative emotional current generated by annoying group behaviors may activate memories of similar prior incidents, including the emotions that had been associated with those historical peer group incidents. • The allergenic behavioral stimulus then triggers increasing negative emotional responses to the peer behavior "allergen" when it next happens. • Peers may trigger social allergies in others by their group behavior without being aware that they are doing so, since some people make an effort to present positive face through self-control during public events, even over long periods of time, in which the negative behavior is repeated. • Social allergens in peer group relationships may include unwanted teasing, lack of gratitude, derogatory comments, exclusion, or coercion, to name a few.
Peer group behaviors are continually judged by the members. Peers continually evaluate the value of group membership in a particular group as being either rewarding or costly.
In some situations, the presence of peers or teammates may trigger enhanced performance by other members of the peer group.

(Continued)

Appendix (Continued)

Theory/Concept	Assumptions
Social Loafing	The reduction in motivation or effort of some group members who are working on a task collectively, compared to the work or effort that the individual expends when working alone.[39] Social loafing may be mindless (the individual is not aware he or she is doing less) or mindful (the person believes that less effort is needed since the rest of the group is available to do the work).
Social Penetration Theory	Social penetration is the process of relationship intimacy where people move from superficial communication to more intimate communication, as self-disclosures increase by breadth and depth.[40] Self-disclosure involves the intentional sharing of significant information about oneself that would not otherwise be known. People feel closer to those who self-disclose more in breadth and depth.
Social Proof	The tendency to see acts as more appropriate, valid, and desirable when others are seen doing them.[41] Also referred to as the "sheep factor."
Sucker Effect	When someone suspects that other group members may be slacking off while other group members are working. Rather than be a "sucker" who does all the work, a group member slacks off in order to match the level of work done by others (see "free ride effect").[42]
Symbolic Interaction Theory	People interact with one another by creating symbolic rituals, objects, and language, which, in turn, shapes their self-concepts, influences their behaviors with other people, and makes their social worlds meaningful.[43]

Application to Peer Groups
• Suggests that the mere presence of others and perception of the effort needed by each member may trigger less effort than a peer group needs. • Suggests that, contrary to the motivational effect of the presence of peers, in some situations peer members slack off. • Offers a variable from which to understand peer group members who are frustrated with working on tasks in their group, since they may find it more difficult or socially painful to criticize a peer member than to criticize someone over whom they have legitimate power or status.
• The ability to successfully offer or decode social group cues helps people make more satisfying behavioral decisions. • Less satisfying group memberships are more likely to occur when the breadth and depth of self-disclosure between peers is more superficial. • More satisfying peer group memberships are more likely to occur when self-disclosure between peers is broader and deeper. • Self-disclosure in peer groups affects the intimacy other members feel toward one another. • When self-disclosure is unbalanced between peers, some members will feel less or more connection to others.
• Explains the child's refrain, "But Mom, everyone else is doing it!" • Suggests that peer group members are using the behavior of other members as persuasive data to support their own desires or choices. • Explains the powerful covert persuasion of peer groups on the values and behavior of members.
Under some circumstances, the presence of other peers may trigger less effort and commitment on the part of group members, especially where it is perceived that others are getting away with doing less work.
• All peer groups are embedded in symbolic rituals (simple or elaborate) that have relational meaning for the group members who participate in them. • When peers do not share the meaning of symbolic rituals or objects, the success or value of a peer group to its members is threatened. • Greater understanding of historic, cultural, and personal meaning embedded in objects, occasions, and rituals for others increases group satisfaction. • Lack of understanding of historic, cultural, and personal meaning embedded in gift objects, occasions, and ritual for others produces dissatisfaction with relationships. • Peer groups use symbols to enhance the value of their group's identity to members and make it meaningful. • Peer groups use symbolic interaction processes to shape their group identity and influence the behaviors of members.

(Continued)

Appendix (Continued)

Theory/Concept	Assumptions
Synergy	The result that occurs when a group's performance surpasses the capabilities of any single member in terms of quantity, quality, creativity, protection, support, or some other measure that is relevant to those group members.
Theory of Thin-Slicing	Thin-slicing involves the natural human tendency to engage in rapid thinking when confronted with novel events. Thin-slicing describes the ability of our brains to find patterns in novel situations and behaviors that are based on narrow slices of experience or information.[44] The social brain loves to leap to conclusions, rather than to wade through unfamiliar new data, so people make quick judgments based on little information. The Theory of Thin-Slicing explains how our frugal brains are willing to let a little knowledge go a long way.
Tipping Point	A sociological principle that describes the process by which the status quo appears to change suddenly. More recently applied to describe the manner in which a small influential group causes a product, style, music, or behavior to become popular.[45]
Zero History	Describes the first moments of a group whose members may or may not know one another, but who have not worked together in *this particular group* before. Prior to the zero history moment, this group did not exist. At the zero history moment, group members may experience initial social or task anxiety and are immediately faced with organizing themselves and creating group identity.[46]

Application to Peer Groups
• Offers one variable to explain why members are committed to their peer groups. • Casts light on the desirability of membership in particular groups. • Suggests a factor for study of peer groups in which scholars examine a member's perception of group synergy, outsiders' perception of the synergy of other groups, and the connection between perceived group synergy and group satisfaction or dissatisfaction.
Many group events or behaviors (pre-, during, or post-) tend to produce rapid evaluations and snap judgments about: • The appropriateness of a peer's behavior. • The desirability or value of a group member. • The effort put into group tasks. • Whether a nonmember seeking entry is worthy of peer group membership. • The more novel any aspects of the decision or event are, the more likely that decision or event will be to stimulate thin-sliced thinking and judgment. Even when based on little information, some of those rapid judgments will be correct, while some will produce errors, since the brain is willing to let a little knowledge go a long way. Peer group decisions and behaviors may be based on one peer's thin-slicing of the data.
• Offers a useful perspective from which to examine a peer group's influence on outsiders, from a BFGP. • When combined with "reference group," offers a dual tool for explaining a particular peer group's influence on the behaviors of outside others. • From a sociological macro standpoint, offers language useful for investigating the changing relationships, trends, status, and power of specific peer groups in communities or organizations. • Suggests that "tipping point influence" of a peer group may not always be something of which the group or its peer members are aware. • Suggests an examination of key influential peer groups within schools, neighborhoods, or communities, through the process of looking at the contagious effect of their behaviors, dress, language, or preferences.
• When a new member enters an existing peer group, zero history for that member creates an awkwardness that may not be shared by the group. • When groups that are expected to super-task are first assembled, zero history creates a need for immediately facing a social dilemma rather than proceeding to task. • Zero history makes it awkward for strangers selected as jurors to begin the deliberative task until they have surpassed social anxiety. • The anxiety of zero history will be differently experienced and last longer for some group members than for others.

(Continued)

Appendix (Continued)

[1] For a general discussion, see Aronson, E., Wilson, T. D., & Akert, R. M. (1999). *Social psychology* (3rd ed.). New York: Longman.

Matlin, M. W. (1994). *Cognition* (4th ed.). Fort Worth, TX: Harcourt Brace & Company.

For a classic study, see Kahneman, D., & Tversky, A. (1984). Choices, values, and frames. *American Psychologist, 39,* 341–350.

[2] Heider, F. (1958). *The psychology of interpersonal relations*. New York: Wiley. See subsequent theoretical development of Heider's work: Kelley, H. H. (1972). Attribution in social interaction. In E. E. Jones, D. E. Kanouse, H. H. Kelley, R. E. Nisbett, S. Valins, & B. Weiner (Eds.), *Attribution: Perceiving the causes of behavior* (pp. 151–174). Morristown, NJ: General Learning Press.

[3] For attributional biases in romantic relationships, see Fincham, F. D., Beach, S. R., & Baucom, D. H. (1987). Attribution processes in distressed and nondistressed couples: 4. Self-Partner attribution differences. *Journal of Personality and Social Psychology, 52,* 739–748.

Grigg, F., Fletcher, G. J. O., & Fitness, J. (1989). Spontaneous attributions in happy and unhappy dating relationships. *Journal of Social and Personal Relationships, 6,* 61–68.

Vangelisti, A. L. (1992). Communication problems in committed relationships: An attributional analysis. In J. H. Harvey, T. L. Orbuch, & A. L. Weber (Eds.), *Attributions, accounts, and close relationships* (pp. 144–164). New York: Springer-Verlag.

[4] Festinger, L. (1957). *A theory of cognitive dissonance*. Stanford, CA: Stanford University Press.

[5] Folger, J. P., & Poole, M. S. (1984). *Working through conflict: A communication perspective* (Glenview, IL: Scott, Foresman), p. 84.

[6] Locke, E. A., Tirnauer, D., Roberson, Q., Goldman, B., Latham, M. E, & Weldon, E. (2001). The importance of the individual in an age of groupism. In M. E. Turner (Ed.), *Groups at work: Theory and research* (pp. 501–528). Mahwah, NJ: Lawrence Erlbaum.

[7] Festinger, L., Pepitone, A., & Newcomb, T. (1952). Some consequences of deindividuation in a group. *Journal of Abnormal Social Psychology, 47,* 382–389.

[8] For an excellent discussion of the effects of deviants in a small group, see Adams, K. & Galanes, G. J. (2006). *Communicating in groups: Applications and skills* (6th ed.). Boston, MA: McGraw Hill, Chapter 7, "Becoming a Group."

[9] This term was originally used by the Catholic Church. When someone was nominated for sainthood, a priest would be assigned by the Church the role of Advocate for the Devil. That priest's role was to investigate all possible reasons the saint-nominee should not be given sainthood.

[10] Goleman, D. (1995). *Emotional intelligence: Why it can matter more than I.Q.* New York: Bantam. See also a study in which a two-minute exposure of people waiting together resulted in the less-expressive person's mood coming to resemble the mood of the more-expressive person: Anderson, C., Keltner, D., & John, O. P. (2003). Emotional convergence between people over time. *Journal of Personality and Social Psychology, 84,* 1054–1068.

[11] Hatfield, E., & Traupmann, J. (1981). Intimate relationships: A perspective from equity theory. In S. W. Duck & R. Gilmour (Eds.), *Personal relationships: Vol. 1. Studying personal relationships* (pp. 165–178). London: Academic Press.

Hatfield, E., Traupmann, J., Sprecher, S., Utne, M., & Hay, J. (1985). Equity and intimate relations: Recent research. In W. Ickes (Ed.), *Compatible and incompatible relationships* (pp. 912–117). New York: Springer-Verlag.

Hatfield, E., Utne, M. K., & Traupmann, J. (1979). Equity theory and intimate relationships. In R. L. Burgess & T. L. Huston (Eds.), *Social exchange in developing relationships* (pp. 99–133). New York: Academic Press.

[12] Burgoon, J. K. (1978). A communication model of personal space violations: Explication and an initial test. *Human Communication Research, 4*, 129–142.

Burgoon, J. K., Buller, D. B., & Woodall, W. G. (1996). *Nonverbal communication: The unspoken dialogue*. New York: McGraw-Hill.

Burgoon, J. K., & Hale, J. L. (1988). Nonverbal expectancy violations: Model elaboration and application to immediacy behaviors. *Communication Monographs, 55*, 58–79.

[13] Facework includes both face-saving tactics and face restoration strategies.

Brown, P., & Levinson, S. (1978). Universals in language usage: Politeness phenomenon. In E. Goody (Ed.), *Questions and politeness* (pp. 56–89). Cambridge: Cambridge University Press.

Cupach, W. R., & Metts, S. (1994). *Facework*. Thousand Oaks, CA: Sage.

Ting-Toomey, S. (1994). Face and facework: An introduction. In S. Ting-Toomey (Ed.), *The challenge of facework* (pp. 1–14). Albany, NY: SUNY Press.

[14] Domenici, K., & Littlejohn, S. W. (2006). *Facework: Bridging theory and practice*. Thousand Oaks, CA: Sage, p. 11 (full definition).

[15] Karau, S. J., & Williams, K. D. (2001). Understanding individual motivation in groups: The collective effort model. In M. E. Turner (Ed.), *Groups at work: Theory and research, Applied social research* (pp. 113–141). Mahwah, NJ: Lawrence Erlbaum.

[16] Heider, F. (1958). *The psychology of interpersonal relations*. New York: Wiley.

[17] Ross, L. (1977). The intuitive psychologist and his shortcomings: Distortions in the attribution process. In L. Berkowitz (Ed.), *Advances in experimental social psychology* (Vol. 10, pp. 174–221). New York: Academic Press.

Ross, L., Amabile, T. M., & Steinmetz, J. L. (1977). Social roles, social control, and biases in social perception processes. *Journal of Personality and Social Psychology, 35*, 485–494.

Taylor, S. E., & Koivumaki, J. H. (1976). The perception of self and others: Acquaintanceship, affect, and actor-observer differences. *Journal of Personality and Social Psychology, 33*, 403–408.

Miller, A. G., Jones, E. E., & Hinkle, S. (1981). A robust attribution error in the personality domain. *Journal of Experimental Social Psychology, 17*, 587–600.

[18] Maltz, D. N., & Borker, R. (1982). A cultural approach to male-female miscommunication. In J. J. Gumpertz (Ed.), *Language and social identity* (pp. 196–216). Cambridge: Cambridge University Press.

[19] Wood, J. T. (2005). *Gendered lives: Communication, gender, and culture* (6th ed.). Belmont, CA: Thomson Wadsworth Learning.

Doyle, J. A. (1997). *The male experience* (3rd ed.). Dubuque, IA: Brown & Benchmark.

Aronson, J. (1992). Women's sense of responsibility for the care of old people: "But who else is going to do it?" *Gender and Society, 6*, 8–29.

Wood, J. T. (1994). *Who cares: Women, care, and culture*. Carbondale: Southern Illinois University Press.

Nolen-Hoeksma, S., & Rusting, C. L. (1999). Gender differences in well-being. In D. Kahneman, E. Diener, & N. Schwarz (Eds.), *Well-being: Foundations of hedonic psychology* (pp. 330–351). New York: Russell Sage Foundation.

[20] SunWolf (2002). Getting to "GroupAha!": Provoking creative processes in task groups. In L. R. Frey (Ed.), *New directions in group communication* (pp. 203–217). Thousand Oaks, CA: Sage.

(Continued)

Appendix (Continued)

[21] SunWolf. (2006). Decisional regret theory: Reducing the anxiety about uncertain outcomes during group decision making through shared counterfactual storytelling. *Communication Studies, 57(2)*, 1–29.

[22] Lipman-Blumen, J., & Leavitt, H. J. (1999). *Hot groups: Seeding them, feeding them, and using them to ignite your organization*. New York: Oxford University Press.

[23] Infante, D. A., Rancer, A. S., & Womack, D. F. (1990). *Building communication theory* (3rd ed.). Prospect Heights, IL: Waveland Press.

West, R., & Turner, L. H. (2004). *Introducing communication theory: Analysis and application* (2nd ed.). New York: McGraw-Hill.

[24] Thibaut, J. W., & Kelley, H. H. (1959). *The social psychology of groups*. New York: John Wiley.

[25] Rusbult, C. E. (1980). Commitment and satisfaction in romantic associations: A test of the investment model. *Journal of Experimental Social Psychology, 16*, 172–186.

Rusbult, C. E. (1980). Satisfaction and commitment in friendships. *Representative Research in Social Psychology, 11*, 96–105.

[26] "Peer-suasion" was usefully coined by Gass & Seiter (2007).

Gass, R. H., & Seiter, J. S. (2007). *Persuasion, social influence, and compliance gaining* (3rd ed.). Boston, MA: Pearson, p. 130.

[27] Byrne, D. (1971). *The attraction paradigm*. New York: Academic Press.

[28] SunWolf, & Leets, L. (2003). Communication paralysis during peer group exclusion: Social dynamics that prevent children and adolescents from expressing disagreement. *Journal of Language and Social Psychology, 22*, 355–384.

[29] Baxter, L. A., & Montgomery, B. M. (1997). Rethinking communication in personal relationships from a dialectical perspective. In S. Duck (Ed.), *Handbook of personal relationships* (2nd ed.). New York: John Wiley & Sons.

[30] Nettle, D. (2005). *Happiness: The science behind your smile*. New York: Oxford University Press.

Seligman, M. E. P. (2002). *Authentic happiness*. New York: The Free Press.

Argyle, M. (1987). *The psychology of happiness*. London: Routledge.

Frank, R. H. (1999). *Luxury fever: Why money fails to satisfy in an era of excess*. New York: The Free Press.

Kahneman, D. (1999). Objective happiness. In D. Kahneman, E. Diener, & N. Schwarz (Eds.), *Well-being: Foundations of hedonic psychology* (pp. 3–25). New York: Russell Sage Foundation.

Marar, Z. (2003). *The happiness paradox*. London: Reaktion Books.

[31] Berns, G. (2005). *Satisfaction: The science of finding true fulfillment*. New York: Henry Holt.

[32] Layard, R. (2005). *Happiness: Lessons from a new science*. New York: Penguin Press.

[33] Fiske, S. T., & Taylor, S. E. (1991). *Social cognition* (2nd ed.). New York: McGraw-Hill.

[34] Cunningham, M. R., Barbee, A. P., & Druen, P. B. (1997). Social allergens and the reactions they produce: Escalation of love and annoyance in love and work. In R. M. Kowalski (Ed.), *Aversive interpersonal behaviors* (pp. 189–214). New York: Plenum Press.

[35] Hess, J. A. (2000). Maintaining nonvoluntary relationships with disliked partners. An investigation into the use of distancing behaviors. *Human Communication Research, 26*, 458–488.

[36] Cunningham, M. R., Shamblen, S. R., Barbee, A. P., & Ault, L. K. (2005). Social allergies in romantic relationships: Behavioral repetition, emotional sensitization, and dissatisfaction in dating couples. *Personal Relationships, 12*, 273–295.

[37] Roloff, M. E. (1981). *Interpersonal communication: The social exchange approach*. Beverly Hills, CA: Sage.

[38] Gagne, M., & Zuckerman, M. (1999). Performance and learning goal orientations as moderators of social loafing and social facilitation. *Small Group Research, 30(5)*, 524–544.

[39] Karau, S. J., & Williams, K. D. (1993). Social loafing: A meta-analytic review and theoretical integration. *Journal of Personality and Social Psychology, 65(4)*, 681–706.

[40] Altman, I., & Taylor, D. A. (1973). *Social penetration: The development of interpersonal relationships*. New York: Holt, Rinehart & Winston.

[41] Cialdini, R. B. (1993). *Influence: The psychology of persuasion* (Rev. ed.). New York: Morrow.

From a sociological standpoint, Gladwell, M. (2002). *The tipping point*. New York: Little, Brown and Company.

[42] Locke, E. A., Tirnauer, D., Roberson, Q., Goldman, B., Latham, M. E, & Weldon, E. (2001). The importance of the individual in an age of groupism. In M. E. Turner (Ed.), *Groups at work: Theory and research* (pp. 501–528). Mahwah, NJ: Lawrence Erlbaum.

[43] Mead, G. H. (1934). *Mind, self and society: From the standpoint of a social behaviorist*. Chicago: University of Chicago Press.

Blumer, H. (1969). *Symbolic interactionism: Perspective and method*. Englewood Cliffs, NJ: Prentice Hall.

Denzin, N. K. (Ed.) (1994). *Studies in symbolic interaction*. Greenwich, CT: JAI Press.

[44] Gladwell, M. (2005). *Blink: The power of thinking without thinking*. New York: Little, Brown & Company.

[45] Gladwell, M. (2002). *The tipping point*. New York: Little, Brown and Company.

[46] SunWolf. (2006). Empathic attunement facilitation: Stimulating immediate task engagement in zero-history training groups of helping professionals. In L. R. Frey (Ed.), *Facilitating group communication: Innovations and applications with natural groups: Vol. 1: Facilitating group creation, conflict, and conversation* (pp. 3–32). Cresskill, NJ: Hampton Press.

Notes

❖ NOTES TO PROLOGUE

1. Lipman-Blumen, J., & Leavitt, H. J. (1999). *Hot groups: Seeding them, feeding them, and using them to ignite your organization.* New York: Oxford University Press, p. 9.

2. *Workin' from can't to can't: African-American cowboys in Texas,* produced by The University of Texas Institute of Texan Cultures at San Antonio, and available at store.the-museum-store.org/wofrcatocaaf.html. Excerpted from transcript, p. 7.

3. Retrieved March 3, 2004, from *The Oregonian* newspaper Web site, www.oregonlive.com

4. SunWolf, & Leets, L. (2004). Being left out: Rejecting outsiders and communicating group boundaries in childhood and adolescent peer groups. *Journal of Applied Communication Research, 32(3),* 195–223, p. 207.

5. Asher, S. R. (1990). Recent advances in the study of peer rejection. In S. R. Asher & J. D. Coie (Eds.), *Peer rejection in childhood* (pp. 3–14). New York: Cambridge University Press.

6. Asher, S. R. (1990). Recent advances in the study of peer rejection. In S. R. Asher & J. D. Coie (Eds.), *Peer rejection in childhood* (pp. 3–14). New York: Cambridge University Press, p. 4.

7. SunWolf, & Leets, L. (2004). Being left out: Rejecting outsiders and communicating group boundaries in childhood and adolescent peer groups. *Journal of Applied Communication Research, 32(3),* 195–223.

8. Hayden, L., Taruulli, D., & Hymel, S. (1988, May). *Children talk about loneliness.* Paper presented at the biennial meeting of the University of Waterloo Conference on Child Development, Waterloo, Ontario.

Asher, S. R., Parkhurst, J. T., Hymel, S., & Williams, G. A. (1990). Peer rejection and loneliness in childhood. In S. R. Asher & J. D. Coie (Eds.), *Peer rejection in childhood* (pp. 253–273). New York: Cambridge University Press, p. 253.

❖ NOTES TO CHAPTER 1

1. Baldwin, J. R., Perry, S. D., & Moffitt, M. A. (2004). *Communication theories for everyday life.* Boston, MA: Pearson Education.

2. SunWolf. (2006). Decisional regret theory: Reducing the anxiety about uncertain outcomes during group decision making through shared counterfactual storytelling. *Communication Studies, 57(2),* 1–29.

3. Poole, M. S., & Hollingshead, A. B. (Eds.) (2005). *Theories of small groups: Interdisciplinary perspectives.* Thousand Oaks, CA: Sage, p. 2.

4. Frey, L. R., & SunWolf. (2005). The symbolic-interpretive perspective on group life. In M. S. Poole & A. Hollingshead (Eds.), *Theories of small groups: Interdisciplinary perspectives* (pp. 185–239). Thousand Oaks, CA: Sage.

Frey, L. R., & SunWolf. (2004). A symbolic-interpretive perspective on group dynamics. *Small Group Research, 35(3),* 277–306.

5. Frey, L. R., & SunWolf. (2004). A symbolic-interpretive perspective on group dynamics. *Small Group Research, 35(3),* 277–306.

6. Burke, K. (1966). *Language as symbolic action: Essays on life, literature, and method.* Berkeley: University of California Press, p. 16.

7. MacIntyre, A. (1981). *After virtue: A study in moral theory* (2nd ed.). Notre Dame, IN: University of Notre Dame Press, p. 201.

8. Fisher, W. R. (1987). *Human communication as narration: Toward a philosophy of reason, value, and action.* Columbia: University of South Carolina Press.

9. Wegner, D. M. (1987). Transactive memory: A contemporary analysis of the group mind. In B. Mullen & G. R. Goethals (Eds.), *Theories of group behavior* (pp. 185–208). New York: Springer.

10. Rouse, W., & Morris, N. (1986). On looking into the black box: Prospects and limits in the search for mental models. *Psychological Bulletin, 100,* 359–363.

11. Strauss, A. (1978). *Negotiations: Varieties, contexts, processes, and social order.* San Francisco: Jossey-Bass.

Strauss, A. (1994). *Continual permutations of action.* Cambridge: Cambridge University Press.

12. Frey, L. R., & SunWolf. (2004). A symbolic-interpretive perspective on group dynamics. *Small Group Research, 35(3),* 277–306.

Frey, L. R., & SunWolf. (2005). The symbolic-interpretive perspective on group life. In M. S. Poole & A. Hollingshead (Eds.), *Theories of small groups: Interdisciplinary perspectives* (pp. 185–239). Thousand Oaks, CA: Sage.

13. Frey, L. R., & SunWolf. (2005). The symbolic-interpretive perspective on group life. In M. S. Poole & A. Hollingshead (Eds.), *Theories of small groups: Interdisciplinary perspectives* (pp. 185–239). Thousand Oaks, CA: Sage (Figure 6.1, p. 190).

14. Frey, L. R., & SunWolf. (2004). A symbolic-interpretive perspective on group dynamics. *Small Group Research, 35(3),* 277–306.

15. Frey, L. R., & SunWolf. (2004). A symbolic-interpretive perspective on group dynamics. *Small Group Research, 35(3),* 277–306.

16. Adelman, M. B., & Frey, L. R. (1997). *The fragile community: Living together with AIDS.* Mahwah, NJ: Lawrence Erlbaum.

Adelman, M. B., & Frey, L. R. (1994). The pilgrim must embark: Creating and sustaining community in a residential facility for people with AIDS. In L. R. Frey (Ed.), *Group communication in context: Studies of natural groups* (pp. 3–22). Hillsdale, NJ: Lawrence Erlbaum.

17. Meyer, J. C. (1997). Humor and member narratives: Uniting and dividing at work. *Western Journal of Communication, 61,* 188–208.

18. Fine, G. A. (1987). *With the boys: Little League baseball and preadolescent culture.* Chicago: University of Chicago Press.

19. See http://www.commondreams.org/views06/0204-28.htm.

20. Festinger, L. (1957). *A theory of cognitive dissonance.* Stanford, CA: Stanford University Press.

21. Oetzel, J. G., & Robbins, J. (2003). Multiple identities in teams in a cooperative supermarket. In L. R. Frey (Ed.), *Group communication in context: Studies of bona fide groups* (2nd ed., pp. 183–208). Mahwah, NJ: Lawrence Erlbaum.

22. Longitudinal study of 143 groups: Duffy, M. K., & Shaw, J. D. (2000). The Salieri syndrome: Consequences of envy in groups. *Small Group Research, 31,* 3–23.

23. Felicio, D. M., & Miller, C. T. (1994). Social comparison in medical school: What students say about gender and similarity. *Basic and Applied Social Psychology, 15,* 277–297.

24. Sinclair-James, L., & Stohl, C. (1997). Group endings and new beginnings. In L. R. Frey & J. K. Barge (Eds.), *Managing group life: Communicating in decision-making groups* (pp. 308–334). Boston: Houghton Mifflin.

25. Poole, M. S., Seibold, D. R., & McPhee, R. D. (1996). The structuration of group decisions. In R. Y. Hirokawa & M. S. Poole (Eds.), *Communication and group decision making* (2nd ed., pp. 114–146). Thousand Oaks, CA: Sage.

26. Poole, M. S., Seibold, D. R., & McPhee, R. D. (1996). The structuration of group decisions. In R. Y. Hirokawa & M. S. Poole (Eds.), *Communication and group decision making* (2nd ed., pp. 114–146). Thousand Oaks, CA: Sage, p. 117.

27. Witmer, D. F. (1997). Communication and recovery: Structuration as an ontological approach to organizational culture. *Communication Monographs, 64,* 324–349.

28. DeSanctis, G., & Poole, M. S. (1994). Capturing the complexity in advanced technology use: Adaptive structuration theory. *Organization Science, 5,* 121–147.

Poole, M. S., & DeSanctis, G. (1990). Understanding the use of group decision support systems: The theory of adaptive structuration. In J. Fulk & C. Steinfield (Eds.), *Organizations and communication technology* (pp. 175–195). Newbury Park, CA: Sage.

Poole, M. S., & DeSanctis, G. (1992). Microlevel structuration in computer-supported group decision-making. *Human Communication Research, 19*, 5–49.

Poole, M. S., Holmes, M., & DeSanctis, G. (1991). Conflict management in a computer-supported meeting environment. *Management Science, 37*, 926–953.

29. Poole, M. S., & DeSanctis, G. (1992). Microlevel structuration in computer-supported group decision-making. *Human Communication Research, 19*, 5–49.

30. Poole, M. S., DeSanctis, G., Kirsch, L., & Jackson, M. (1995). Group decision support systems as facilitators of quality team efforts. In L. R. Frey (Ed.), *Innovations in group facilitation techniques: Applications in natural settings* (pp. 299–320). Cresskill, NJ: Hampton Press.

31. Canary, D. J., Brossman, B. G., & Seibold, D. R. (1987). Argument structures in decision-making groups. *Southern Communication Journal, 53*, 18–37.

Seibold, D. R., McPhee, R. D., Poole, M. S., Tanita, N. E., & Canary, D. J. (1981). Argument, group influence, and decision outcomes. In G. Ziegelmuller & J. Rhodes (Eds.), *Dimensions of argument: Proceedings of the second summer conference on argumentation* (pp. 663–692). Annandale, VA: Speech Communication Association.

32. Meyers, R. A., & Seibold, D. R. (1990). Perspectives on group argument: A critical review of persuasive arguments theory and an alternative structurational view. In J. A. Anderson (Ed.), *Communication yearbook* (Vol. 13, pp. 268–302). Newbury Park, CA: Sage

33. SunWolf, & Seibold, D. R. (1998). Jurors' intuitive rules for deliberations: A structurational approach to communication in jury decision making. *Communication Monographs, 65*, 282–307.

34. Landman, J. (1993). *Regret: The persistence of the possible.* New York: Oxford University Press.

35. Landman, J., & Petty, R. (2000). "It could have been you": How states exploit counterfactual thought to market lotteries. *Psychology and Marketing, 17*, 299–321.

36. McConnell, A. R., Niedermeier, K. E., Leibold, J. M., El-Alayli, A. G., Chin, P. P., & Kuiper, N. M. (2000). What if I find it cheaper someplace else?: Role of prefactual thinking and anticipated regret in consumer behavior. *Psychology and Marketing, 17*, 281–298.

37. Roese, N. J., & Olson, J. M. (1995). Counterfactual thinking: A critical overview. In N. J. Roese & J. M. Olson (Eds.), *What might have been: The social psychology of counterfactual thinking* (pp. 1–55). Mahwah, NJ: Lawrence Erlbaum.

Roese, N. J., & Olson, J. M. (1995). Functions of counterfactual thinking. In N. J. Roese & J. M. Olson (Eds.), *What might have been: The social psychology of counterfactual thinking* (pp. 169–198). Mahwah, NJ: Lawrence Erlbaum.

38. DERT acknowledges and draws on some constructs offered by Uncertainty Reduction Theory (Berger, 1979), the Narrative Paradigm (Fisher, 1987, 1997), Symbolic Convergence Theory (Bormann, 1985, 1994, 1996), and Structuration Theory (Poole, Seibold, & McPhee, 1985, 1996).

Berger, C. R. (1979). Beyond initial interactions: Uncertainty, understanding and the development of interpersonal relationships. In H. Giles & R. Sinclair (Eds.), *Language and social psychology* (pp. 122–144). Oxford, England: Basil Blackwell.

Fisher, W. R. (1987). *Human communication as narration: Toward a philosophy of reason, value, and action.* Columbia: University of South Carolina Press.

Fisher, W. R. (1997). Narration, reason, and community. In L. P. Hinchman & S. K. Hinchman (Eds.), *Memory, identity, community: The idea of narrative in the human sciences* (pp. 307–327). Albany, NY: State University of New York Press.

Bormann, E. G. (1985). Symbolic convergence theory: A communication formulation. *Journal of Communication, 35,* 128–138.

Bormann, E. G. (1994). In defense of symbolic convergence theory: A look at the theory and its criticisms after two decades. *Communication Theory, 4,* 259–294.

Bormann, E. G. (1996). Symbolic convergence theory and communication in group decision making. In R. Y. Hirokawa & M. S. Poole (Eds.), *Communication and group decision making* (2nd ed., pp. 81–113). Thousand Oaks, CA: Sage.

Poole, M. S., Seibold, D. R., & McPhee, R. D. (1985). Group decision-making as a structurational process. *Quarterly Journal of Speech, 71,* 74–102.

Poole, M. S., Seibold, D. R., & McPhee, R. D. (1996). The structuration of group decisions. In R. Y. Hirokawa & M. S. Poole (Eds.), *Communication and group decision making* (2nd ed., pp. 114–146). Thousand Oaks, CA: Sage.

39. SunWolf. (2006). Decisional regret theory: Reducing the anxiety about uncertain outcomes during group decision making through shared counterfactual storytelling. *Communication Studies, 57(2),* 1–29.

40. Davis, C. G., & Lehman, D. R. (1995). Counterfactual thinking and coping with traumatic life events. In N. J. Roese & J. M. Olson (Eds.), *What might have been: The social psychology of counterfactual thinking* (pp. 353–374). Mahwah, NJ: Lawrence Erlbaum.

41. Seelau, E. P., Seelau, S. M., Wells, G. L., & Windschitl, P. D. (1995). Counterfactual constraints. In N. J. Roese & J. M. Olson (Eds.), *What might have been: The social psychology of counterfactual thinking* (pp. 57–79). Mahwah, NJ: Lawrence Erlbaum.

42. Kasimatis, M., & Wells, G. L. (1995). Individual differences in counterfactual thinking. In N. J. Roese & J. M. Olson (Eds.), *What might have been: The social psychology of counterfactual thinking* (pp. 81–101). Mahwah, NJ: Lawrence Erlbaum.

43. Dunning, D., & Madey, S. F. (1995). Comparison processes in counterfactual thought. In N. J. Roese & J. M. Olson (Eds.), *What might have been: The social psychology of counterfactual thinking* (pp. 103–132). Mahwah, NJ: Lawrence Erlbaum.

44. McMullen, M. N., Markman, K. D., & Gavanski, I. (1995). Living in neither the best nor worst of all possible worlds: Antecedents and consequences of upward and downward counterfactual thinking. In N. J. Roese & J. M. Olson (Eds.), *What might have been: The social psychology of counterfactual thinking* (pp. 133–168). Mahwah, NJ: Lawrence Erlbaum.

45. Sherman, S. J., & McConnell, A. R. (1995). Dysfunctional implications of counterfactual thinking: When alternatives to reality fail us. In N. J. Roese & J. M. Olson (Eds.), *What might have been: The social psychology of counterfactual thinking* (pp. 199–231). Mahwah, NJ: Lawrence Erlbaum.

46. Gleicher, F., Boninger, D. S., Strathman, A., Armor, D., Hetts, J., & Ahn, M. (1995). With an eye toward the future: The impact of counterfactual thinking on affect, attitudes, and behavior. In N. J. Roese & J. M. Olson (Eds.), *What might have been: The social psychology of counterfactual thinking* (pp. 283–304). Mahwah, NJ: Lawrence Erlbaum.

47. Miller & Taylor, 1995.

48. McGill, A. L., & Klein, J. G. (1995). Counterfactual and contrasting reasoning in explanations for performance: Implications for gender bias. In N. J. Roese & J. M. Olson (Eds.), *What might have been: The social psychology of counterfactual thinking* (pp. 333–352). Mahwah, NJ: Lawrence Erlbaum.

49. Sanna, L. J., Meier, S., & Wegner, E. A. (2001). Counterfactuals and motivation: Mood as input to affective enjoyment and preparation. *British Journal of Social Psychology, 40,* 235–256.

50. SunWolf. (2006). Decisional regret theory: Reducing the anxiety about uncertain outcomes during group decision making through shared counterfactual storytelling. *Communication Studies, 57(2),* 1–29.

51. Tajfel, H. (1982). *Social identity and intergroup relations.* Cambridge: Cambridge University Press.

52. Tajfel, H., & Turner, J. C. (1986). The social identity theory of intergroup behavior. In S. Worchel & W. Austin (Eds.), *The psychology of intergroup relations* (pp. 7–24). Chicago: Nelson Hall.

53. Tajfel, H. (1982). *Social identity and intergroup relations.* Cambridge: Cambridge University Press.

54. SunWolf. (2006). *Juror competency juror compassion.* Charlottesville, VA: LexisNexis Publishing.

55. Darley, J. M., & Batson, C. D. (1973). From Jerusalem to Jericho: A study of situational and dispositional variables in helping behavior. *Journal of Personality and Social Psychology, 27,* 100–108.

Darley, J. M., & Latané, B. (1968). Bystander intervention in emergencies: Diffusion of responsibility. *Journal of Personality and Social Psychology, 8,* 377–383.

56. Sprecher, S., & Fehr, B. (2005). Compassionate love for close others and humanity. *Journal of Social and Personal Relationships, 22,* 629–651.

57. Dodge, M. K. (1984). Learning to care: Developing prosocial behavior among one- and two-year-olds in group settings. *Journal of Research and Development in Education, 17,* 26–30.

58. Batson, C. D. (1991). *The altruism question: Toward a social-psychological answer.* Hillsdale, NJ: Lawrence Erlbaum.

Batson, C. D. (1998). Altruism and prosocial behvior. In D. Gilbert, S. Fiske, & G. Lindzey (Eds.), *The handbook of social psychology* (4th ed., Vol. 2, pp. 282–316). New York: McGraw-Hill.

59. Of the 7,000 people who received medals from the Carnegie Hero Fund Commission for risking their lives to save a stranger, 91 percent were men.

60. Eagly, A. H. (1991). Explaining sex differences in social behavior: A meta-analytic perspective. Special Issue: Meta-analysis in personality and social psychology. *Personality and Social Psychology Bulletin, 17,* 306–315.

Eagly, A. H. (1995). The science and politics of comparing women and men. *American Psychologist, 50,* 145–158.

Eagly, A. H., & Crowley, M. (1986). Gender and helping behavior: A meta-analytic review of the social psychological literature. *Psychological Bulletin, 100,* 283–308.

61. Isen, A. M., & Levin, P. A. (1972). Effect of feeling good on helping: Cookies and kindness. *Journal of Personality and Social Psychology, 21,* 384–388.

62. Harris, M. B., Benson, S. M., & Hall, C. (1975). The effects of confession on altruism. *Journal of Social Psychology, 96,* 187–192.

63. Hsu, S. S. (1995, April 8). Fredericksburg searches its soul after clerk is beaten as 6 watch. *Washington Post,* pp. A1, A13.

64. Latané, B., & Darley, J. M. (1968). Group inhibition of bystander intervention. *Journal of Personality and Social Psychology, 10,* 215–221.

Latané, B., & Darley, J. M. (1970). *The unresponsive bystander: Why doesn't he help?* Englewood Cliffs, NJ: Prentice Hall

65. Norris wrote, "Just the knowledge that a good book is awaiting one at the end of a long day makes that day happier."

Norris, K. (1931/1988). *Hands Full of Living.* Mattituck, NY: Amereon.

66. Kramer, M. W. (2004). Toward a communication theory of group dialectics: An ethnographic study of a community theater group. *Communication Monographs, 71,* 311–332.

67. Baxter, L. A., & Montgomery, B. M. (1996). *Relating: Dialogues and dialectics.* New York: Guilford Press.

Baxter, L. A., & Montgomery, B. M. (1998). A guide to dialectical approaches to studying personal relationships. In B. M. Montgomery & L. A. Baxter (Eds.), *Dialectical approaches to studying personal relationships* (pp. 1–16). Mahwah, NJ: Lawrence Erlbaum.

Baxter, L. A., & Montgomery, B. M. (1997). Rethinking communication in personal relationships from a dialectical perspective. In S. Duck (Ed.), *Handbook of personal relationships* (2nd ed.). New York: John Wiley & Sons.

68. Kramer, M. W. (2004). Toward a communication theory of group dialectics: An ethnographic study of a community theater group. *Communication Monographs, 71*, 311–332.

69. Kramer, M. W. (2004). Toward a communication theory of group dialectics: An ethnographic study of a community theater group. *Communication Monographs, 71*, 311–332, 328.

70. Lesch, C. L. (1994). Observing theory in practice: Sustaining consciousness in a coven. In L. R. Frey (Ed.), *Group communication in context: Studies of natural groups* (pp. 57–82). Hillsdale, NJ: Lawrence Erlbaum.

71. Kramer, M. W. (2004). Toward a communication theory of group dialectics: An ethnographic study of a community theater group. *Communication Monographs, 71*, 311–332.

72. Kramer, M. W. (2004). Toward a communication theory of group dialectics: An ethnographic study of a community theater group. *Communication Monographs, 71*, 311–332 (p. 321).

73. SunWolf, & Leets, L. (2003). Communication paralysis during peer group exclusion: Social dynamics that prevent children and adolescents from expressing disagreement. *Journal of Language and Social Psychology, 22*, 355–384.

74. Putnam, L. L., & Stohl, C. (1990). Bona fide groups: A reconceptualization of groups in context. *Communication Studies, 41*, 248–265.

Putnam, L. L., & Stohl, C. (1996). Bona fide groups: An alternative perspective for communication and small group decision making. In R. Y. Hirokawa & M. S. Poole (Eds.), *Communication and group decision making* (2nd ed., pp. 179–214). Thousand Oaks, CA: Sage.

75. Putnam, L. L., & Stohl, C. (1990). Bona fide groups: A reconceptualization of groups in context. *Communication Studies, 41*, 248–265.

Putnam, L. L., & Stohl, C. (1996). Bona fide groups, an alternative perspective for communication and small group decision making. In R. Y. Hirokawa & M. S. Poole (Eds.), *Communication and group decision making* (2nd ed., pp. 147–178). Thousand Oaks, CA: Sage.

76. SunWolf, & Leets, L. (2004). Being left out: Rejecting outsiders and communicating group boundaries in childhood and adolescent peer groups. *Journal of Applied Communication Research, 32(3)*, 195–223.

77. Stohl, C., & Putnam, L. L. (2003). Communication in bona fide groups: A retrospective and prospective account. In L. R. Frey (Ed.), *Group communication in context: Studies of bona fide groups* (2nd ed., pp. 399–414). Mahwah, NJ: Lawrence Erlbaum.

78. Berteotti, C. R., & Seibold, D. R. (1994). Coordination and role-definition problems in health-care teams: A hospice case study. In L. R. Frey (Ed), *Group communication in context: Studies of natural groups* (pp. 107–131). Hillsdale, NJ: Lawrence Erlbaum.

❖ NOTES TO CHAPTER 2

1. Paley, V. G. (1992). *You can't say you can't play.* Cambridge, MA: Harvard University Press.

2. Asher, S. R., & Coie, J. D. (Eds.). (1990). *Peer rejection in childhood.* New York: Cambridge University Press.

Asher, S. R., Parkhurst, J. T., Hymel, S., & Williams, G. A. (1990). Peer rejection and loneliness in childhood. In S. R. Asher & J. D. Coie (Eds.), *Peer rejection in childhood* (pp. 253–273). New York: Cambridge University Press.

3. Keyton, J. (1994). Going forward in group communication research may mean going back: Studying the groups of children. *Communication Studies, 45,* 40–51.

4. Socha, T. J., & Socha, D. M. (1994). Children's task-group communication: Did we learn it all in kindergarten? In L. R. Frey (Ed.), *Group communication in context: Studies of natural groups* (pp. 227–246). Hillsdale, NJ: Lawrence Erlbaum.

5. Killen, M., Pisacane, K., Lee-Kim, J., & Ardila-Rey, A. (2001). Fairness or stereotypes? Young children's priorities when evaluating group exclusion and inclusion. *Developmental Psychology, 37,* 587–596.

6. Theimer, C. E., Killen, M., & Stangor, C. (2001). Young children's evaluations of exclusion in gender-stereotypic peer contexts. *Developmental Psychology, 37,* 18–27.

7. Arnold, D. H., Homrok, S., Ortiz, C., & Stowe, R. M. (1999). Direct observation of peer rejection acts and their temporal relation with aggressive acts. *Early Childhood Research Quarterly, 14,* 183–196.

8. Paley, V. G. (1992). *You can't say you can't play.* Cambridge, MA: Harvard University Press.

9. Sapon-Shevin, M., Dobbelaere, A., Corrigan, C., Goodman, K., & Mastin, M. (1998). Everyone here can play. *Educational Leadership, 56,* 42–45.

10. Gigliotti, R. J. (1988). Sex differences in children's task-group performance: Status/norm or ability? *Small Group Behavior, 19,* 273–293.

11. Martin, C. L., Fabes, R. A., Evans, S. M., & Wyman, H. (1999). Social cognition on the playground: Children's beliefs about playing with girls versus boys and their relations to sex segregated play. *Journal of Social and Personal Relationships, 16,* 751–771.

12. Maltz, D. N., & Borker, R. (1982). A cultural approach to male-female miscommunication. In J. J. Gumpertz (Ed.), *Language and social identity* (pp. 196–216). Cambridge: Cambridge University Press.

13. Phillips, E. L., Shenker, S., & Revitz, P. (1951). The assimilation of the new child into the group. *Psychiatry, 14,* 319–325.

14. Malley, H. (1935). A study of some of the techniques underlying the establishment of successful social contacts at the preschool level. *Journal of Genetic Psychology, 47,* 431–457.

15. Dodge, K. A., Schlundt, D. G., Schocken, I., & Delugach, J. D. (1983). Social competence and children's sociometric status: The role of peer group entry strategies. *Merrill-Palmer Quarterly, 29,* 309–336.

Putallaz, M., & Gottman, J. M. (1981). An interactional model of children's entry into peer groups. *Child Development, 52,* 986–994.

16. Forbes, D. L., Katz, M. M., Paul, B., & Lubin, D. (1982). Children's plans for joining play: An analysis of structure and function. In D. Forbes & M. T. Greenberg (Eds.), *New directions for child development: Children's planning strategies* (pp. 61–79). San Francisco: Jossey Bass.

17. Pope, A. W., Bierman, K. L., & Mumma, G. H. (1991). Aggression, hyperactivity, and inattention-immaturity: Behavior dimensions associated with peer rejection in elementary school boys. *Developmental Psychology, 27,* 663–671.

18. Putallaz, M., & Wasserman, A. (1990). Children's entry behavior. In S. R. Asher, & J. D. Coie (Eds.), *Peer rejection in childhood* (pp. 60–89). New York: Cambridge University Press.

19. French, D. C., & Stright, A. L. (1991). Emergent leadership in children's small groups. *Small Group Research, 22,* 187–199.

20. Yamaguchi, R. (2001). Children's learning groups: A study of emergent leadership, dominance, and group effectiveness. *Small Group Research, 32,* 671–697.

21. Buhs, E., & Ladd, G. W. (2001). Peer rejection as an antecedent of young children's school adjustment: An examination of mediating processes. *Developmental Psychology, 37,* 550–560.

22. Wood, J. J., Cowan, P. A., & Baker, B. L. (2002). Behavior problems and peer rejection in preschool boys and girls. *Journal of Genetic Psychology, 163,* 72–89.

23. Asher, S. R., & Coie, J. D. (Eds.). (1990). *Peer rejection in childhood.* New York: Cambridge University Press.

Asher, S. R., Parkhurst, J. T., Hymel, S., & Williams, G. A. (1990). Peer rejection and loneliness in childhood. In S. R. Asher & J. D. Coie (Eds.), *Peer rejection in childhood* (pp. 253–273). New York: Cambridge University Press.

Berndt, T. J. (1996). Exploring the effects of friendship quality on social development. In W. M. Bukowski, A. F. Newcomb, & W. W. Hartup (Eds.), *The company they keep: Friendship in childhood and adolescence* (pp. 346–365). Cambridge: Cambridge University Press.

Greenspan, S. I. (1993). *Playground politics: Understanding the emotional life of your school-age child.* Reading, MA: Addison-Wesley.

Kupersmidt, J. B., Coie, J. D., & Dodge, K. A. (1990). The role of poor peer relationships in the development of disorder. In S. R. Asher & J. D. Coie (Eds.), *Peer rejection in childhood* (pp. 274–305). New York: Cambridge University Press.

Newcomb, A. F., & Bagwell, C. L. (1996). The developmental significance of children's friendship relations. In W. M. Bukowski, A. F. Newcomb, & W. W. Hartup (Eds.), *The company they keep: Friendship in childhood and adolescence* (pp. 289–321). Cambridge: Cambridge University Press.

24. Matthews, M. W. (1996). Addressing issues of peer rejection in child-centered classrooms. *Early Childhood Education Journal, 24,* 93–97.

25. Wood, J. J., Cowan, P. A., & Baker, B. L. (2002). Behavior problems and peer rejection in preschool boys and girls. *Journal of Genetic Psychology, 163,* 72–89.

26. Parker, J. G., & Asher, S. R. (1993). Friendship and friendship quality in middle childhood: Links with peer group acceptance and feelings of loneliness and social dissatisfaction. *Developmental Psychology, 29,* 611–621.

27. Bagwell, C. L., Newcomb, A. F., & Bukowski, W. M. (1998). Preadolescent friendship and peer rejection as predictors of adult adjustment. *Child Development, 69,* 140–153.

28. Aboud, F. E., & Mendelson, M. J. (1996). Determinants of friendship selection and quality: Developmental perspectives. In W. M. Bukowski, A. F. Newcomb, & W. W. Hartup (Eds.), *The company they keep: Friendship in childhood and adolescence* (pp. 87–112). Cambridge: Cambridge University Press.

Koeppl, G. K. (1990). Adapting intervention to the problems of aggressive and disruptive rejected children. In S. R. Asher & J. D. Coie (Eds.), *Peer rejection in childhood* (pp. 309–337). New York: Cambridge University Press.

29. Matthews, M. W. (1996). Addressing issues of peer rejection in child-centered classrooms. *Early Childhood Education Journal, 24,* 93–97.

30. Hodges, E. V., Malone, M. J., & Perry, D. G. (1997). Individual risk and social risk as interacting determinants of victimization in the peer group. *Developmental Psychology, 33,* 1032–1039.

31. Downey, G., Lebolt, A., Rincon, C., & Freitas, A. L. (1998). Rejection sensitivity and children's interpersonal difficulties. *Child Development, 69,* 1074–1091.

32. Dodge, K. A., Lansford, J. E., Burks, V. S., Bates, J. E., Pettit, G. S., Fontaine, R., & Price, J. M. (2003). Peer rejection and social information-processing factors in the development of aggressive behavior problems in children. *Child Development, 74,* 374–393.

33. Buhs, E., & Ladd, G. W. (2001). Peer rejection as an antecedent of young children's school adjustment: An examination of mediating processes. *Developmental Psychology, 37,* 550–560.

34. Wentzel, K. R., & Erdley, C. A. (1993). Strategies for making friends: Relations to social behavior and peer acceptance in early adolescence. *Developmental Psychology, 29,* 819–826.

35. Sapon-Shevin, M., Dobbelaere, A., Corrigan, C., Goodman, K., & Mastin, M. (1998). Everyone here can play. *Educational Leadership, 56,* 42–45.

Sapon-Shevin, M., Dobbelaere, A., Corrigan, C., Goodman, K., & Mastin, M. (1998). Promoting inclusive behavior in inclusive classrooms: "You can't say you can't play." In I. H. Meyer, H. S. Park, M. Grenot-Scheyer, I. S. Schwartz, & B. Harry (Eds.), *Making friends: The influences of culture and development* (pp. 105–132). Baltimore: Paul H. Brookes.

36. Rosenberg, S. L., McKeon, L. M., & Dinero, T. E. (1999). Positive peer groups reclaim rejected kids. *The Education Digest, 65,* 22–27.

37. Frederickson, N., & Turner, J. (2003). Utilizing the classroom peer group to address children's social needs: An evaluation of the Circle of Friends intervention approach. *The Journal of Special Education, 36,* 234–245.

38. Bowers, F. E., McGinnis, C., Ervin, R. A., & Friman, P. C. (1999). Merging research and practice: The example of positive peer reporting applied to social rejection. *Education and Treatment of Children, 22,* 218–226.

39. Sapon-Shevin, M., Dobbelaere, A., Corrigan, C., Goodman, K., & Mastin, M. (1998). Everyone here can play. *Educational Leadership, 56,* 42–45.

40. Sapon-Shevin, M., Dobbelaere, A., Corrigan, C., Goodman, K., & Mastin, M. (1998). Everyone here can play. *Educational Leadership, 56,* 42–45, p. 44.

❖ NOTES TO CHAPTER 3

1. SunWolf, & Leets, L. (2004). Being left out: Rejecting outsiders and communicating group boundaries in childhood and adolescent peer groups. *Journal of Applied Communication Research, 32(3),* 195–223.

2. Simmons, R. (2002). *Odd girl out: The hidden culture of aggression in girls.* New York: Harcourt.

3. Simmons, R. (2002). *Odd girl out: The hidden culture of aggression in girls.* New York: Harcourt.

4. Hudson, D. A. (Executive Producer). (2002, February 18). Inside your child's social life: The Oprah Winfrey show. Chicago: ABC.

5. Stossel, J. (Executive Producer). (2002, February 15). The "in" crowd and social cruelty. New Hudson, MI: ABC News.

6. Giannetti, C. C., & Sagarese, M. (2001). *Cliques: Eight steps to help your child survive the social jungle.* New York: Broadway Books.

7. Giannetti, C. C., & Sagarese, M. (2001). *Cliques: Eight steps to help your child survive the social jungle.* New York: Broadway Books, p. 5

8. Thompson, M., & Grace, C. O. (2001). *Best friends, worst enemies: Understanding the social lives of children.* New York: Ballantine Books.

9. Horn, S. S. (2003). Adolescents' reasoning about exclusion from social groups. *Developmental Psychology, 39,* 71–84.

10. Buhs, E., & Ladd, G. W. (2001). Peer rejection as an antecedent of young children's school adjustment: An examination of mediating processes. *Developmental Psychology, 37*, 550–560.

11. Socha, T. J., & Socha, D. M. (1994). Children's task-group communication: Did we learn it all in kindergarten? In L. R. Frey (Ed.), *Group communication in context: Studies of natural groups* (pp. 227–246). Hillsdale, NJ: Lawrence Erlbaum.

12. Sapon-Shevin, M., Dobbelaere, A., Corrigan, C., Goodman, K., & Mastin, M. (1998). Promoting inclusive behavior in inclusive classrooms: "You can't say you can't play." In I. H. Meyer, H. S. Park, M. Grenot-Scheyer, I. S. Schwartz, & B. Harry (Eds.), *Making friends: The influences of culture and development* (pp. 105–132). Baltimore: Paul H. Brookes.

13. Thompson, M., & Grace, C. O. (with Cohen, L. J.). (2001). *Best friends, worst enemies: Understanding the social lives of children*. New York: Ballantine Books.

14. Simmons, R. (2002). *Odd girl out: The hidden culture of aggression in girls*. New York: Harcourt.

Thompson, M., & Grace, C. O. (2001). *Best friends, worst enemies: Understanding the social lives of children*. New York: Ballantine Books.

Eisenberger, N. I., Lieberman, M. D., & Williams, K. D. (2003). Does rejection hurt? An fMRI study of social exclusion. *Science, 302*, 290–292.

Orenstein, P. (1994). *Schoolgirls: Young women, self-esteem, and the confidence gap*. New York: Doubleday.

15. National Institute of Mental Health (2000). *Suicide facts*. Retrieved May 18, 2003 from http://www.nimh.nih.gov/research/suifact.cfm.

16. Hartup, W. W. (1995). The three faces of friendship. *Journal of Social and Personal Relationships, 12*, 569–574.

Hartup, W. W. (1996). Cooperation, close relationships, and cognitive development. In W. M. Bukowski, A. F. Newcomb, & W. W. Hartup (Eds.), *The company they keep: Friendship in childhood and adolescence* (pp. 213–237). Cambridge: Cambridge University Press.

17. Dodge, K. A., Lansford, J. E., Burks, V. S., Bates, J. E., Pettit, G. S., Fontaine, R., & Price, J. M. (2003). Peer rejection and social information-processing factors in the development of aggressive behavior problems in children. *Child Development, 74*, 374–393.

18. Rejection massively reduces IQ. *New Scientist* (2002, March 15). Retrieved July 1, 2006, from http://www.newscientist.com/news/news.jsp?id=ns99992051

19. Putallaz, M., & Wasserman, A. (1990). Children's entry behavior. In S. R. Asher & J. D. Coie (Eds.), *Peer rejection in childhood* (pp. 60–89). New York: Cambridge University Press.

20. Sinclair-James, L., & Stohl, C. (1997). Group endings and new beginnings. In L. R. Frey & J. K. Barge (Eds.), *Managing group life: Communicating in decision-making groups* (pp. 308–334). Boston: Houghton Mifflin.

Socha, T. J., & Socha, D. M. (1994). Children's task-group communication: Did we learn it all in kindergarten? In L. R. Frey (Ed.), *Group communication in context: Studies of natural groups* (pp. 227–246). Hillsdale, NJ: Lawrence Erlbaum.

21. Bettenhausen, K. L., & Murnighan, J. K. (1991). The development and stability of norms in groups facing interpersonal and structural challenge. *Administrative Science Quarterly, 36*, 20–35.

22. Socha, T. J. (1999). Communication in family units: Studying the first "group." In L. R. Frey , D. S. Gouran, & M. S. Poole (Eds.), *The handbook of group communication theory and research* (pp. 475–492). Thousand Oaks, CA: Sage.

23. French, D. C., & Stright, A. L. (1991). Emergent leadership in children's small groups. *Small Group Research, 22*, 187–199.

24. Moreland, R. L. (1985). Social categorization and the assimilation of "new" group members. *Journal of Personality and Social Psychology, 48*, 1173–1190.

25. Paley, V. G. (1992). *You can't say you can't play*. Cambridge, MA: Harvard University Press.

26. Thompson, M., & Grace, C. O. (with Cohen, L. J.). (2001). *Best friends, worst enemies: Understanding the social lives of children*. New York: Ballantine Books.

27. Sorenson, S. M. (1981, May). *Group-hate: A negative reaction to group work*. Paper presented at the annual meeting of the International Communication Association, Minneapolis, MN.

28. Keyton, J., & Frey, L. R. (2002). The state of traits: Predispositions and group communication. In L. R. Frey (Ed.), *New directions in group communication* (pp. 99–120). Thousand Oaks, CA: Sage.

29. Orenstein, P. (1994). *Schoolgirls: Young women, self-esteem, and the confidence gap*. New York: Doubleday.

30. Orenstein, P. (1994). *Schoolgirls: Young women, self-esteem, and the confidence gap*. New York: Doubleday, p. 100.

31. SunWolf, & Leets, L. (2003). Communication paralysis during peer group exclusion: Social dynamics that prevent children and adolescents from expressing disagreement. *Journal of Language and Social Psychology, 22*, 355–384.

32. Oetzel, J. G. (2002). The effects of culture and cultural diversity on communication to work groups: Synthesizing vertical and cultural differences with a face-negotiation perspective. In L. R. Frey (Ed.), *New directions in group communication* (pp. 121–137). Thousand Oaks, CA: Sage.

33. McAlister, A. L. (1995). Behavioral journalism: Beyond the marketing model for health communication. *American Journal of Health Promotion, 9*, 417–420.

34. McAlister, A. L., Ama, E., Barroso, C., Peters, R. J., & Kelder, S. (2000). Promoting tolerance and moral engagement through peer modeling. *Cultural Diversity and Ethnic Minority Psychology, 6,* 363–373.

35. McAlister, A. L., Ama, E., Barroso, C., Peters, R. J., & Kelder, S. (2000). Promoting tolerance and moral engagement through peer modeling. *Cultural Diversity and Ethnic Minority Psychology, 6,* 363–373.

36. Riera, M. (2004). *Uncommon sense for parents with teenagers* (rev. ed.). Berkeley, CA: Celestial Arts Publishing.

❖ NOTES TO CHAPTER 4

1. Egley, A., & Ritz, C. E. (2006). Highlights of the 2004 National Youth Gang Survey. *National Youth Gang Center.* Retrieved January 30, 2007, from http://www.iir.com/nygc/publications/fs200601.pdf

2. Lyddane, D. (2006). Understanding gangs and gang mentality: Acquiring evidence of the gang conspiracy. *United States Attorneys' Bulletin (May 2006,* 1–14). Retrieved December 1, 2006, from http://www.usdoj.gov/usao/eousa/foia_reading_room/usab5403.pdf

3. Conquergood, D. (1994). For the Nation! How street gangs problematize patriotism. In H. W. Simons & M. Billig (Eds.), *After postmodernism: Reconstructing ideology critique* (pp. 200–221). Thousand Oaks, CA: Sage.

4. Conquergood, D. (1994). Homeboys and hoods: Gangs and cultural space. In L. R. Frey (Ed.), *Group communication in context: Studies of natural groups* (pp. 23–52). Hillsdale, NJ: Lawrence Erlbaum.

Conquergood cited in Padilla, F. (1992). *The gang as an American enterprise.* New Brunswick, NJ: Rutgers University Press.

5. Conquergood, D. (1994). Homeboys and hoods: Gangs and cultural space. In L. R. Frey (Ed.), *Group communication in context: Studies of natural groups* (pp. 23–52). Hillsdale, NJ: Lawrence Erlbaum.

6. Conquergood, D. (1994). Homeboys and hoods: Gangs and cultural space. In L. R. Frey (Ed.), *Group communication in context: Studies of natural groups* (pp. 23–52). Hillsdale, NJ: Lawrence Erlbaum, p. 40.

7. Conquergood, D. (1994). Homeboys and hoods: Gangs and cultural space. In L. R. Frey (Ed.), *Group communication in context: Studies of natural groups* (pp. 23–52). Hillsdale, NJ: Lawrence Erlbaum, p. 27.

8. Conquergood, D. (1994). Homeboys and hoods: Gangs and cultural space. In L. R. Frey (Ed.), *Group communication in context: Studies of natural groups* (pp. 23–52). Hillsdale, NJ: Lawrence Erlbaum, p. 41.

9. Conquergood, D. (1994). Homeboys and hoods: Gangs and cultural space. In L. R. Frey (Ed.), *Group communication in context: Studies of natural groups* (pp. 23–52). Hillsdale, NJ: Lawrence Erlbaum, p. 43.

10. Conquergood, D. (1994). Homeboys and hoods: Gangs and cultural space. In L. R. Frey (Ed.), *Group communication in context: Studies of natural groups* (pp. 23–52). Hillsdale, NJ: Lawrence Erlbaum.

11. Conquergood, D. (1994). Homeboys and hoods: Gangs and cultural space. In L. R. Frey (Ed.), *Group communication in context: Studies of natural groups* (pp. 23–52). Hillsdale, NJ: Lawrence Erlbaum, p. 27.

12. Conquergood, D. (1994). Homeboys and hoods: Gangs and cultural space. In L. R. Frey (Ed.), *Group communication in context: Studies of natural groups* (pp. 23–52). Hillsdale, NJ: Lawrence Erlbaum, p.40.

13. Ganz, N. (2004). *Graffiti world: Street art from five continents.* New York: Harry N. Abrams, Inc.

14. Ganz, N. (2004). *Graffiti world: Street art from five continents.* New York: Harry N. Abrams, Inc.

15. Rodriguez, A., & Clair, R. P. (1999). Graffiti as communication: Exploring the discursive tensions of anonymous texts. *Southern Communication Journal, 65,* 1–15.

16. Rodriguez, A., & Clair, R. P. (1999). Graffiti as communication: Exploring the discursive tensions of anonymous texts. *Southern Communication Journal, 65,* 1–15.

17. Newall, V. (1986–1987) The moving spray can: A collection of some contemporary English graffiti. *The International Journal of Verbal Aggression, 9,* 39–47.

Reisner, R., & Wechsler, L. (1974). *Encyclopedia of graffiti.* New York: MacMillan.

18. Damian, D. (2005). Playing the dozens. Retrieved February 14, 2007, from http://darkdamian.blogspot.com/2005/04/playing-dozens.html

19. Slang of the Week, January 8, 2004. snaps (noun). *Slang City.* Retrieved January 10, 2007, from http://www.slangcity.com/email_archive/1_08_04.htm

20. Damian, D. (2005). Playing the dozens. Retrieved February 14, 2007, from http://darkdamian.blogspot.com/2005/04/playing-dozens.html

21. Garner, T. (1983). Playing the dozens: Folklore as strategies for living. *Quarterly Journal of Speech, 69,* 47–57.

22. Garner, T. (1983). Playing the dozens: Folklore as strategies for living. *Quarterly Journal of Speech, 69,* 47–57, p. 51.

23. Office of Juvenile Justice and Delinquency Prevention, U.S. Department of Justice, March 2001, "Female gangs: A focus on research." Retrieved October 1, 2006 from http://www.ncjrs.org/html/ojjdp/jjbu12001_3_3/contents.html

24. Office of Juvenile Justice and Delinquency Prevention, U.S. Department of Justice, March 2001, "Female gangs: A focus on research." Retrieved October 1, 2006 from http://www.ncjrs.org/html/ojjdp/jjbu12001_3_3/contents.html

25. Miller, J. (2000). Gender dynamics in youth gangs: A comparison of males' and females' accounts. *Justice Quarterly, 17,* 419–448.

See also, Miller, J. (1998). Gender and victimization risk among young women in youth gangs. *Journal of Research in Crime and Delinquency, 35,* 429–453.

26. Quicker, J. (1983). *Homegirls: Characterizing Chicana gangs.* San Pedro, CA: International Universities Press.

27. Chin, K. (1996). Gang violence in Chinatown. In, C. R. Huff (Ed.), *Gangs in America.* Newbury Park, CA: Sage.

28. Campbell, A. (1987). Self definition by rejection. *Social Problems, 34,* 451–466.

Campbell, A. (1990). Female participation in gangs. In, C. R. Huff (Ed.), *Gangs in America.* Newbury Park, CA: Sage.

❖ NOTES TO CHAPTER 5

1. Lipman-Blumen, J., & Leavitt, H. J. (1999). *Hot groups: Seeding them, feeding them, and using them to ignite your organization.* New York: Oxford University Press, p. 3.

2. Lipman-Blumen, J., & Leavitt, H. J. (1999). *Hot groups: Seeding them, feeding them, and using them to ignite your organization.* New York: Oxford University Press, p. 9.

3. Ellingson, L. L. (2003). Interdisciplinary health care teamwork in the clinic backstage. *Journal of Applied Communication Research, 31,* 93–117.

4. Lipman-Blumen, J., & Leavitt, H. J. (1999). *Hot groups: Seeding them, feeding them, and using them to ignite your organization.* New York: Oxford University Press, p. 50.

5. Roberts, N. C., & King, P. J. (1996). *Transforming public policy: Dynamics of policy entrepreneurship and innovation.* San Francisco: Jossey-Bass.

6. Roberts, N. C., & King, P. J. (1996). *Transforming public policy: Dynamics of policy entrepreneurship and innovation.* San Francisco: Jossey-Bass, p. 132.

7. Quade, A. (2007, March 19). Elite team rescues troops behind enemy lines. *CNN World News.* Retrieved March 19, 2007, from http://www.cnn.com/2007/WORLD/meast/03/15/search.rescue/index.html

8. Quade, A. (2007, March 19). Elite team rescues troops behind enemy lines. *CNN World News.* Retrieved March 19, 2007, from http://www.cnn.com/2007/WORLD/meast/03/15/search.rescue/index.html

9. Quade, A. (2007, March 19). Elite team rescues troops behind enemy lines. *CNN World News.* Retrieved March 19, 2007, from http://www.cnn.com/2007/WORLD/meast/03/15/search.rescue/index.html

10. Katz, W. L. (1986). *Black Indians: A hidden heritage.* New York: Simon Pulse, p. 169.

11. Durham, P., & Jones, E. L. (1965). *The Negro cowboys.* Lincoln, NE: University of Nebraska Press. p. 3

12. Katz, W. L. (1986). *Black Indians: A hidden heritage.* New York: Simon Pulse, p. 170.

13. Durham, P., & Jones, E. L. (1965). *The Negro cowboys.* Lincoln, NE: University of Nebraska Press.

14. "Workin' from can't to can't: African-American cowboys in Texas." Transcript and videotape produced by the University of Texas, Institute of Texan Cultures at San Antonio, and available at store.the-museum-store.org/wofrcatocaaf.html. Excerpted from transcript of Nathaniel Youngblood's dialogue, p. 7.

15. Durham, P., & Jones, E. L. (1965). *The Negro cowboys.* Lincoln, NE: University of Nebraska Press, p. 12.

The life and adventures of Nat Love, written by Nat Love (1854–1921), known in the cattle country as "Deadwood Dick" (originally published in 1907 by Wayside Press, Los Angeles; reissued 1995, University of Nebraska Press), the only book written by an African American cowboy.

16. Katz, W. L. (1986). *Black Indians: A hidden heritage.* New York: Simon Pulse, p. 3.

17. "Black Indians: An American story, narrated by James Earl Jones." DVD produced by Rich-Meade Films, Inc. (2000) and available at www.richheape.com.

18. "Workin' from can't to can't: African-American cowboys in Texas." Transcript and videotape produced by the University of Texas, Institute of Texan Cultures at San Antonio, and available at store.the-museum-store.org/wofrcatocaaf.html

19. "Workin' from can't to can't: African-American cowboys in Texas," transcript and videotape produced by the University of Texas, Institute of Texan Cultures at San Antonio, and available for purchase at store.the-museum-store.org/wofrcatocaaf.html. Excerpted from transcript, p. 3.

20. "Workin' from can't to can't: African-American cowboys in Texas." Transcript and videotape produced by the University of Texas, Institute of Texan Cultures at San Antonio, and available at store.the-museum-store.org/wofrcatocaaf.html. Excerpted from transcript, p. 4.

21. *The life and adventures of Nat Love,* written by Nat Love (1854–1921), known in the cattle country as "Deadwood Dick."

Love, N. *The life and adventures of Nat Love.* (1907 [Wayside Press, Los Angeles]/1995 [University of Nebraska Press]). 1995 edition, introduction by Brackette F. Williams, p. iii.

22. "Workin' from can't to can't: African-American cowboys in Texas," transcript and videotape produced by the University of Texas, Institute of Texan Cultures at San Antonio, and available at store.the-museum-store.org/wofrcatocaaf.html. Excerpted from transcript, p. 7.

23. "Workin' from can't to can't: African-American cowboys in Texas," transcript and videotape produced by the University of Texas, Institute of

Texan Cultures at San Antonio, and available at store.the-museum-store.org/wofrcatocaaf.html. Excerpted from transcript, p. 4.

❖ NOTES TO CHAPTER 6

1. First defined in SunWolf. (2006). *Practical jury dynamics2: From one juror's trial perceptions to the group's decision-making processes.* Charlottesville, VA: LexisNexis Publishing.

2. Kalven, H., & Zeisel, H. (1966). *The American jury.* Boston: Little Brown.

3. Magna Carta of Great Britain, 1215. Translation prepared by Xavier Hildegarde, November 2001. Retrieved January 29, 2008, from http://www.magnacartaplus.org/magnacarta/

4. Burnett, D. G. (2001). *A trial by jury.* New York: Alfred A. Knopf.

5. Chapman, G. (2003). Rancor in the jury room. Retrieved October 3, 2003, from http://www.oaklandtribune.com/Stories/0,1413,82%257E1865%257E1671066,00.html

6. Finkelstein, K. E. (2001). Tempers seem to be growing shorter in many jury rooms. *The New York Times,* p. B1.

7. SunWolf. (2004). *Practical jury dynamics: From one juror's trial perceptions to the group's decision-making processes.* Charlottesville, VA: LexisNexis Publishing. Expanded in 2nd ed.: SunWolf. (2006). *Practical jury dynamics2: From one juror's trial perceptions to the group's decision-making processes.* Charlottesville, VA: LexisNexis Publishing.

8. Kalven, H., Jr., & Zeisel, H. (with Thomas Callahan, T., & Philip Ennis, P.). (1966). *The American jury.* Boston: Little Brown.

9. Pritchard, M. E., & Keenan, J. M. (1999). Memory monitoring in mock jurors. *Journal of Experimental Psychology: Applied, 5,* 152–168.

10. Cooley, A., Bass, C., Rubin-Jackson, M., Byrnes, T., & Walker, M. (1995). *Madam foreman: A rush to judgment.* Beverly Hills, CA: Dove Books.

11. *U.S.* v. *Leahy,* 82 F.3d 624 (1996).

12. *U.S.* v. *Morris,* 977 F.2d 677 (1992).

13. *U.S.* v. *Thai,* 29 F.3d 785 (1994).

14. *U.S.* v. *Martinez,* 14 F.3d 543 (1994).

15. *U.S.* v. *Console,* 13 F.3d 641 (1993).

16. Marder, N. S. (2003). Introduction to the jury at a crossroad: the American experience. *Chicago-Kent Law Review, 78,* 909–933.

17. Sommer, R. (1961). Leadership and group geography. *Sociometry, 24,* 99–110.

18. Strodtbeck, F. L., & Hook, L. H. (1961). The social dimensions of a twelve-man jury table. *Sociometry, 24,* 397–415.

19. Strodtbeck, F. L., James, R. M., & Hawkins, C. (1957). Social status in jury deliberations. *American Sociological Review, 22,* 713–719.

20. Hawkins, C. H. (1962). Interaction rates of jurors aligned in factions. *American Sociological Review, 27,* 689–691.

Simon, R. J. (1967). *The jury and the defense of insanity.* Boston, MA: Little, Brown.

21. SunWolf, & Seibold, D. R. (1998). Jurors' intuitive rules for deliberation: A structurational approach to the study of communication in jury decision making. *Communication Monographs, 65,* 282–307.

22. Strodtbeck, F. L., James, R. M., & Hawkins, C. (1957). Social status in jury deliberations. *American Sociological Review, 22,* 713–719.

23. Eakin, B. A. (1975). An empirical study of the effect of leadership influence on decision outcomes in different sized jury panels. *Kansas Journal of Sociology, 11,* 109–126.

24. Boster, F. J., Hunter, J. E., & Hale, J. L. (1991). An information-processing model of jury decision making. *Communication Research, 18,* 524–547.

25. Hastie, R., Penrod, S. D., & Pennington, N. (1983). *Inside the jury.* Cambridge, MA: Harvard University Press.

26. Barge, J. K., & Hirokawa, R. Y. (1989). Toward a communication competency model of group leadership. *Small Group Behavior, 20,* 167–189.

27. Barge, J. K., & Hirokawa, R. Y. (1989). Toward a communication competency model of group leadership. *Small Group Behavior, 20,* 167–189.

28. SunWolf. (2004). *Practical jury dynamics: From one juror's trial perceptions to the group's decision-making processes.* Charlottesville, VA: LexisNexis Publishing.

Now expanded in its second edition, SunWolf. (2006). *Practical jury dynamics2: From one juror's trial perceptions to the group's decision-making processes.* Charlottesville, VA: LexisNexis Publishing.

29. SunWolf, & Seibold, D. R. (1998). Jurors' intuitive rules for deliberation: A structurational approach to the study of communication in jury decision making. *Communication Monographs, 65,* 282–307.

30. Frey, L. R. (1996). Remembering and "re-membering": A history of theory and research on communication and group decision making. In R. Y. Hirokawa & M. S. Poole (Eds.), *Communication and group decision-making* (2nd ed., pp. 19–51). Newbury Park, CA: Sage.

31. James, R. (1959). Status and competence of jurors. *The American Journal of Sociology, 64,* 563–570.

Stasser, G., Kerr, N. L., & Bray, R. M. (1982). The social psychology of jury deliberations: Structure, process, and product. In N. L. Kerr & R. M. Bray, *The psychology of the courtroom* (pp. 221–256). New York: Harcourt Brace Jovanovich.

32. James, R. (1959). Status and competence of jurors. *The American Journal of Sociology, 64,* 563–570.

33. Nemeth, C. (1976). Rules governing jury deliberations: A consideration of recent changes. In G. Bermant, C. Nemeth, & N. Vidmar (Eds.), *Psychology and the law* (pp. 169–184). Lexington, MA: Lexington.

34. Hawkins, C. H. (1962). Interaction rates of jurors aligned in factions. *American Sociological Review, 27,* 689–691.

35. Strodtbeck, F. (1962). Social process, the law, and jury functioning. In W. M. Evan (Ed.), *Law and Sociology* (pp. 144–164). New York: The Free Press of Glencoe.

36. Hans, V. P., & Vidmar, N. (1986). *Judging the jury.* New York: Plenum Press.

37. Schultz, B. (1982). Argumentativeness: Its effect in group decision-making and its role in leadership perception. *Communication Quarterly, 30,* 368–375.

38. Ng, S. H., Bell, D., & Brooke, M. (1993). Gaining turns and achieving high influence ranking in small conversational groups. *British Journal of Social Psychology, 32,* 265–275.

39. Diamond, S. S. (1997). Illuminations and shadows from jury simulations. *Law and Human Behavior, 21,* 561–571.

40. MacCoun, R. J., & Kerr, N. L. (1988). A symmetric influence in mock jury deliberation: Jurors' bias for leniency. *Journal of Personality and Social Psychology, 54,* 21–33.

41. Strodtbeck, F. (1962). Social process, the law, and jury functioning. In W. M. Evan (Ed.), *Law and Sociology* (pp. 144–164). New York: The Free Press of Glencoe.

42. Dann, B. M. (1993). "Learning lessons" and "speaking rights": Creating educated and democratic juries. *Indiana Law Journal, 68,* 1229–1279.

43. Chester, G. (1970). *The ninth juror.* New York: Random House.

44. SunWolf. (2004). *Practical jury dynamics: From one juror's trial perceptions to the group's decision-making processes.* Charlottesville, VA: LexisNexis Publishing. Expanded in 2nd ed.: SunWolf. (2006). *Practical jury dynamics2: From one juror's trial perceptions to the group's decision-making processes.* Charlottesville, VA: LexisNexis Publishing.

45. Mulgrew, I. (2002, November 13). Guilty or not? Might as well flip a coin: What jurors don't know alarms researchers. *The Vancouver Sun,* p. B6.

46. SunWolf. (2004). *Practical jury dynamics: From one juror's trial perceptions to the group's decision-making processes.* Charlottesville, VA: LexisNexis Publishing. Expanded in 2nd ed.: SunWolf (2006). *Practical jury dynamics2: From one juror's trial perceptions to the group's decision making processes.* Charlottesville, VA: LexisNexis Publishing.

47. Kerr, N. L., & MacCoun, R. J. (1985). The effects of jury size and polling method on the process and product of jury deliberation. *Journal of Personality and Social Psychology, 48,* 349–363.

48. MSNBC's *Rita Cosby: Live and Direct,* August 8, 2005.

49. Aronson, E., Wilson, T. D., & Akert, R. M. (1999). *Social psychology* (3rd ed.). New York: Longman.

50. Kahneman, D. (1995). Varieties of counterfactual thinking. In N. J. Roese & J. M. Olson (Eds.), *What might have been: The social psychology of counterfactual thinking* (pp. 375–396). Mahwah, NJ: Lawrence Erlbaum.

51. Gastil, J. (1992). A definition of small group democracy. *Small Group Research, 23,* 278–301. Gastil, J. (1993). Identifying obstacles to small group democracy. *Small Group Research, 24,* 5–27.

52. Dann, B. M. (1993). "Learning lessons" and "speaking rights": Creating educated and democratic juries. *Indiana Law Journal, 68,* 1229–1279.

❖ NOTES TO EPILOGUE

1. "Workin' from can't to can't: African-American cowboys in Texas." Transcript and videotape produced by the University of Texas, Institute of Texan Cultures at San Antonio, and available at store.the-museum-store.org/wofrcatocaaf.html. Excerpted from transcript, p. 7.

References

Aboud, F. E., & Mendelson, M. J. (1996). Determinants of friendship selection and quality: Developmental perspectives. In W. M. Bukowski, A. F. Newcomb, & W. W. Hartup (Eds.), *The company they keep: Friendship in childhood and adolescence* (pp. 87–112). Cambridge: Cambridge University Press.

Adelman, M. B., & Frey, L. R. (1994). The pilgrim must embark: Creating and sustaining community in a residential facility for people with AIDS. In L. R. Frey (Ed.), *Group communication in context: Studies of natural groups* (pp. 3–22). Hillsdale, NJ: Lawrence Erlbaum.

Adelman, M. B., & Frey, L. R. (1997). *The fragile community: Living together with AIDS.* Mahwah, NJ: Lawrence Erlbaum.

Arnold, D. H., Homrok, S., Ortiz, C., & Stowe, R. M. (1999). Direct observation of peer rejection acts and their temporal relation with aggressive acts. *Early Childhood Research Quarterly, 14,* 183–196.

Aronson, E., Wilson, T. D., & Akert, R. M. (1999). *Social psychology* (3rd ed.). New York: Longman.

Asher, S. R. (1990). Recent advances in the study of peer rejection. In S. R. Asher & J. D. Coie (Eds.), *Peer rejection in childhood* (pp. 3–14). New York: Cambridge University Press.

Asher, S. R., & Coie, J. D. (Eds.). (1990). *Peer rejection in childhood.* New York: Cambridge University Press.

Asher, S. R., Parkhurst, J. T., Hymel, S., & Williams, G. A. (1990). Peer rejection and loneliness in childhood. In S. R. Asher & J. D. Coie (Eds.), *Peer rejection in childhood* (pp. 253–273). New York: Cambridge University Press.

Bagwell, C. L., Newcomb, A. F., & Bukowski, W. M. (1998). Preadolescent friendship and peer rejection as predictors of adult adjustment. *Child Development, 69,* 140–153.

Baldwin, J. R., Perry, S. D., & Moffitt, M. A. (2004). *Communication theories for everyday life.* Boston, MA: Pearson Education.

Barge, J. K., & Hirokawa, R. Y. (1989). Toward a communication competency model of group leadership. *Small Group Behavior, 20,* 167–189.

Batson, C. D. (1991). *The altruism question: Toward a social-psychological answer.* Hillsdale, NJ: Lawrence Erlbaum.

Batson, C. D. (1998). Altruism and prosocial behvior. In D. Gilbert, S. Fiske, & G. Lindzey (Eds.), *The handbook of social psychology* (4th ed., Vol. 2, pp. 282–316). New York: McGraw-Hill.

Baxter, L. A., & Montgomery, B. M. (1996). *Relating: Dialogues and dialectics.* New York: Guilford Press.

Baxter, L. A., & Montgomery, B. M. (1997). Rethinking communication in personal relationships from a dialectical perspective. In S. Duck (Ed.), *Handbook of personal relationships* (2nd ed.). New York: John Wiley.

Baxter, L. A., & Montgomery, B. M. (1998). A guide to dialectical approaches to studying personal relationships. In B. M. Montgomery & L. A. Baxter (Eds.), *Dialectical approaches to studying personal relationships* (pp. 1–16). Mahwah, NJ: Lawrence Erlbaum.

Berger, C. R. (1979). Beyond initial interactions: Uncertainty, understanding and the development of interpersonal relationships. In H. Giles & R. Sinclair (Eds.), *Language and social psychology* (pp. 122–144). Oxford, UK: Basil Blackwell.

Berndt, T. J. (1996). Exploring the effects of friendship quality on social development. In W. M. Bukowski, A. F. Newcomb, & W. W. Hartup (Eds.), *The company they keep: Friendship in childhood and adolescence* (pp. 346–365). Cambridge: Cambridge University Press.

Berns, G. S., Chappelow, J., Zink, C. F., Pagnoni, G., Martin-Skurski, M. E., & Richards, J. (2005). Neurobiological correlates of social conformity and independence during mental rotation. *Biological Psychiatry, 58(3)*, 245–253.

Berteotti, C. R., & Seibold, D. R. (1994). Coordination and role-definition problems in health-care teams: A hospice case study. In L. R. Frey (Ed), *Group communication in context: Studies of natural groups* (pp. 107–131). Hillsdale, NJ: Lawrence Erlbaum.

Bettenhausen, K. L., & Murnighan, J. K. (1991). The development and stability of norms in groups facing interpersonal and structural challenge. *Administrative Science Quarterly, 36*, 20–35.

Blumer, H. (1969). *Symbolic interactionism: Perspective and method.* Englewood Cliffs, NJ: Prentice-Hall.

Bormann, E. G. (1985). Symbolic convergence theory: A communication formulation. *Journal of Communication, 35*, 128–138.

Bormann, E. G. (1994). In defense of symbolic convergence theory: A look at the theory and its criticisms after two decades. *Communication Theory, 4*, 259–294.

Bormann, E. G. (1996). Symbolic convergence theory and communication in group decision making. In R. Y. Hirokawa & M. S. Poole (Eds.), *Communication and group decision making* (2nd ed., pp. 81–113). Thousand Oaks, CA: Sage.

Boster, F. J., Hunter, J. E., & Hale, J. L. (1991). An information-processing model of jury decision making. *Communication Research, 18*, 524–547.

Bowers, F. E., McGinnis, C., Ervin, R. A., & Friman, P. C. (1999). Merging research and practice: The example of positive peer reporting applied to social rejection. *Education and Treatment of Children, 22*, 218–226.

Buhs, E., & Ladd, G. W. (2001). Peer rejection as an antecedent of young children's school adjustment: An examination of mediating processes. *Developmental Psychology, 37*, 550–560.

Burke, K. (1966). *Language as symbolic action: Essays on life, literature, and method.* Berkeley: University of California Press.

Burnett, D. G. (2001). *A trial by jury.* New York: Alfred A. Knopf.

Campbell, A. (1987). Self definition by rejection. *Social Problems, 34*, 451–466.

Campbell, A. (1990). Female participation in gangs. In, C. R. Huff (Ed.), *Gangs in America.* Newbury Park, CA: Sage.

Canary, D. J., Brossman, B. G., & Seibold, D. R. (1987). Argument structures in decision-making groups. *Southern Communication Journal, 53*, 18–37.

Chapman, G. (2003). Rancor in the jury room. Retrieved October 3, 2003 from http://www.oaklandtribune.com/Stories/0,1413,82%257E1865%257E1671066,00.html

Chester, G. (1970). *The ninth juror.* New York: Random House.

Chin, K. (1996). Gang violence in Chinatown. In C. R. Huff (Ed.), *Gangs in America.* Newbury Park, CA: Sage.

Conquergood, D. (1994). For the Nation! How street gangs problematize patriotism. In H. W. Simons & M. Billig (Eds.), *After postmodernism: Reconstructing ideology critique* (pp. 200–221). Thousand Oaks, CA: Sage.

Conquergood, D. (1994). Homeboys and hoods: Gangs and cultural space. In L. R. Frey (Ed.), *Group communication in context: Studies of natural groups* (pp. 23–52). Hillsdale, NJ: Lawrence Erlbaum.

Cooley, A., Bass, C., Rubin-Jackson, M., Byrnes, T., & Walker, M. (1995). *Madam foreman: A rush to judgment.* Beverly Hills, CA: Dove Books.

Damian, D. (2005). Playing the dozens. Retrieved February 14, 2007, from http://darkdamian.blogspot.com/2005/04/playing-dozens.html

Dann, B. M. (1993). "Learning lessons" and "speaking rights": Creating educated and democratic juries. *Indiana Law Journal, 68*, 1229–1279.

Darley, J. M., & Batson, C. D. (1973). From Jerusalem to Jericho: A study of situational and dispositional variables in helping behavior. *Journal of Personality and Social Psychology, 27*, 100–108.

Darley, J. M., & Latané, B. (1968). Bystander intervention in emergencies: Diffusion of responsibility. *Journal of Personality and Social Psychology, 8*, 377–383.

Davis, C. G., & Lehman, D. R. (1995). Counterfactual thinking and coping with traumatic life events. In N. J. Roese & J. M. Olson (Eds.), *What might have been: The social psychology of counterfactual thinking* (pp. 353–374). Mahwah, NJ: Lawrence Erlbaum.

DeSanctis, G., & Poole, M. S. (1994). Capturing the complexity in advanced technology use: Adaptive structuration theory. *Organization Science, 5*, 121–147.

Diamond, S. S. (1997). Illuminations and shadows from jury simulations. *Law and Human Behavior, 21*, 561–571.

Dodge, K. A., Lansford, J. E., Burks, V. S., Bates, J. E., Pettit, G. S., Fontaine, R., & Price, J. M. (2003). Peer rejection and social information-processing factors in the development of aggressive behavior problems in children. *Child Development, 74,* 374–393.

Dodge, K. A., Schlundt, D. G., Schocken, I., & Delugach, J. D. (1983). Social competence and children's sociometric status: The role of peer group entry strategies. *Merrill-Palmer Quarterly, 29,* 309–336.

Dodge, M. K. (1984). Learning to care: Developing prosocial behavior among one- and two-year-olds in group settings. *Journal of Research and Development in Education, 17,* 26–30.

Downey, G., Lebolt, A., Rincon, C., & Freitas, A. L. (1998). Rejection sensitivity and children's interpersonal difficulties. *Child Development, 69,* 1074–1091.

Duffy, M. K., & Shaw, J. D. (2000). The Salieri syndrome: Consequences of envy in groups. *Small Group Research, 31,* 3–23.

Dunning, D., & Madey, S. F. (1995). Comparison processes in counterfactual thought. In N. J. Roese & J. M. Olson (Eds.), *What might have been: The social psychology of counterfactual thinking* (pp. 103–132). Mahwah, NJ: Lawrence Erlbaum.

Durham, P., & Jones, E. L. (1965). *The Negro cowboys.* Lincoln, NE: University of Nebraska Press.

Eagly, A. H. (1991). Explaining sex differences in social behavior: A meta-analytic perspective. [Special Issue: Meta-analysis in personality and social psychology]. *Personality and Social Psychology Bulletin, 17,* 306–315.

Eagly, A. H. (1995). The science and politics of comparing women and men. *American Psychologist, 50,* 145–158.

Eagly, A. H., & Crowley, M. (1986). Gender and helping behavior: A meta-analytic review of the social psychological literature. *Psychological Bulletin, 100,* 283–308.

Eakin, B. A. (1975). An empirical study of the effect of leadership influence on decision outcomes in different sized jury panels. *Kansas Journal of Sociology, 11,* 109–126.

Egley, A., & Ritz, C. E. (2006). Highlights of the 2004 National Youth Gang Survey. *National Youth Gang Center.* Retrieved January 30, 2007, from http://www.iir.com/nygc/publications/fs200601.pdf

Eisenberger, N. I., Lieberman, M. D., & Williams, K. D. (2003). Does rejection hurt? An fMRI study of social exclusion. *Science, 302,* 290–292.

Ellingson, L. L. (2003). Interdisciplinary health care teamwork in the clinic backstage. *Journal of Applied Communication Research, 31,* 93–117.

Felicio, D. M., & Miller, C. T. (1994). Social comparison in medical school: What students say about gender and similarity. *Basic and Applied Social Psychology, 15,* 277–297.

Festinger, L. (1957). *A theory of cognitive dissonance.* Stanford, CA: Stanford University Press.

Fine, G. A. (1987). *With the boys: Little League baseball and preadolescent culture.* Chicago: University of Chicago Press.

Finkelstein, K. E. (2001). Tempers seem to be growing shorter in many jury rooms. *The New York Times,* p. B1.

Fisher, W. R. (1987). *Human communication as narration: Toward a philosophy of reason, value, and action.* Columbia: University of South Carolina Press.

Fisher, W. R. (1997). Narration, reason, and community. In L. P. Hinchman & S. K. Hinchman (Eds.), *Memory, identity, community: The idea of narrative in the human sciences* (pp. 307–327). Albany, NY: State University of New York Press.

Forbes, D. L., Katz, M. M., Paul, B., & Lubin, D. (1982). Children's plans for joining play: An analysis of structure and function. In D. Forbes & M. T. Greenberg (Eds.), *New directions for child development: Children's planning strategies* (pp. 61–79). San Francisco: Jossey Bass.

Frederickson, N., & Turner, J. (2003). Utilizing the classroom peer group to address children's social needs: An evaluation of the Circle of Friends intervention approach. *The Journal of Special Education, 36,* 234–245.

French, D. C., & Stright, A. L. (1991). Emergent leadership in children's small groups. *Small Group Research, 22,* 187–199.

Frey, L. R. (1996). Remembering and "re-membering": A history of theory and research on communication and group decision making. In R. Y. Hirokawa & M. S. Poole (Eds.), *Communication and group decision-making* (2nd ed., pp. 19–51). Newbury Park, CA: Sage.

Frey, L. R., & SunWolf. (2004). A symbolic-interpretive perspective on group dynamics. *Small Group Research, 35(3),* 277–306.

Frey, L. R., & SunWolf. (2005). The symbolic-interpretive perspective on group life. In M. S. Poole & A. Hollingshead (Eds.), *Theories of small groups: Interdisciplinary perspectives* (pp. 185–239). Thousand Oaks, CA: Sage.

Frey, L. R., & SunWolf. (2005). The symbolic-interpretive perspective on group life. In M. S. Poole & A. Hollingshead (Eds.), *Theories of small groups: Interdisciplinary perspectives* (pp. 185–239). Thousand Oaks, CA: Sage.

Frey, L. R., & SunWolf. (2004). A symbolic-interpretive perspective on group dynamics. *Small Group Research, 35(3),* 277–306.

Frey, L. R., & SunWolf. (2005). The symbolic-interpretive perspective on group life. In M. S. Poole & A. Hollingshead (Eds.), *Theories of small groups: Interdisciplinary perspectives* (pp. 185–239). Thousand Oaks, CA: Sage.

Ganz, N. (2004). *Graffiti world: Street art from five continents.* New York: Harry N. Abrams Inc.

Garner, T. (1983). Playing the dozens: Folklore as strategies for living. *Quarterly Journal of Speech, 69,* 47–57.

Gastil, J. (1992). A definition of small group democracy. *Small Group Research, 23,* 278–301.

Gastil, J. (1993). Identifying obstacles to small group democracy. *Small Group Research, 24,* 5–27.

Giannetti, C. C., & Sagarese, M. (2001). *Cliques: Eight steps to help your child survive the social jungle.* New York: Broadway Books.

Gigliotti, R. J. (1988). Sex differences in children's task-group performance: Status/norm or ability? *Small Group Behavior, 19,* 273–293.

Gladwell, Malcolm (2005). *Blink: The power of thinking without thinking.* New York: Little, Brown & Company.

Gleicher, F., Boninger, D. S., Strathman, A., Armor, D., Hetts, J., & Ahn, M. (1995). With an eye toward the future: The impact of counterfactual thinking on affect, attitudes, and behavior. In N. J. Roese & J. M. Olson (Eds.), *What might have been: The social psychology of counterfactual thinking* (pp. 283–304). Mahwah, NJ: Lawrence Erlbaum.

Greenspan, S. I. (1993). *Playground politics: Understanding the emotional life of your school-age child.* Reading, MA: Addison-Wesley.

Hans, V. P., & Vidmar, N. (1986). *Judging the jury.* New York: Plenum Press.

Harris, M. B., Benson, S. M., & Hall, C. (1975). The effects of confession on altruism. *Journal of Social Psychology, 96,* 187–192.

Hartup, W. W. (1995). The three faces of friendship. *Journal of Social and Personal Relationships, 12,* 569–574.

Hartup, W. W. (1996). Cooperation, close relationships, and cognitive development. In W. M. Bukowski, A. F. Newcomb, & W. W. Hartup (Eds.), *The company they keep: Friendship in childhood and adolescence* (pp. 213–237). Cambridge: Cambridge University Press.

Hastie, R., Penrod, S. D., & Pennington, N. (1983). *Inside the jury.* Cambridge, MA: Harvard University Press.

Hawkins, C. H. (1962). Interaction rates of jurors aligned in factions. *American Sociological Review, 27,* 689–691.

Hayden, L., Taruulli, D., & Hymel, S. (1988, May). *Children talk about loneliness.* Paper presented at the biennial meeting of the University of Waterloo Conference on Child Development, Waterloo, Ontario.

Hodges, E. V., Malone, M. J., & Perry, D. G. (1997). Individual risk and social risk as interacting determinants of victimization in the peer group. *Developmental Psychology, 33,* 1032–1039.

Horn, S. S. (2003). Adolescents' reasoning about exclusion from social groups. *Developmental Psychology, 39,* 71–84.

Hsu, S. S. (1995, April 8). Fredericksburg searches its soul after clerk is beaten as 6 watch. *Washington Post,* pp. A1, A13.

Hudson, D. A. (Executive Producer). (2002, February 18). Inside your child's social life: The Oprah Winfrey show. Chicago: ABC.

Isen, A. M., & Levin, P. A. (1972). Effect of feeling good on helping: Cookies and kindness. *Journal of Personality and Social Psychology, 21,* 384–388.

James, R. (1959). Status and competence of jurors. *The American Journal of Sociology, 64,* 563–570.

Kahneman, D. (1995). Varieties of counterfactual thinking. In N. J. Roese & J. M. Olson (Eds.), *What might have been: The social psychology of counterfactual thinking* (pp. 375–396). Mahwah, NJ: Lawrence Erlbaum.

Kalven, H., Jr., & Zeisel, H. (with Thomas Callahan, T., & Philip Ennis, P.). (1966). *The American jury.* Boston: Little Brown.

Kasimatis, M., & Wells, G. L. (1995). Individual differences in counterfactual thinking. In N. J. Roese & J. M. Olson (Eds.), *What might have been: The social psychology of counterfactual thinking* (pp. 81–101). Mahwah, NJ: Lawrence Erlbaum.

Katz, W. L. (1986). *Black Indians: A hidden heritage.* New York: Simon Pulse.

Kerr, N. L., & MacCoun, R. J. (1985). The effects of jury size and polling method on the process and product of jury deliberation. *Journal of Personality and Social Psychology, 48,* 349–363.

Keyton, J. (1994). Going forward in group communication research may mean going back: Studying the groups of children. *Communication Studies, 45,* 40–51.

Keyton, J., & Frey, L. R. (2002). The state of traits: Predispositions and group communication. In L. R. Frey (Ed.), *New directions in group communication* (pp. 99–120). Thousand Oaks, CA: Sage.

Killen, M., Pisacane, K., Lee-Kim, J., & Ardila-Rey, A. (2001). Fairness or stereotypes? Young children's priorities when evaluating group exclusion and inclusion. *Developmental Psychology, 37,* 587–596.

Koeppl, G. K. (1990). Adapting intervention to the problems of aggressive and disruptive rejected children. In S. R. Asher & J. D. Coie (Eds.), *Peer rejection in childhood* (pp. 309–337). New York: Cambridge University Press.

Kramer, M. W. (2004). Toward a communication theory of group dialectics: An ethnographic study of a community theater group. *Communication Monographs, 71,* 311–332.

Kupersmidt, J. B., Coie, J. D., & Dodge, K. A. (1990). The role of poor peer relationships in the development of disorder. In S. R. Asher & J. D. Coie (Eds.), *Peer rejection in childhood* (pp. 274–305). New York: Cambridge University Press.

Landman, J. (1993). *Regret: The persistence of the possible.* New York: Oxford University Press.

Landman, J., & Petty, R. (2000). "It could have been you": How states exploit counterfactual thought to market lotteries. *Psychology and Marketing, 17,* 299–321.

Latané, B., & Darley, J. M. (1968). Group inhibition of bystander intervention. *Journal of Personality and Social Psychology, 10,* 215–221.

Latané, B., & Darley, J. M. (1970). *The unresponsive bystander: Why doesn't he help?* Englewood Cliffs, NJ: Prentice Hall

Lesch, C. L. (1994). Observing theory in practice: Sustaining consciousness in a coven. In L. R. Frey (Ed.), *Group communication in context: Studies of natural groups* (pp. 57–82). Hillsdale, NJ: Lawrence Erlbaum.

Lipman-Blumen, J., & Leavitt, H. J. (1999). *Hot groups: Seeding them, feeding them, and using them to ignite your organization.* New York: Oxford University Press.

Lyddane, D. (2006). Understanding gangs and gang mentality: Acquiring evidence of the gang conspiracy. *United States Attorneys' Bulletin (May 2006,* 1–14). Retrieved December 1, 2006, from http://www.usdoj.gov/usao/eousa/foia_reading_room/usab5403.pdf

MacCoun, R. J., & Kerr, N. L. (1988). A symmetric influence in mock jury deliberation: Jurors' bias for leniency. *Journal of Personality and Social Psychology, 54,* 21–33.

MacIntyre, A. (1981). *After virtue: A study in moral theory* (2nd ed.). Notre Dame, IN: University of Notre Dame Press.

Magna Carta of Great Britain, 1215. Translation prepared by Xavier Hildegarde, November 2001. Retrieved January 29, 2008, from http://www.magnacartaplus.org/magnacarta/

Malley, H. (1935). A study of some of the techniques underlying the establishment of successful social contacts at the preschool level. *Journal of Genetic Psychology, 47,* 431–457.

Maltz, D. N., & Borker, R. (1982). A cultural approach to male-female miscommunication. In J. J. Gumpertz (Ed.), *Language and social identity* (pp. 196–216). Cambridge: Cambridge University Press.

Marder, N. S. (2003). Introduction to the jury at a crossroad: the American experience. *Chicago-Kent Law Review, 78,* 909–933.

Martin, C. L., Fabes, R. A., Evans, S. M., & Wyman, H. (1999). Social cognition on the playground: Children's beliefs about playing with girls versus boys and their relations to sex segregated play. *Journal of Social and Personal Relationships, 16,* 751–771.

Matthews, M. W. (1996). Addressing issues of peer rejection in child-centered classrooms. *Early Childhood Education Journal, 24,* 93–97.

McAlister, A. L. (1995). Behavioral journalism: Beyond the marketing model for health communication. *American Journal of Health Promotion, 9,* 417–420.

McAlister, A. L., Ama, E., Barroso, C., Peters, R. J., & Kelder, S. (2000). Promoting tolerance and moral engagement through peer modeling. *Cultural Diversity and Ethnic Minority Psychology, 6,* 363–373.

McConnell, A. R., Niedermeier, K. E., Leibold, J. M., El-Alayli, A. G., Chin, P. P., & Kuiper, N. M. (2000). What if I find it cheaper someplace else? Role of prefactual thinking and anticipated regret in consumer behavior. *Psychology and Marketing, 17,* 281–298.

McGill, A. L., & Klein, J. G. (1995). Counterfactual and contrasting reasoning in explanations for performance: Implications for gender bias. In N. J. Roese & J. M. Olson (Eds.), *What might have been: The social psychology of counterfactual thinking* (pp. 333–352). Mahwah, NJ: Lawrence Erlbaum.

McMullen, M. N., Markman, K. D., & Gavanski, I. (1995). Living in neither the best nor worst of all possible worlds: Antecedents and consequences of upward and downward counterfactual thinking. In N. J. Roese & J. M. Olson (Eds.), *What might have been: The social psychology of counterfactual thinking* (pp. 133–168). Mahwah, NJ: Lawrence Erlbaum.

Mead, G. H. (1934). *Mind, self, and society.* Chicago: University of Chicago Press.

Meyer, J. C. (1997). Humor and member narratives: Uniting and dividing at work. *Western Journal of Communication, 61,* 188–208.

Meyers, R. A., & Seibold, D. R. (1990). Perspectives on group argument: A critical review of persuasive arguments theory and an alternative structurational view. In J. A. Anderson (Ed.), *Communication yearbook* (Vol. 13, pp. 268–302). Newbury Park, CA: Sage

Miller, J. (1998). Gender and victimization risk among young women in youth gangs. *Journal of Research in Crime and Delinquency, 35,* 429–453.

Miller, J. (2000). Gender dynamics in youth gangs: A comparison of males' and females' accounts. *Justice Quarterly, 17,* 419–448.

Moreland, R. L. (1985). Social categorization and the assimilation of "new" group members. *Journal of Personality and Social Psychology, 48,* 1173–1190.

Mulgrew, I. (2002, November 13). Guilty or not? Might as well flip a coin: What jurors don't know alarms researchers. *The Vancouver Sun,* p. B6.

National Institute of Mental Health (2000). *Suicide facts.* Retrieved May 18, 2003 from http://www.nimh.nih.gov/research/suifact.cfm.

Nemeth, C. (1976). Rules governing jury deliberations: A consideration of recent changes. In G. Bermant, C. Nemeth, & N. Vidmar (Eds.), *Psychology and the law* (pp. 169–184). Lexington, MA: Lexington.

Newall, V. (1986–1987) The moving spray can: A collection of some contemporary English graffiti. *The International Journal of Verbal Aggression, 9,* 39–47.

Newcomb, A. F., & Bagwell, C. L. (1996). The developmental significance of children's friendship relations. In W. M. Bukowski, A. F. Newcomb, & W. W. Hartup (Eds.), *The company they keep: Friendship in childhood and adolescence* (pp. 289–321). Cambridge: Cambridge University Press.

Ng, S. H., Bell, D., & Brooke, M. (1993). Gaining turns and achieving high influence ranking in small conversational groups. *British Journal of Social Psychology, 32,* 265–275.

Norris, K. (1931/1988). *Hands full of living.* Mattituck, NY: Amereon.

Oetzel, J. G. (2002). The effects of culture and cultural diversity on communication to work groups: Synthesizing vertical and cultural differences with a face-negotiation perspective. In L. R. Frey (Ed.), *New directions in group communication* (pp. 121–137). Thousand Oaks, CA: Sage.

Oetzel, J. G., & Robbins, J. (2003). Multiple identities in teams in a cooperative supermarket. In L. R. Frey (Ed.), *Group communication in context: Studies of bona fide groups* (2nd ed., pp. 183–208). Mahwah, NJ: Lawrence Erlbaum.

Office of Juvenile Justice and Delinquency Prevention, U.S. Department of Justice, March 2001, "Female gangs: A focus on research." Retrieved October 1, 2006 from http://www.ncjrs.org/html/ojjdp/jjbu12001_3_3/contents.html

Orenstein, P. (1994). *Schoolgirls: Young women, self-esteem, and the confidence gap.* New York: Doubleday.

Padilla, F. (1992). *The gang as an American enterprise.* New Brunswick, NJ: Rutgers University Press.

Paley, V. G. (1992). *You can't say you can't play.* Cambridge, MA: Harvard University Press.

Parker, J. G., & Asher, S. R. (1993). Friendship and friendship quality in middle childhood: Links with peer group acceptance and feelings of loneliness and social dissatisfaction. *Developmental Psychology, 29,* 611–621.

Phillips, E. L., Shenker, S., & Revitz, P. (1951). The assimilation of the new child into the group. *Psychiatry, 14,* 319–325.

Poole, M. S., & DeSanctis, G. (1990). Understanding the use of group decision support systems: The theory of adaptive structuration. In J. Fulk & C. Steinfield (Eds.), *Organizations and communication technology* (pp. 175–195). Newbury Park, CA: Sage.

Poole, M. S., & DeSanctis, G. (1992). Microlevel structuration in computer-supported group decision-making. *Human Communication Research*, 19, 5–49.

Poole, M. S., DeSanctis, G., Kirsch, L., & Jackson, M. (1995). Group decision support systems as facilitators of quality team efforts. In L. R. Frey (Ed.), *Innovations in group facilitation techniques: Applications in natural settings* (pp. 299–320). Cresskill, NJ: Hampton Press.

Poole, M. S., & Hollingshead, A. B. (Eds.) (2005). *Theories of small groups: Interdisciplinary perspectives.* Thousand Oaks, CA: Sage.

Poole, M. S., Holmes, M., & DeSanctis, G. (1991). Conflict management in a computer-supported meeting environment. *Management Science, 37,* 926–953.

Poole, M. S., Seibold, D. R., & McPhee, R. D. (1985). Group decision-making as a structurational process. *Quarterly Journal of Speech, 71,* 74–102.

Poole, M. S., Seibold, D. R., & McPhee, R. D. (1996). The structuration of group decisions. In R. Y. Hirokawa & M. S. Poole (Eds.), *Communication and group decision making* (2nd ed., pp. 114–146). Thousand Oaks, CA: Sage.

Pope, A. W., Bierman, K. L., & Mumma, G. H. (1991). Aggression, hyperactivity, and inattention-immaturity: Behavior dimensions associated with peer rejection in elementary school boys. *Developmental Psychology, 27,* 663–671.

Pritchard, M. E., & Keenan, J. M. (1999). Memory monitoring in mock jurors. *Journal of Experimental Psychology: Applied, 5,* 152–168.

Putallaz, M., & Gottman,J. M. (1981). An interactional model of children's entry into peer groups. *Child Development, 52,* 986–994.

Putallaz, M., & Wasserman, A. (1990). Children's entry behavior. In S. R. Asher, & J. D. Coie (Eds.), *Peer rejection in childhood* (pp. 60–89). New York: Cambridge University Press.

Putnam, L. L., & Stohl, C. (1990). Bona fide groups: A reconceptualization of groups in context. *Communication Studies, 41,* 248–265.

Putnam, L. L., & Stohl, C. (1996). Bona fide groups, an alternative perspective for communication and small group decision making. In R. Y. Hirokawa & M. S. Poole (Eds.), *Communication and group decision making* (2nd ed., pp. 147–178). Thousand Oaks, CA: Sage.

Quade, A. (2007, March 19). Elite team rescues troops behind enemy lines. *CNN World News.* Retrieved March 19, 2007, from http://www.cnn.com/2007/WORLD/meast/03/15/search.rescue/index.html

Quicker, J. (1983). *Homegirls: Characterizing Chicana gangs.* San Pedro, CA: International Universities Press.

Reisner, R. ., & Wechsler, L. (1974). *Encyclopedia of graffiti.* New York: MacMillan.

Rejection massively reduces IQ. *New Scientist* (2002, March 15). Retrieved July 1, 2006, from http://www.newscientist.com/news/news.jsp?id=ns99992051

Riera, M. (2004). *Uncommon sense for parents with teenagers* (rev. ed.). Berkeley, CA: Celestial Arts Publishing.

Roberts, N. C., & King, P. J. (1996). *Transforming public policy: Dynamics of policy entrepreneurship and innovation.* San Francisco: Jossey-Bass.

Rodriguez, A., & Clair, R. P. (1999). Graffiti as communication: Exploring the discursive tensions of anonymous texts. *Southern Communication Journal, 65,* 1–15.

Roese, N. J., & Olson, J. M. (1995). Counterfactual thinking: A critical overview. In N.J. Roese & J.M. Olson (Eds.), *What might have been: The social psychology of counterfactual thinking* (pp. 1–55). Mahwah, NJ: Lawrence Erlbaum.

Roese, N. J., & Olson, J. M. (1995). Functions of counterfactual thinking. In N.J. Roese & J.M. Olson (Eds.), *What might have been: The social psychology of counterfactual thinking* (pp. 169–198). Mahwah, NJ: Lawrence Erlbaum.

Rosenberg, S. L., McKeon, L. M., & Dinero, T. E. (1999). Positive peer groups reclaim rejected kids. *The Education Digest, 65,* 22–27.

Rouse, W., & Morris, N. (1986). On looking into the black box: Prospects and limits in the search for mental models. *Psychological Bulletin, 100,* 359–363.

Sanna, L. J., Meier, S., & Wegner, E. A. (2001). Counterfactuals and motivation: Mood as input to affective enjoyment and preparation. *British Journal of Social Psychology, 40,* 235–256.

Sapon-Shevin, M., Dobbelaere, A., Corrigan, C., Goodman, K., & Mastin, M. (1998). Everyone here can play. *Educational Leadership, 56,* 42–45.

Sapon-Shevin, M., Dobbelaere, A., Corrigan, C., Goodman, K., & Mastin, M. (1998). Promoting inclusive behavior in inclusive classrooms: "You can't say you can't play." In I. H. Meyer, H. S. Park, M. Grenot-Scheyer, I. S. Schwartz & B. Harry (Eds.), *Making friends: The influences of culture and development* (pp. 105–132). Baltimore: Paul H. Brookes.)

Schultz, B. (1982). Argumentativeness: Its effect in group decision-making and its role in leadership perception. *Communication Quarterly, 30,* 368–375.

Seelau, E. P., Seelau, S. M., Wells, G. L., & Windschitl, P. D. (1995). Counterfactual constraints. In N. J. Roese & J. M. Olson (Eds.), *What might have been: The social psychology of counterfactual thinking* (pp. 57–79). Mahwah, NJ: Lawrence Erlbaum.

Seibold, D. R., McPhee, R. D., Poole, M. S., Tanita, N. E., & Canary, D. J. (1981). Argument, group influence, and decision outcomes. In G. Ziegelmuller & J. Rhodes (Eds.), *Dimensions of argument: Proceedings of the second summer conference on argumentation* (pp. 663–692). Annandale, VA: Speech Communication Association.

Sherman, S. J., & McConnell, A. R. (1995). Dysfunctional implications of counterfactual thinking: When alternatives to reality fail us. In N. J. Roese & J. M. Olson (Eds.), *What might have been: The social psychology of counterfactual thinking* (pp. 199–231). Mahwah, NJ: Lawrence Erlbaum.

Simmons, R. (2002). *Odd girl out: The hidden culture of aggression in girls.* New York: Harcourt.

Simon, R. J. (1967). *The jury and the defense of insanity.* Boston, MA: Little, Brown.

Sinclair-James, L., & Stohl, C. (1997). Group endings and new beginnings. In L. R. Frey & J. K. Barge (Eds.), *Managing group life: Communicating in decision-making groups* (pp. 308–334). Boston: Houghton Mifflin.

Slang of the Week, January 8, 2004. snaps (noun). *Slang City.* Retrieved January 10, 2007, from http://www.slangcity.com/email_archive/1_08_04.htm

Socha, T. J. (1999). Communication in family units: Studying the first "group." In L. R. Frey , D. S. Gouran, & M. S. Poole (Eds.), *The handbook of group communication theory and research* (pp. 475–492). Thousand Oaks, CA: Sage.

Socha, T. J., & Socha, D. M. (1994). Children's task-group communication: Did we learn it all in kindergarten? In L. R. Frey (Ed.), *Group communication in context: Studies of natural groups* (pp. 227–246). Hillsdale, NJ: Lawrence Erlbaum.

Socha, T. J., & Socha, D. M. (1994). Children's task-group communication: Did we learn it all in kindergarten? In L. R. Frey (Ed.), *Group communication in context: Studies of natural groups* (pp. 227–246). Hillsdale, NJ: Lawrence Erlbaum.

Sommer, R. (1961). Leadership and group geography. *Sociometry, 24,* 99–110.

Sorenson, S. M. (1981, May). *Group-hate: A negative reaction to group work.* Paper presented at the annual meeting of the International Communication Association, Minneapolis, MN.

Sprecher, S., & Fehr, B. (2005). Compassionate love for close others and humanity. *Journal of Social and Personal Relationships, 22,* 629–651.

Stasser, G., Kerr, N. L., & Bray, R. M. (1982). The social psychology of jury deliberations: Structure, process, and product. In N. L. Kerr & R. M. Bray, *The psychology of the courtroom* (pp. 221–256). New York: Harcourt Brace Jovanovich.

Stohl, C., & Putnam, L. L. (2003). Communication in bona fide groups: A retrospective and prospective account. In L. R. Frey (Ed.), *Group communication in context: Studies of bona fide groups* (2nd ed., pp. 399–414). Mahwah, NJ: Lawrence Erlbaum.

Stossel, J. (Executive Producer). (2002, February 15). The "in" crowd and social cruelty. New Hudson, MI: ABC News.

Strauss, A. (1978). *Negotiations: Varieties, contexts, processes, and social order.* San Francisco: Jossey-Bass.

Strauss, A. (1994). *Continual permutations of action.* Cambridge: Cambridge University Press.

Strodtbeck, F. (1962). Social process, the law, and jury functioning. In W. M. Evan (Ed.), *Law and sociology* (pp. 144–164). New York: The Free Press of Glencoe.

Strodtbeck, F. L., & Hook, L. H. (1961). The social dimensions of a twelve-man jury table. *Sociometry, 24,* 397–415.

Strodtbeck, F. L., James, R. M., & Hawkins, C. (1957). Social status in jury deliberations. *American Sociological Review, 22,* 713–719.

SunWolf. (2004). *Practical jury dynamics: From one juror's trial perceptions to the group's decision-making processes.* Charlottesville, VA: LexisNexis Publishing.

SunWolf. (2006). *Juror competency, juror compassion.* Charlottesville, VA: LexisNexis Publishing.

SunWolf. (2006). *Practical jury dynamics2: From one juror's trial perceptions to the group's decision-making processes.* Charlottesville, VA: LexisNexis Publishing.

SunWolf. (2006). Decisional regret theory: Reducing the anxiety about uncertain outcomes during group decision making through shared counterfactual storytelling. *Communication Studies, 57(2),* 1–29.

SunWolf, & Leets, L. (2003). Communication paralysis during peer group exclusion: Social dynamics that prevent children and adolescents from expressing disagreement. *Journal of Language and Social Psychology, 22,* 355–384.

SunWolf, & Leets, L. (2004). Being left out: Rejecting outsiders and communicating group boundaries in childhood and adolescent peer groups. *Journal of Applied Communication Research, 32(3),* 195–223.

SunWolf, & Seibold, D. R. (1998). Jurors' intuitive rules for deliberation: A structurational approach to the study of communication in jury decision making. *Communication Monographs, 65,* 282–307.

Tajfel, H. (1982). *Social identity and intergroup relations.* Cambridge: Cambridge University Press.

Tajfel, H., & Turner, J. C. (1986). The social identity theory of intergroup behavior. In S. Worchel & W. Austin (Eds.), *The psychology of intergroup relations* (pp. 7–24). Chicago: Nelson Hall.

Theimer, C. E., Killen, M., & Stangor, C. (2001). Young children's evaluations of exclusion in gender-stereotypic peer contexts. *Developmental Psychology, 37,* 18–27.

Thompson, M., & Grace, C. O. (with Cohen, L. J.). (2001). *Best friends, worst enemies: Understanding the social lives of children.* New York: Ballantine Books.

Wegner, D. M. (1987). Transactive memory: A contemporary analysis of the group mind. In B. Mullen & G. R. Goethals (Eds.), *Theories of group behavior* (pp. 185–208). New York: Springer.

Wentzel, K. R., & Erdley, C. A. (1993). Strategies for making friends: Relations to social behavior and peer acceptance in early adolescence. *Developmental Psychology, 29,* 819–826.

West, R., & Turner, L. H. (2007). *Introducing communication theory: Analysis and application* (3rd ed., Chapter 12). Boston: McGraw Hill.

Witmer, D. F. (1997). Communication and recovery: Structuration as an ontological approach to organizational culture. *Communication Monographs, 64,* 324–349.

Wood, J. J., Cowan, P. A., & Baker, B. L. (2002). Behavior problems and peer rejection in preschool boys and girls. *Journal of Genetic Psychology, 163,* 72–89.

Workin' from can't to can't: African-American cowboys in Texas, produced by The University of Texas Institute of Texan Cultures at San Antonio, and available at store.the-museum-store.org/wofrcatocaaf.html.

Yamaguchi, R. (2001). Children's learning groups: A study of emergent leadership, dominance, and group effectiveness. *Small Group Research, 32,* 671–697.

Index

About the Author

Dr. SunWolf is an enthusiastic observer of everyday communication acts, a survivor of many peer groups, and a juryologist. She has been fascinated with jurors and their imperfect worlds since her first trial, in 1975. A veteran of many roles within the American justice system (law school faculty, litigation attorney, Training Director for Colorado's Public Defender System, and trial consultant), she has represented and advocated on behalf of many members of street gangs. A moment of epiphany during a death penalty trial (about how to touch a juror's heart as well as mind) pushed her back to graduate school, where she completed both Master's and Doctoral degrees in Interpersonal and Group Communication from the University of California, Santa Barbara. Dr. SunWolf is an Associate Professor of Communication at Santa Clara University, where she teaches relationships, group dynamics, conflict, and social persuasion.

Professor SunWolf is also a performing storyteller, with corresponding research investigating the pedagogical and persuasive effects of multicultural tales. Dr. SunWolf's coauthored study with Dr. David Seibold on jurors' intuitive rules for deliberation received the Dennis S. Gouran Research Award from the Group Communication Division of the National Communication Association (NCA) as most outstanding scholarly journal article in the previous two years. Her coauthored article with Dr. Laura Leets, "Being Left Out" was awarded Most Outstanding Scholarly Article by NCA's Applied Communication

Division for its significant contribution to scholarship in theory, research, and practice. She serves on the editorial boards of *Small Group Research, Journal of Applied Communication Research,* and *Review of Communication.* An active translator of social science research for practitioners, she lectures at continuing legal education programs throughout the country. She is the originator of Decisional Regret Theory, which explains how jurors attempt to reduce the anxiety of anticipated *verdict-regret* by first imagining (and later arguing) with counterfactual "what if" stories. She is Visiting Professor at Santa Clara University School of Law, teaching "Jury Law & Strategies," —a class devoted to thinking about the persuasion and behaviors of juries.

Dr. SunWolf's previous books include *Practical Jury Dynamics, Jury Thinking*, and *Juror Competency Juror Compassion*. Her scholarship has appeared in *Communication Monographs, Howard Journal of Communications, Journal of Language and Social Psychology, Journal of Moral Education, Journal of Applied Communication Research, Communication Studies, Small Group Research, Communication Research Trends, Facilitating Group Communication in Context, The Handbook of Language and Social Psychology, The Handbook of Group Communication Theories and Research, New Directions in Group Communication, Theories of Small Groups, and The Handbook of Group Research and Practice.*

Dr. SunWolf is currently studying and writing about the bio-cognitive thinking processes of our moral minds and our religious beliefs. What happens when people are making decisions in groups with people who do not share their moral thinking?